Gardens of Awakening

Gardens
of Awakening

A Guide to the Aesthetics, History, and Spirituality of Kyōto's Zen Landscapes

Kazuaki Tanahashi
Photography by Mitsue Nagase

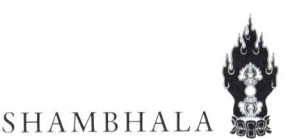

SHAMBHALA

Shambhala Publications, Inc.
2129 13th Street
Boulder, Colorado 80302
www.shambhala.com

Cover art: Mitsue Nagase
Cover design: Gopa & Ted2, Inc
Interior design: Gopa & Ted2, Inc
The image of Musō Soseki on p. 21 is courtesy of Tenryū-ji.
The Sūtra on the Heart of Realizing Wisdom beyond Wisdom translated by
Kazuaki Tanahashi and Joan Halifax on p. 131 is in public domain.

First Edition
Printed in Malaysia

Shambhala Publications makes every effort to print on acid-free,
recycled paper. Shambhala Publications is distributed worldwide
by Penguin Random House, Inc., and its subsidiaries.

Library of Congress Cataloging-in-Publication Data
Names: Tanahashi, Kazuaki, 1933– author. | Nagase, Mitsue, other.
Title: Gardens of awakening: a guide to the aesthetics, history,
and spirituality of Kyōto's Zen landscapes /
Kazuaki Tanahashi; photos by Mitsue Nagase.
Description: Boulder: Shambhala, 2024. | Includes bibliographical
references and index.
Identifiers: LCCN 2023011365 | ISBN 9781645472056 (hardback)
Subjects: LCSH: Zen Buddhism—Doctrines. | Gardening—
Religious aspects—Buddhism. | Aesthetics—Religious aspects—Zen Buddhism.
Classification: LCC BQ9268.6 .T36 2024 | DDC 294.3/927—dc23/eng/20230508
LC record available at https://lccn.loc.gov/2023011365

For Bernd Schellhorn
who savors the world
with joy and wonder

Contents

APPENDICES

Preface

WELCOME TO THE GARDENS OF AWAKENING! This book sees Zen Buddhist practice as a pursuit of inner reality, something genuine that is not bound by outer forms. Yet from the perspective of truth within, it becomes possible to envision and form an environment for a rigorous, continuous practice. That environment includes a Zen garden.

With photographs and commentary, this book will guide you through a series of Zen gardens, most of which were created during the fourteenth through seventeenth centuries. Some are teeming with plants and flowing water, while others have only sand and stones. But they are all associated with particular Zen temples, and they all share certain Zen aesthetics related to the cultivation of awakening. Photographer Mitsue Nagase and I focus on examples from Kyōto, as the city is exceptionally full of Zen landscape masterpieces.

In part one of this book, "The Landscape Within," I discuss the cultural and historical background of Zen gardens with some photographs related to the topics covered.

In part two, "Aesthetics and Stories," we arrange photographs to reveal the seven prominent qualities of Zen art: direct, ordinary, vigorous, gleaming, pivotal, nondual, and inexhaustible. On each spread the photo to the right highlights the quality, and the photo to the left presents a larger view of the setting. Nagase's more than seventy wondrous photographs thus convey the diverse visual impacts of Zen and Zen art.

These gardens offer a great variety of symbolism, history, culture, and anecdote. I hope the stories I tell in this part will help you get to know these gardens intimately.

In this book we focus on Zen gardens in the traditional sense, meaning those that support meditation practice at temples. But nowadays there are Zen-inspired gardens in private homes, museums, and corporate buildings worldwide. I am sure they all help viewers to calm down, contemplate, and refresh their lives.

Enjoy. And remember: Every stone, plant, and structure points you to awakening.

Kazuaki Tanahashi

x

Photographer's Words

Late one January afternoon, I was at Kennin-ji, a Zen monastery in Kyōto. After an hour of photographing for this book, I was ready to leave—I had packed up my camera equipment and was walking toward the exit. But something caught my eye and made me turn back.

It was the sand—its ordinary, plain, still, gray-and-white pattern. I had just spent a good half-hour photographing it, but now it appeared so different.

It was dancing. The gentle yellow wash of the day's last rays of sunlight illumined its surface, and the sand was reflecting this—flickering, it was transformed. I stood there, simply taking in what was so unexpectedly unfolding in front of my eyes. The sand was telling me about impermanence, manifesting the NOW, the joy of being right here, and nothing else mattered in that moment. I felt the light within me, the sand, and a sublime feeling of all boundaries dissolving between us. I knew what I was seeing would be gone in just a few moments. What a gift!

This experience changed my relationship with Zen gardens. I started to listen more closely and became more patient. I now spend more time with the gardens and go back again and again to meet them each time anew. Sometimes they feel hushed; sometimes they are astonishingly vivid. The seasons transform them. Sometimes a garden will seem aggressive, and another time the same garden may radiate tranquility. I have learned that one day I may feel barely any connection while in the space, and the next there may be beauty everywhere I look.

In traditional Zen temples, often a wide wooden veranda faces the garden. I just sit there and take in what is present. Wind passing through the trees. Rocks and sand reflecting the light in endless varieties. Spring rain moistening the path . . . Sometimes *shakkei*—the borrowed scenery of mountains in the far distance—completes the garden view by counterbalancing it. Slightly turning my head may bring out entirely different dimensions, relationships, and expressions.

I watch birds and lizards, and how flowers come and go according to seasonal changes. In winter, snow covers everything in white, yet some shapes still show through. The first flowers of spring ignite a spark of color. The pale white and dark pink petals of *sakura*—cherry blossoms—may illuminate the entire garden. By early May, you can feel the full life force of the trees, in the incandescent fresh green of the maples. In summer, strong sunlight creates an intense contrast between light and shadow, and everything seems so solid. A sudden downpour in the afternoon can change the landscape entirely, and when it stops, cicadas renew their chanting. Autumn foliage adds a painter's touch to the garden—with their different shades of yellow, orange, and red, the leaves seem even more intense against the dark wooden pillars and floors of temple buildings. Then, winter comes again . . . so cold. Sitting and gazing at an icy pond and frozen moss, one second can feel like an eternity.

What exactly am I looking at? I ask myself. It is not rock, sand, trees, moss, a pond, or a bridge . . . I slow my breath and remind myself that the quieter my mind is, the more the garden reflects, radiates, and unfolds within me.

Mitsue Nagase

Notes to the Reader

DATES AND SEASONS

Gardens of Awakening follows the lunar calendar traditionally used in East Asia. The first to third months correspond to spring, and the other seasons follow in three-month periods. The fifteenth day of the month is the day of the full moon.

AGES

When referring to people born before 1868, the beginning of the Meiji Period, we follow the traditional East Asian way of counting ages, where a person is one year old at birth and gains a year on New Year's Day instead of on the day of their birth. We use the Western way of counting ages after 1868.

NAMES

Every layperson's name is presented in the Western way—a given name, poetic name, or title followed by a family name, whereas a Japanese name has the opposite sequence. Buddhist names are not reversed.

KEY TERMS

We give a romanized Japanese word along with ideographic (*kanji*) and syllabic characters (*kana*) for some key terms. For kanji, we use simplified Japanese characters (*tōyō kanji*). The Japanese terms in *kanji* and *kana* may be helpful to you either for further study or in visiting the gardens as well as to familiarize yourself with some basic concepts in Japanese.

MACRONS

Macrons indicating long vowels are used in the main text on all Japanese words, including such common names as Kyōto. Macrons are largely omitted from the names in the acknowledgments, the bibliography, and in quoted texts.

Apostrophes

An apostrophe after *n* is used to signify that it is an independent syllable and not affected by the following vowel. For example, *n'a* is pronounced as *n* plus *a*, but not as *na*.

Italicization

We will italicize all words of Japanese origin—including those adopted as English words such as *haiku*—for consistency. However, proper names will not be italicized.

Zen and Chan

The type of Buddhism we are discussing here started in China, where it is called Chan 禅, and then was introduced to Korea, Vietnam, and Japan. It is called Zen in Japan, and this name became common in English and other languages in the twentieth century. Consequently, Chan is sometimes referred to as "Chinese Zen." I generally follow this convention with apologies to Chinese speakers.

Temple Accessibility

This book presents some of the most renowned Zen temples in Kyōto. Their availability for public viewing is shown in "Zen Temples in Kyōto Selected" in the appendices. These are still a small portion of those worth exploring. We also recommend Kyōto guidebooks in the bibliography for more information.

Chronology

Periods	Years of Reign for Emperors	Regents/*Shōguns* in Office	Zen Masters
Hcian, 794–1185			
			Myōan Eisai, 1141–1215
Kamakura, 1185–1333	Gosaga, 1242–1246	Tokiyori Hōjō, 1246–1256	Eihei Dōgen, 1200–1253
		Tokimune Hōjō, 1268-1284	Enni Ben'en, 1202–1280
			Lanxi Daolong, 1213–1278
	Kameyama, 1259–1274	Sadatoki Hōjō, 1284-1301	Yining Yishan, 1247–1317
	Hanazono, 1308–1318	Takatoki Hōjō, 1316–1326	Kōhō Kennichi, 1241–1316
Muromachi, 1336–1573 [Southern and Northern Dynasties, 1336–1392]	Godaigo, 1318–1336, 1336-1339	Takauji Ashikaga, 1338–1358	Musō Soseki, 1275–1351
			Shūhō Myōchō, 1282–1337
	Kōgen, 1332–1333	Yoshiakira Ashikaga, 1358–1367	Kanzan Egen, 1277–1360
	Kōmyō, 1337–1348		Zekkai Chūshin, 1336–1405
	Gokomatsu, 1392–1412	Yoshimitsu Ashikaga, 1368–1394	
		Yoshimochi Ashikaga, 1323–1425	
	Gohanazono, 1429–1464		Tokuhō Zenketsu, 1419–1506
[Warring States, 1467–1603]	Gotsuchimikado, 1465–1500	Yoshimasa Ashikaga, 1443–1473	
		Yoshihisa Ashikaga, 1473–1489	
Azuchi-Momoyama, 1573–1600		Hideyoshi Toyotomi, 1585–1591	
Edo, 1603–1867		Ieyasu Tokugawa, 1603–1605	Yinyuan Longqi, 1592–1673
			Hakuin Ekaku, 1685–1768

Part One
The Landscape Within

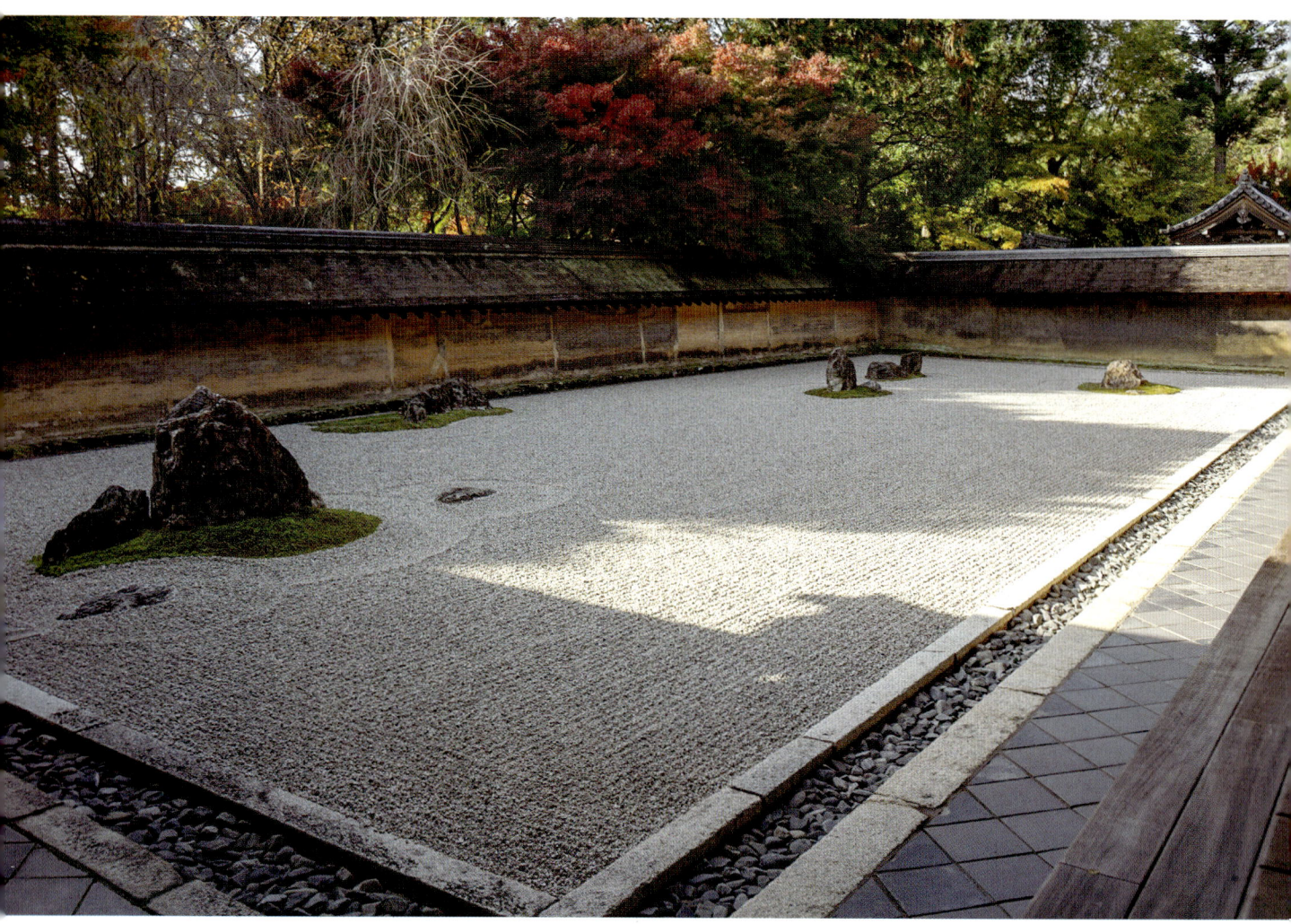

Fig. 1. Ryōan-ji

Experiencing the Zen Gardens

IMAGINE THAT YOU have traveled to Kyōto, Japan. In front of you lies an ocean of sand. Scattered islands of moss appear to float in the sand, several rocks standing upon them. You might picture in your mind a tigress escorting her cubs, trying to paddle through the water to a shore ahead. The rectangular space of the garden is surrounded by archaic roofed walls of oiled clay. Trees stand outside of the compound. However, the garden has no trees and also no path to stroll on, no brooks, no ponds with swimming fish, no grass, no flowers, and no humans walking around. You face a vast nothingness. It's like the plain wooden wall in the meditation hall that helps you to face inward and go within yourself—you see yourself through the emptiness of the garden.

Forget about any fellow visitors sitting, chatting, and taking photographs to send through cyberspace. You are in the midst of an enigma. All your expectations about what a garden is are thrown over. You have flown all this way to be immersed in wonderment at this popular tourist site. And yet you see no seasonal flowers here to greet you, nothing pleasing at all. What a paradox! You may find yourself wondering: *Why is this garden here? How was it created? What were those who created it thinking? And what we can learn from it?*

The name of the designer of the *sekitei* 石庭 or "stone garden" of the Ryōan-ji (Dragon Ease Monastery) is unknown. Perhaps it was created at the time the community was led by Zen master Tokuhō Zenketsu (1419–1506), who dedicated himself to the reconstruction of the temple and was given the title of the founder (*kaisan* 開山) of the revived monastery in 1488. We don't know how much Zenketsu was involved in planning the garden. At any rate, whoever created this antigarden was a conceptual artist, as well as an abstract expressionist and minimalist of the late fifteenth century. And this designer, though skilled and innovative, was drawing from deep wells of tradition. Indeed, the Ryōan-ji garden is a product of centuries of Zen thinking and the evolution of Zen architecture and landscaping. (Note that the term *temple*—*tera* or *-ji* 寺— includes a monastery, which is a residential training center—*semmon dōjō* 専門道場 —but *monastery* does not necessarily mean temple in general.)

Whether or not you have extensive knowledge of Zen, your fresh and direct impression of the garden, along with your enjoyment and inquiry, is valuable. But putting the gardens in the context of the history, practice, and the thinking (or non-thinking) of Zen, which has brought about the unique forms of these architectural and cultivated wonders, may help you to experience the landscape within yourself.

Function of Zen Gardens

THE PRIMARY PURPOSE of Zen architecture and landscaping is to provide an environment for the communal practice of Zen meditation and other rituals of Zen monasticism. Within a Zen temple compound, all the buildings and their surroundings have their particular function. The monasteries were originally for training practitioners and were not open to the public for viewing until recent times. In other words, there used to be no tourists—none of us.

A compound in a large Zen monastery consists of seven main components: the mountain (temple) gate typically to the south, the Buddha hall in the center, and the dharma hall to the north—and these three usually all line up—then the kitchen and the bath hall on one side and the monks' hall and wash hall on the other. (See in the appendices, "Temple Plan Example: Tōfuku-ji.")

Monks practice meditation, take formal breakfast and lunch, and sleep in the monks' hall. Services are held at the Buddha hall, and lectures are given at the dharma hall. There are also the abbot's quarters, office buildings, and guest quarters. In addition, there are subtemples called *tatchū* 塔頭, originally built as residences for retired abbots or as a site for their tombs. (*Tatchū* literally means "*stūpa* center.") Subtemples may be adjacent to or set away from their main temples.

The term for the abbot's quarters, *hōjō* 方丈, originally meant "ten feet square." Though such buildings likely started out with these small dimensions, they later became a larger independent building in major monasteries. The abbot's quarters consist of a front area for receiving guests and conducting ceremonies and a private back area for the abbot to reside in. The front gardens of the *hōjōs* are often the main landscaped areas within monasteries.

Monastics' daily schedule includes periods of *zazen* (meditation in sitting posture), walking meditation, study, and work practice called *samu*. In Japan the Sōtō School emphasizes just sitting, and the Rinzai School emphasizes *kōan* practice: a step-by-step investigation, under the guidance of masters, of enigmatic questions derived mostly from dialogues between the ancient Chinese Zen masters and students. (The Sōtō School came from the Caodong School, founded by Dongshan and his successor

Caoshan in China, and the Rinzai School was named after the Chinese Linji School, founded by Linji.)

To reside in a quiet place on a remote mountain is ideal for Zen life; a number of monks and nuns in China retreated into the mountains and practiced in such isolation. But it was also important for practitioners to be accessible to city dwellers. So they built places for practice on the outskirts of cities as well. For this reason, monasteries and temples have so-called "mountain names" in addition to their temple names. A community of practitioners is called a "forest." Thus, Zen gardens represent that crucial component of nature as it exists within the compound of facilities for meditation practice.

Originally, in semitropical India, Buddhist monks and nuns were required to practice begging and renounce activities to support their livelihood. They were prohibited from engaging in labor. But in China, with its severe climate along with its cultural reverence for daily activities, monastics were required to work, including cleaning, farming, gardening, and temple management. As eighth- to ninth-century master Baizhang famously said, "A day without labor is a day without eating."

Thus, daily labor became an essential part of Zen practice. Tending to gardens—weeding, trimming, sweeping, raking, and watering—is part of enlightened action in nature for nature. Thus, nature and the self become inseparable. Tending the plants and the sand is no other than polishing one's own character. Gardens are an essential instrument for awakening.

Nonself as a Keynote

ZEN SCHOOLS emphasize their total attention to meditation, and so the major characteristics we find at Zen monasteries are silence, stillness, isolation, plainness, austerity, sternness, purity, and emptiness.

The stone garden of the Ryoan-ji in front of the abbot's quarters is an outstanding example of these characteristics. With its lack of color and visual attractors, the garden is not noisy, but rather silent. With no branches or flowers moving in the wind, the garden is as still as meditation. The garden is not for social gatherings but for practice in retreat from worldly affairs. With sand, rocks, and moss as its sole elements, the garden is not gaudy or showy, but plain. There is reverence for each element: space, stones, and sand patterns, in which all things become somber. The garden was built and is maintained by those who participate in rigorous training, so it is polished to the point

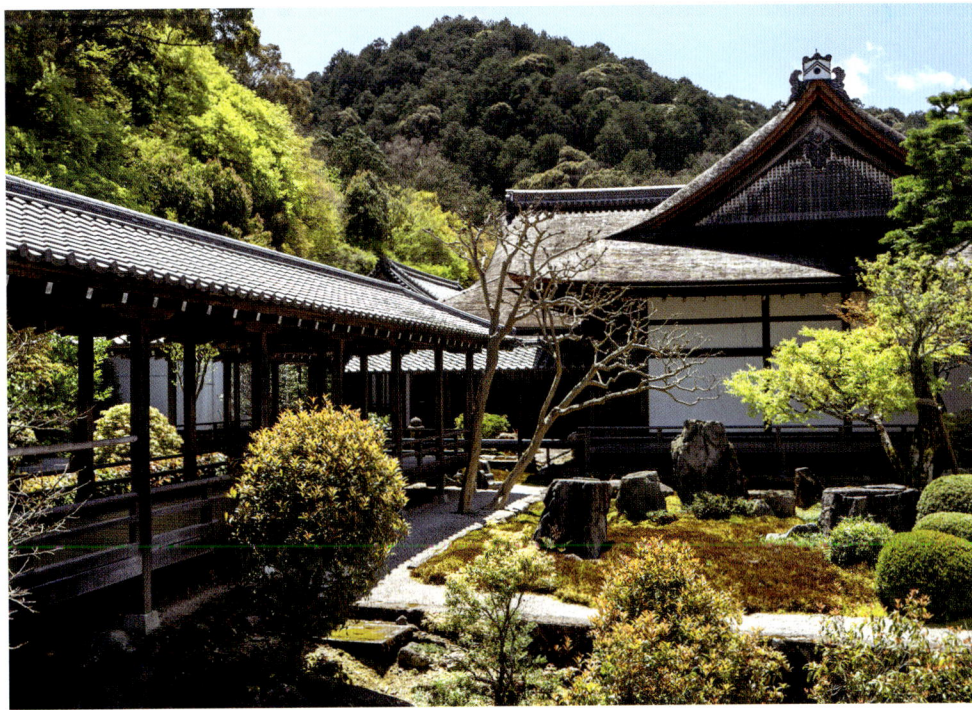

Fig. 2.
Nanzen-ji

of freshness and invigoration. The buildings are spotless, and the gardens are cleaned wholeheartedly with reverence and dedication, reflecting spirituality. And, above all its remarkable features, the whole garden represents emptiness.

The *Heart Sūtra* is recited every morning in Zen monasteries, temples, and centers. It is chanted in services in almost all Zen rituals. In its short form, the text summarizes the selfless experience of reality in meditation and how this transcends our usual way of thinking.

One of the common English translations by Edward Conze says:

> Whatever is form, that is emptiness; whatever is emptiness, that is form; the same is true of feelings, perceptions, impulses, and consciousness. Here, O Sariputra, all dharmas are marked with emptiness; they are not produced or stopped, not defiled or immaculate, not deficient or complete. Therefore, O Sariputra, in emptiness there is no form, nor feeling, nor perception, nor impulse, nor consciousness. No eye, ear, nose, tongue, body, mind.[*]

As you see, emptiness is central in this scripture. It is so not only in Zen but in all of Mahāyāna Buddhism. What is emptiness then? Let me present the corresponding passages of the scripture translated by Joan Halifax Rōshi and myself:

> Form is boundlessness; boundlessness is form. Feelings, perceptions, inclinations, and discernment are also like this. O Shariputra, boundlessness is the nature of all things. It neither arises nor perishes, neither stains nor purifies, neither increases nor decreases. Boundlessness is not limited by form, nor by feelings, perceptions, inclinations, or discernment. It is free of the eyes, ears, nose, tongue, body, and mind.

In this translation of the *Heart Sūtra*—the entirety of which is presented in the appendices—Rōshi Joan and I wanted to demonstrate that "no eye, ear, nose, tongue, body, and mind" does not mean they don't exist, but instead that there is freedom from such a distinction by experiencing the oneness of all things. We translated the Sanskrit word *shūnyatā*, which literally means "zeroness," as "boundlessness." In Mahāyāna Buddhism, *zeroness* means the lack of distinctions or boundaries. From the perspective of nonduality, all things are seen as one, without having definite and everlasting boundaries and self-identity. *Empty* means "nonself," not in the usual sense of "self-effacing,"

---

[*] Edward Conze, *Buddhist Wisdom Books: The Diamond Sutra, The Heart Sutra* (New York: Harper & Row, 1978).

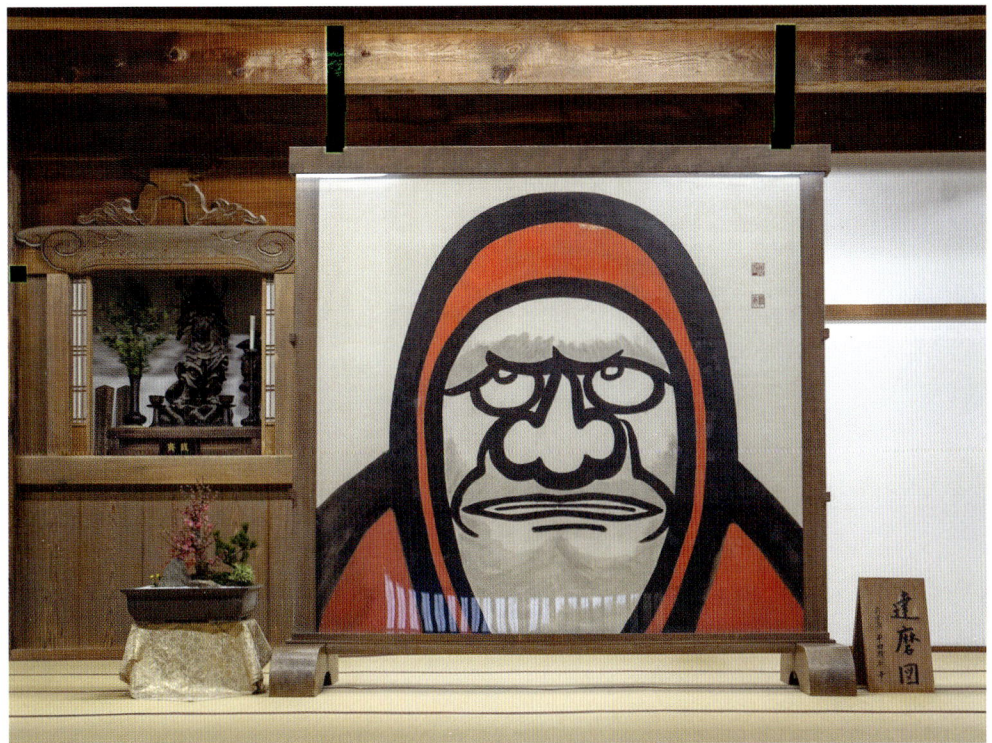

Fig. 3.
Bodhidharma,
Tenryū-ji

but as dropping the boundaries of the self. This is the greater sense of what is usually called "emptiness"—*kū* 空 in Japanese.

There is another seemingly negative concept in Zen, which is *mu* 無 (*wu* in Chinese). It means "not," "there is no," or "nothing." It often means "no thinking," "nothing to possess," or "nothing to achieve." Again, this single-syllable word, regarded as expressing transcendence and freedom in Zen practice and insight, should not be taken literally. I sometimes translate *mu* as "beyond" or "beyondness." Some Zen masters may insist that everything about Zen is *mu*, and some scholars may argue that the art and craft of Zen are those of *mu*.

According to the first case of the *Blue Cliff Record*, the most revered collection of *kōans*, Bodhidharma, regarded as the First Ancestor of Chan Buddhism in China, spoke in terms of "no merit," "nothing sacred," and "not knowing."

Hakuin Ekaku, the seventeenth- to eighteenth-century monk, regarded as the restorer of the Japanese Rinzai School, gave a certificate with his own painting of a dragon-shaped staff to one of his *kōan* study students. (The dragon is a symbol of an outstanding Zen practitioner.) It included the words: "Nihei Tanaka has passed my barrier against dualism, called 'the sound of one hand.' This is to certify it—a heavy prize indeed for a courageous person!"

In summary, *emptiness* or *boundlessness* is a Mahāyāna Buddhist concept from India, while *mu* is a Zen Buddhist concept that originated in China. Both terms represent nonduality, with some linguistic and cultural differences in their nuances.

Much of Zen training is about trying to *experience* nonduality by going beyond the boundary of self-identity while still being based in the duality of all things, with the aim of actualizing this synthesis with stability in daily activities.

Body of Paradoxes

ZEN GARDENS REFLECT the state of meditation.

When you sit on a cushion, you may first check your posture and your balance and see how you feel. You check your environment and sense your fellow practitioners. Thoughts about your situation or your actions may still remain. It's still all about you—which is normal. You in your daily life function as yourself with body, heart, and mind in relationships and in work, and you need to fulfill your responsibilities.

After sitting for a while, your body, heart, and mind settle, and you become more selfless. Eventually, the distinction between large and small, long and short, right and wrong, you and others becomes obscure and insignificant. Practice and enlightenment, process and goal, momentary and timeless, life and death merge. This is the state of nonduality. All becomes one in meditation. This is a nonintellectual, experiential event, a mystical experience. Then, when the bell rings, you go back to the realm of distinctions and boundaries.

Zen master Dōgen of thirteenth-century Japan says in his first essay, "On the Endeavor of the Way":

> The zazen of even one person at one moment imperceptibly accords with all things and fully resonates through all time. Thus, in the past, future, and present of the limitless universe this zazen carries on the buddha's transformation endlessly and timelessly. Each moment of zazen is equally the wholeness of practice, equally the wholeness of realization.

The experience of oneness in meditation, however, is entwined with practical applications of duality, or discerning differences. To engage in meditation in the Zen style, you need to be on time, be at your designated position, and do things in an exactly predetermined way and together with others. You may have a role in running the meditation hall, such as ringing a bell, opening windows to allow air in, or making announcements. In other words, nonduality is supported by duality and vice versa.

This is a dilemma. But our life is full of dilemmas; it's a dynamic interaction of dualism and nondualism. Dōgen calls it *genjō kōan* 現成公案 (actualizing the fundamental point). It's a dance conducted between conventional wisdom and transcendental wisdom (wisdom beyond wisdom). These two are invariably important to make our life and practice of dharma whole and ethical.

The Zen method of training is not to intellectually explain the wisdom beyond wisdom, which is regarded as a great matter of life and death, but rather to let each practitioner experience it with body, heart, and mind. Zen people use "intimate language" (*mitsugo* 密語), which is words beyond words—gesture, hitting, shouting, and silence. Words, therefore, if they are employed, tend to be enigmatic.

The sign in front of the *hōjō* at the Ginkaku-ji (Silver Pavilion Temple) says, "The East mountain walks on water." This is a world of enigma. A mountain's walking does not happen in the actual world, but in poetry everything is possible. So too in meditation. Zen gardens are full of such paradoxes: The extremely minute is enormous; the extremely large is small. What is empty is inexhaustible. What is lifeless is vital. (The first definition of *paradox* in the *American Heritage Dictionary* is "a seemingly contradictory statement that may nonetheless be true.")

Zen has favored paradoxes for centuries. This tendency may be traced to the enlightenment poem "Engraving Trust in the Heart," attributed to the Third Ancestor of the Chan tradition, Jianzhi Sengcan (d. 606). It is a greatly revered text among Zen practitioners.

"Engraving Trust in the Heart" is a lengthy and comprehensive treasure house of paradoxes such as:

"There is nothing lacking, nothing extra"

"Let the way be invisible"

"Stillness turns into motion"

"Free from words and thoughts, returning to the source"

"Object is object because of the subject"

"Surrender with ease"

"In the ultimate freedom, there are no doctrines"

"Space illuminates itself"

"One moment is ten thousand years"

"One is inseparable from all"

"Go beyond past, present, and future."

(My translation of "Engraving Trust in the Heart" with Joan Halifax Rōshi is presented in the appendices.)

As you can see, Zen paradoxes are multifaceted. Zen gardens seem to be quite direct and straightforward; they are simple, full of negative space, and self-revealing. In contrast—or possibly because of all that—the thought behind them is so complex!

The Historical Emergence of Zen Gardens in Japan

Japanese Zen architecture developed under the direct influence of its Chinese predecessor. From the time when schools of Zen were introduced in the twelfth century, monks in Japan made considerable efforts to import floor plans from China, and they constructed their buildings with curved slate roofs with close and purposeful imitation.

One remarkable characteristic of Chinese temples and monastery buildings is that they are colorful, with yellow plaster walls and red—and sometimes green—painted wooden elements. The Mampuku Monastery in Uji, south of Kyōto, of the Ōbaku (Chinese Huangpo) School of Zen, which was founded by the Chinese monk Yinyuan Longqi (Japanese name Ingen Ryūki) in 1661, retains the Chinese style of that time, although its plaster walls are white.

Just as Japanese Zen practices evolved their own flavor over time, Zen architecture developed its own distinctive characteristics. For example, a majority of Japanese temple buildings used plain wood, probably influenced by the style of indigenous Shintō shrines. For walls, builders stuck to white plaster.

In terms of gardens, the Chinese examples tend to form a mysterious, out-of-this-world atmosphere. They emphasize artificiality with eccentric-shaped stones, such as slim standing ones like flames, which give the impression of defying gravity. Some of these stones feature round holes and wrinkles. Many of them come from hills near Lake Tai (Taihu) in Suzhou and are sometimes characterized as Taihu stones or scholars' stones. Japanese monks, by contrast, seem to have shown little interest in such stones with unreal shapes. They preferred the natural look of stable, solid rocks.

Whereas a great number of well-known gardens in Japan belong to Zen temples, most of the famous gardens in China are secular, commissioned either by imperial courts or literati. The Chan temples commonly have gardens, but the country does not seem to share the Japanese cultural tradition of visitors coming to enjoy them.

In the Heian Period (794–1185), a pre-Zen time in Japan, there was already an established art of garden design. Much of gardeners' thinking of this time was compiled in a comprehensive landscape instruction book called *Sakuteiki* (Notes of Garden-Making) by an unknown author, completed around the eleventh century. (There is a translation published as *Sakuteiki: Visions of the Japanese Garden* by Jirō Takei and Marc P. Keane, 2008.)

This period was a time when an elegant and indulgent court culture, centered in the capital city of Kyōto—also called Heian—flourished. The monarchy supported versions of Vajrayāna Buddhism that emphasized elaborate rituals praying for the well-being of elite, upper-class people. Aristocratic families commissioned large-scale gardens. There was also a prevalent sense of living in the Last Age of Dharma—a period that would see Buddhism decline and disappear—and a widespread belief in the Pure Land, a western paradise that would dissolve all sufferings after death. In the late Heian Period, temple designs reflected these Pure Land or the Western Paradise doctrines, where chanting the central deity Amitābha Buddha's name was the single-hearted practice. A temple would have a shrine of Amitābha Buddha to be viewed in the distant west of the gardens beyond ponds.

In 1185, the warrior class seized the military and political control of the nation and established a government in Kamakura, a remote region east of Mount Fuji on the Pacific, while keeping the imperial court's ceremonial authorities in Kyōto. This inaugurated the Kamakura Period (1185–1333). First, *shōguns* (commanding generals) of the Minamoto family ruled, then *shikkens* (regents) of the Hōjō family took over. It was during this period that Zen masters Myōan Eisai (1141–1215) and Eihei Dōgen (1200–1253) brought Zen teachings to Japan from China. Other monks followed and established the Rinzai School in Eisai's lineage and the Sōtō School in Dōgen's. During this time of political unrest and occasional battles, many *samurai* were attracted to Zen due to its intense discipline and its emphasis on the importance of fully facing life and death. *Samurai* leaders liked the fact that many Zen masters were independent of the conventional Buddhism that had been supported by the court establishment.

Tokiyori Hōjō (1227–1263), the fifth regent, was the first important national patron of Zen Buddhism. He invited Dōgen to Kamakura in 1248 and asked him to establish a national Zen monastery there. Dōgen declined, as he preferred his practice center in a quiet mountain area away from political concerns. Tokiyori then found a Chinese master, Lanxi Daolong (Japanese name, Rankei Dōryu, 1213–1278), who was already teaching Rinzai Zen in Japan, and made a similar request. Daolong was more accommodating and founded the Kenchō-ji in Kamakura as the top Zen monastery of Japan. Daolong is regarded as the designer of Japan's first Zen garden, established at the Kenchō-ji in 1253. Unfortunately, the monastery has been destroyed several times since then, and the original garden, along with any descriptions or drawings of it, has been lost. Nevertheless, this was one of the first occasions when prominent Rinzai monks were supported by the *samurai* government. This patronage led to the development of a notably refined Zen culture, including numerous Zen gardens cultivated in the ensuing centuries.

National Teacher Musō Soseki

ALTHOUGH, as we have seen, he was not the first to design one, Musō Soseki (1275–1351) is regarded as the person who established the practice of Zen gardening in Japan. Let's look in some detail at the politics of Japan during Soseki's lifetime, as they were quite turbulent and his work as a Zen teacher and designer of Zen gardens was very much connected to the ebb and flow of Japanese politics and warfare.

Soseki was born in Ise Province in 1275. His given name is unknown. His father is said to have been Tomotsuna Sasaki, a *samurai* of the Minamoto clan. When Soseki was four, his family moved to Kai Province, and his mother died shortly thereafter. He became a monk of the Vajrayāna Shingon School at age nine. Then when he was nineteen, he had a dream about becoming a Zen monk. (Musō means "Dream Window" and Soseki "Spread-out Stones.") In 1294, he became a student of Muin Empan (1230–1307) at the Kennin Monastery of the Rinzai School in Kyōto. In 1295 at age twenty-one, Soseki moved to Kamakura and studied with other masters of the Daolong lineage. Soseki visited the Kenchō-ji several times in later years and was acquainted with Daolong's garden in that monastery.

From 1299 to 1301 Soseki studied with Yining Yishan (Japanese name, Ichinei Issan, 1247–1317), the fifth abbot of the Kenchō-ji who was from China. One day Soseki said to Yishan, "I have not reached *kenshō* (realizing the essential human nature). I would like to request you to directly point to it." Yishan replied, "In my teaching there are no words and there is not a single dharma to give." Soseki further asked, "Please give me an expedient means with compassionate heart." Yishan said, "No expedient means. No compassionate heart." Soseki did not get it.

In 1303, Soseki went to study with Kōhō Kennichi (1241–1316) in Kamakura. Kennichi asked Soseki about his dialogue with Yishan and commented: "Why didn't you say to him, 'How come you have a lot of them?'" With this, Soseki had a glimpse of realization, but that was not enough. He traveled north and, in 1305 on his way to see Kennichi again, he sat under a tree in the garden and went into a hut. In darkness he wanted to lean on a wall but there was no wall and he fell over. He burst out laughing and wrote a poem:

For many years I was digging a hole to look for the sky,
accumulating mediocre hindrances.
One night, tiles and slates are blown up
leisurely crushing the bones of the void.

When he met with Kennichi, they exchanged some words. Then Kennichi stood up, joined his palms together, and bowed to Soseki, acknowledging that he had achieved enlightenment.

In 1307 Soseki had a painter create a portrait of Kennichi and brought it to him, asking him to write a comment (*san* 讃) above the master's image. Kennichi wrote:

Dropping away the body, nothing to depend upon,
sitting through the universe.
A black lacquered bamboo stick
commands buddhas and ancestors.
Attendant monk Seki turns aside
rolling a round stone one thousand feet down
with a dull hatchet in his hands.

"Attendant monk" in Zen is a senior disciple who keeps close to a master and takes care of all matters. "Seki" is an intimate way of referring to Soseki.

Soseki pointed to the word for "dull hatchet" and said, "A good boy wouldn't accept an old man's property." Kennichi then asked, "What do you give to yourself?" Soseki said, "A slap on your palm." Kennichi laughed and transmitted a robe to Soseki—so signifying his entire teaching—who was then thirty-three years old.

Soseki was a powerful calligrapher and an outstanding poet in Chinese style verse—poems written exclusively in ideograms with foot rhyming. Presenting poems in this style was at that time required in Zen rituals. Two books about him in English are *Bokutotsusō: Studies on the Calligraphy of the Zen Master Musō Soseki* by Ildegarda Scheidegger and *Sun at Midnight: Muso Soseki, Poems and Letters*, translated by W. S. Merwin and Soiku Shigematsu.

We can see, then, that Soseki was an elite Zen practitioner. He had studied with renowned Zen masters like Yining Yishan from China, abbot of the most highly respected monastery in Japan. And Soseki was a dharma heir of Kōhō Kennichi, who was a son of Emperor Gosaga and, though a prince, had chosen to become a "home-leaver" or monastic. Even beyond this impressive pedigree, though, there must have been something profound and inspiring about Soseki. He seems not to have been attached to any place, position, or status. Throughout his life, in fact, he tried to move away from reputable positions as soon as possible. Ironically, that led him to be even more sought after. He effortlessly drew many followers and donors, which made his numerous temple and garden buildings possible.

After his enlightenment was verified by Kennichi, Soseki went back to his home province of Kai, north of Mount Fuji, and founded the Jōgo Monastery. Preferring a solo retreat but finding that too many people wanted to study with him, he sneaked out of the monastery and went westward, eventually coming upon an ideally isolated place at the foot of Mount Nagase, Mino Province. The site had a large boulder with a small stream of water falling down over it. At this location he established a temple called the Eihō-ji, where he created a pond, built a bridge over it, and erected an Avalokiteshvara shrine. Again, people rushed to study with him, and so he left once more. In 1318 he engaged in a solo retreat in Tosa Province on Shikoku Island. From 1319 to 1321 he lived in a hut in Miura, near Kamakura. In 1323, he started building a hut in Kazusa Province.

Emperor Godaigo (1288–1339) learned about Soseki's reputation, and in 1325 he asked Soseki to be the abbot of the Nanzen-ji, the most prestigious Rinzai monastery in Kyōto. Soseki, then age fifty-one, declined at first, saying he was not well, but the emperor asked Takatoki Hōjō, the fourteenth regent of the Hōjō government in Kamakura, to convince him. Soseki eventually accepted the position. The emperor, who was well versed in many forms of art, met with Soseki to study dharma three times a month. Soseki does not seem to have been involved in any landscaping at that time.

In 1326, he resigned from the Nanzen-ji and founded the Zuisen'-in in Kamakura at the request of Dōun Nikaidō, a prominent warrior from Kai Province. It seems that conversations with his devoted patron opened up a new direction for him. Soseki was quite involved in garden-making at this temple. Having a waterfall was important to Soseki, but since there were not enough streams flowing on the property, he made a dam to store water and would release it when he had guests.

In 1329, at the repeated request of Takatoki Hōjō, Soseki assumed the position of abbot of the Engaku Monastery in Kamakura. This monastery had been founded by the regent Tokimune Hōjō in 1282 to console the spirits of soldiers on both sides killed during the Mongolian attacks of 1274 and 1281. Soseki's teacher Kōhō Kennichi had been abbot of the temple at one point.

But the following year Soseki stepped down from this honored position and founded the Erin-ji in Enzan, Kai Province—a temple once again sponsored by Dōun Nikaidō. Soseki was passionately involved in both temple and landscape building at the Erin-ji.

In 1331, Takatoki Hōjō once again requested that Soseki become an abbot, this time of the Kenchō Monastery, Kamakura, the top-ranking Zen temple in Japan, but he declined.

In the meantime, there had been a drastic shift in national politics. Emperor Godaigo wanted to take ruling authority back from the Kamakura government. Takauji Ashikaga, a Hōjō retainer who sided with the emperor, defeated Kamakura forces in Kyōto while Godaigo's other forces destroyed the Hōjō government, which brought the Kamakura Period to an end.

In the sixth month of 1333, Emperor Godaigo returned to Kyōto, where he immediately ordered Takauji to summon Soseki from Kamakura. He asked Soseki to resume his position at the Nanzen-ji. Soseki declined, citing sickness and old age. Godaigo said, "The rise of buddha dharma depends upon whether there is a suitable person or not. If you insist on your refusal, I will step down." Faced with something as momentous as the abdication of an emperor, Soseki acquiesced. Two months later, the emperor asked Soseki to reside at the Rinsen Monastery, in the Saga area, west of the capital city. The building had formerly been a palace of the Kameyama Villa, facing the Katsura River.

In 1334, Emperor Godaigo himself received a Buddhist robe from Soseki in the imperial palace and became his student. In 1335, the emperor formally gave the Rinsen Monastery to Soseki and made him the founder. He wrote a letter to bestow upon him the title of national teacher (*kokushi* 国師).

There were other Rinzai monks who had been given this title. For instance, Enni Ben'en, the founder of the Tōfuku-ji, was given the posthumous title of Shōichi Kokushi. But for Soseki to receive the title of national teacher while he was still alive marked recognition that Zen—still a relatively recent arrival in Japan—had achieved an unimaginably high status in the country, right in the midst of all the political upheavals.

Musō Soseki: The Landscaper

IN THE EIGHTH month of 1335, Takauji Ashikaga brought his troops to Kamakura to put down revolts of the remaining Hōjō forces. Afterward, he remained there, intending to initiate his own *samurai* government. In the eleventh month, Emperor Godaigo ordered his troops against Takauji. Takauji in response seized Kyōto in the sixth month of 1336. He concluded a truce with Godaigo, asking him to step down and installing Emperor Kōmyō in the eighth month. Thus, Takauji established his dominance and set up the Ashikaga government to rule the nation. (Later, the base of this government moved from Kamakura to Muromachi Street in Kyōto; therefore, the time in which the Ashikaga government ruled would come to be known as the Muromachi Period, which lasted from 1336 to 1573.) In the autumn of 1336, Takauji became a student of Soseki.

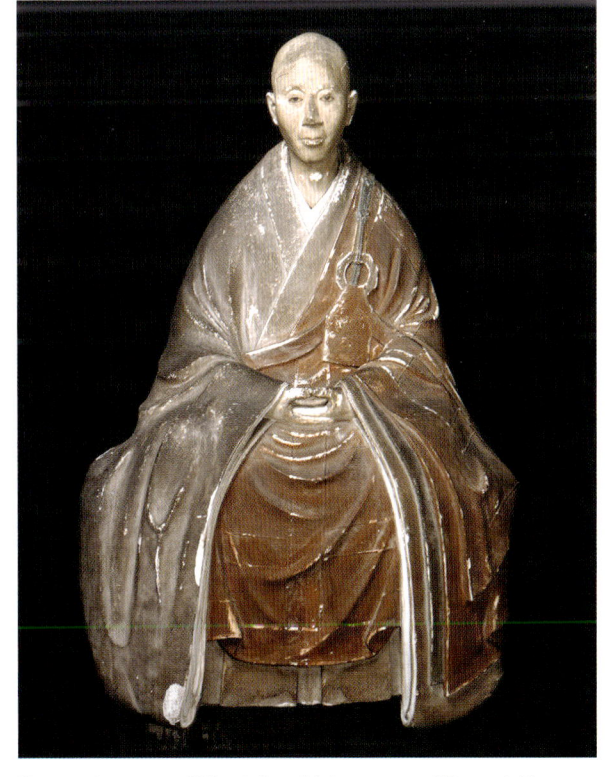

In the twelfth month of the same year, Godaigo, claiming to be still on the throne, moved to Yoshino, Kii Province, to the southeast of Kyōto, to establish his own court. This began an unprecedented era of two ruling emperors known as the Southern and Northern Dynasties Period, which would last for fifty-seven years. Soseki, along with innumerable others who loved Godaigo, must have been heartbroken.

In 1337, Soseki retired from his position at the Rinsen Monastery and began to reside in its subtemple, the Sanne-in. In 1338, Takauji Ashikaga was appointed *shōgun*.

In the following year, Chikahide Fujiwara, a key retainer of Takauji, asked Soseki to found a monastery called the Saihō-ji, which sits in an area that was then west of Kyōto, though

FIG. 4. A statue of Musō Soseki (courtesy of Tenryū-ji).

nowadays is inside the city border. Chikahide was the head priest of the large Matsuo Shintō Shrine, adjacent to two temples that were in disrepair and slated to be converted into the Saihō-ji. Soseki, receiving abundant funding and having access to high craftsmanship, was able to create what is now considered the first full-scale Zen garden. He built Chinese-style temple buildings connected by roofed walkways. He designed a pond called Ōgon Chi (Gold Pond) and a passage around it. Envoys from China and Korea later recorded the beauty of the garden in their journals. But they were not aware of its truly stunning upper part, which was reserved for residential practitioners.

A waterfall is symbolic of Zen practice. The *Blue Cliff Record,* a collection of one hundred *kōans* compiled in China during the Song Period by Xuedou Zhongxian (980–1052) with commentary by Yuanwu Keqin (1063–1135), mentions in Case Eighteen: "Waves in three stages are high, a fish turns into a dragon." This *kōan* is based on a legend of a carp that swims up a waterfall and turns into a dragon. This became a metaphor of a common Zen practitioner turning into an extraordinary one—a dragon who flies freely in the sky.

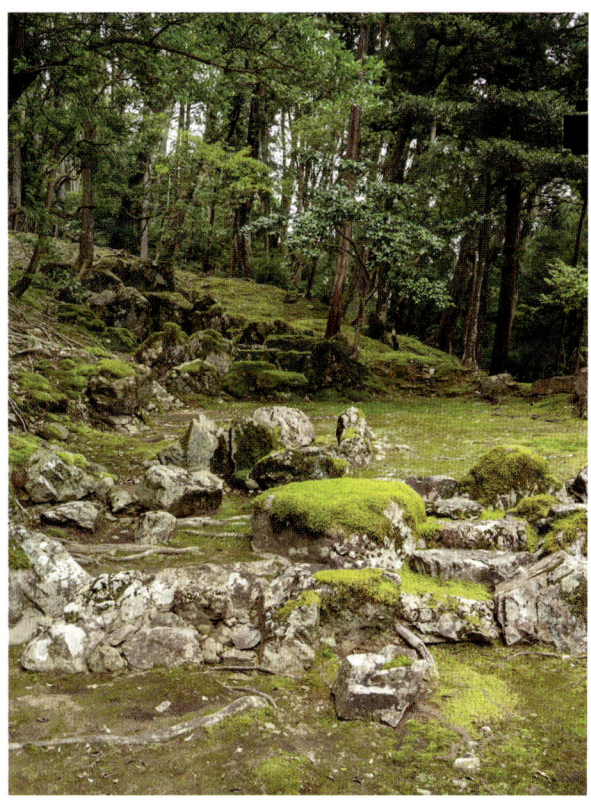

Fig. 5. Dry waterfall, Saihō-ji

Soseki, as we have seen, loved having a waterfall in his gardens, but the northern terrain of the Saihō-ji was mild and there was no possibility of building one. So he turned this limitation around into a breakthrough solution: he would build a waterfall with no water! He set out three stages of stones, with larger stones in higher sections. He called this Ryūmonbaku 龍門瀑, meaning "Dragon Gate Splashes" or "Dragon Gate Waterfall." Near the bottom of the waterfall, there is a *rigyo seki* 鯉魚石, meaning "carp stone." There must have been white sand to represent water. (Since the eighteenth century, a great variety of mosses have covered the entire garden, and now this temple is known as the Koke Dera, or Moss Temple.) The garden also has some *zazen seki* 坐禅石, or "sitting meditation stones," for a master and student to use to meditate and investigate the dharma together. (See "Stone Formations: Dry Waterfall, Saihō-ji" in the appendices.)

This stone formation at the Saihō-ji is regarded as Zen's first *kare sansui* 枯山水, literally meaning "withered mountain and water," usually translated as "dry landscape." From 1339 on, stone formations became central to Japanese Zen garden design, which marked a departure from the traditional style with a pond with an encircling path (*kaiyūshiki teien* 廻遊式庭園). The format influenced the design of other key Zen gardens such as those at the Tenryū-ji, the Rokuon-ji or Golden Pavilion Temple, and the Jishō-ji or Silver Pavilion Temple.

In 1339, the same year that Soseki became the founder of the Saihō-ji, Emperor Godaigo passed away in Yoshino, far away from Kyōto. Also in the same year Shōgun Takauji, who had been remorseful for having fought with Godaigo and thus causing the emperor to flee from the capital city, wanted to build a monastery to console Godaigo's raging spirit. He asked Soseki to lead the project.

In 1340, construction of a new monastery started on the vast, formerly imperial Kameyama Villa where Godaigo had spent most of his youth. It is across the street from the Rinsen-ji. In the following year, former emperor Kōgen named it Tenryū Shisei Zen Monastery. Donations were not enough to fund the construction, so the government allowed trade to resume with Song Dynasty China to raise revenue, granting rights to the temple to send two trading ships each year to China. The first "Tenryū-ji Boat" set

FIG. 6.
Tenryū-ji

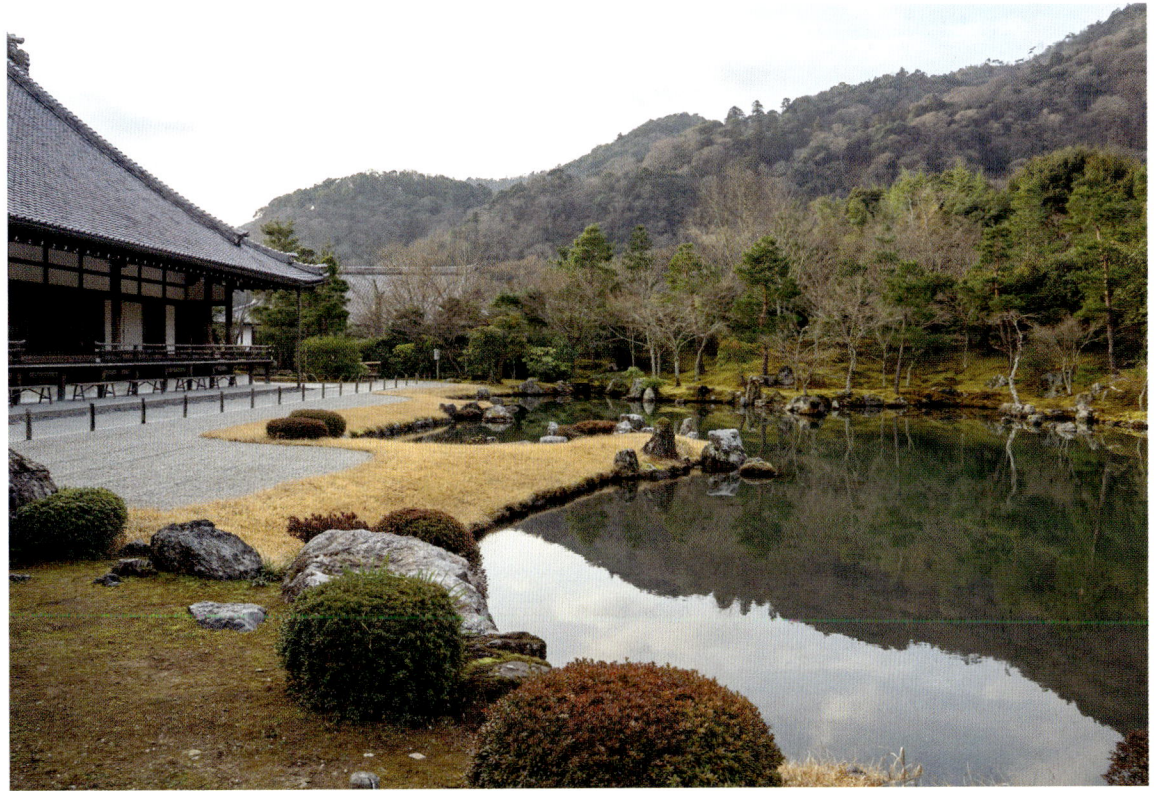

sail in 1342, and this arrangement lasted another 120 years. When the construction of the dharma hall was completed, Soseki conducted a ceremony for the seventh memorial year of Godaigo in 1345, with the former emperor Kōgen in attendance.

Up to this point, Soseki had been building gardens exclusively to aid Zen monastics, but he now began thinking of welcoming lay visitors. With that in mind, he selected ten scenic sites at the monastery in 1346.

In the same year, Emperor Kōmyō became Soseki's student and bestowed upon him an unprecedented second national teacher title: Shōkaku (Authentic Enlightenment) Kokushi. Shōgun Takauji Ashikaga made the Tenryū-ji the first of the highest ranking Five Mountains following the Nanzen-ji, which had been above the Five Mountains. (See the section on "Five Mountains," for more on this.)

While the main buildings in most Zen monasteries face south, most of those at the Tenryū-ji face east, due to the shape of the land. The large *hōjō* faces the west. The view from there includes a pond, many trees, and a stone waterfall formation that in Soseki's time would have had running water. Soseki planted cherry trees from Yoshino, Godaigo's final dwelling place. The Tenryū-ji has amazing background scenery (*shakkei* 借景, literally meaning "borrowed scenery") with a low peak of Mount Arashi. Soseki named the pond Sōgen (Caoxi Source) Pond, after the phrase "a drop of water from the source of Caoxi," where the Sixth Chinese Ancestor Huineng taught. There is a path around the pond with a bridge. Soseki had access to the finest artisans for this garden and was able to bring in huge blue stones from Shikoku Island.

The Tenryū-ji garden represents not only the peak of Soseki's career as a landscape designer but also the peak in the history of Zen garden-making. Given its immense beauty, he must have intended to create a landscape of the western Pure Land for the deceased emperor.

Though perhaps most remembered today for his gardens, Soseki is also known for his Zen teachings. His series of dialogues with Tadayoshi Ashikaga, who was the chief associate of his brother Shōgun Takauji, seem to have taken place after Tadayoshi became Soseki's student in 1349. Tadayoshi asked ninety-one profound dharma questions, and Soseki, with kindness and thoroughness, extensively elucidated the dharma in his replies. These dialogues were later published as *Muchū Mondō* (Questions and Answers in Dreams). There is an English translation of this monumental work by Thomas Yūhō Kirchner called *Dialogues in a Dream: The Life and Zen Teachings of Musō Soseki*.

About garden-making, Soseki said in this dialogue, "Some people wake up with mountains and waters [meaning a "garden" in this case], easing boredom, and use them to help their practice of the way. This is precious, as it is different from those who merely love mountains and waters. But they are not genuine practitioners of the way because they separate mountains and waters from the practice of the way." In other words, for Soseki, garden-making and maintenance were no other than the practice of dharma itself, and the two activities should not be separated from each other.

The monks' hall at the Tenryū-ji was completed in 1351. Former emperor Kōgen gave Soseki the third national teacher title Shinsō (Heart Source) Kokushi, acknowledging that Soseki was truly his guiding master. Soseki also gave the precepts to 1,200 monastics and laypeople.

On the thirtieth day, the ninth month of that year, 1351, Soseki assembled the monks at the Sanne-in of the Rinsen-ji to bid them farewell and passed away on the same day at the age of seventy-seven. Later, four emperors posthumously conferred on Soseki further national teacher titles, in addition to the three he had received in his lifetime. In that way, he has been called the teacher of seven emperors.

Stone Works

THERE ARE FOUR principal elements for garden-making. These are water (*mizu* 水), stones (*ishi* 石), planted material (*shokusai* 植栽), and additional objects for the scenery (*keibutsu* 景物) such as bridges, lanterns, and basins. In Zen gardens, stone placement is primary.

One of Soseki's Chinese-style poems says:

> When no dust forms a peak
> not a drop of water is in the waterfall.
> While a wind blows there is a bright moon night.
> One who is within plays within.

This verse is titled "Tone of *Kare Sansui*." He wrote *kare sansui* as 仮山水, which may be translated as "disguised landscape." Soseki suggests with this verse that only a pure heart can form a mountain peak. There can be a waterfall even with no water. A full moon, symbolizing enlightenment, may exist in the midst of worldly activities. And "one who is within" is someone who contemplates deeply.

There is a story that the mother of Takatoki Hōjō, the fourteenth regent of the Kamakura government, sent a *waka* (a thirty-one-syllable poem) to Soseki asking for guidance.

> Wishing to wait
> for a mountain pass,
> but it has disappeared.
> Even if we don't abandon it
> the world is within a dream.

He replied.

> Abandon the world
> of suffering

27

which you regard as being in a dream,
and hide in a mountain
that is not a mountain.

Perhaps only a Zen master and landscape-maker like Soseki could write such a poem. "A mountain that is not a mountain" must be a stone in a garden functioning as a mountain. Soseki's advice to this highly positioned lady could well be that she free herself from worldly affairs and live in a small hut with a small garden: a whole universe may be found even in one stone.

At the Saihō-ji, in the upper part of the garden Soseki set a group of stones seen as the Nine Mountains and Eight Seas around Mount Sumeru (Shumisen 須弥山), regarded as the center of the world according to ancient Indian mythology. Not far down from the waterfall stones is another group of stones representing a turtle—an animal believed to live for ten thousand years—which may be seen as representing the timelessness of meditation at each moment. Also, a group of stones called *sanzon seki* (三尊石, meaning "triad stones"), symbolizing three Buddhist deities, is found at the southeastern edge of the Gold Pond. In Zen schools, a common symbolic triad consists of Shākyamuni Buddha in the center accompanied by Mañjushrī Bodhisattva and Samantabhadra Bodhisattva.

Stones are silent, still, and plain. It's all up to those who place the stones and the viewers to imagine anything from them. *Sakuteiki*, the eleventh-century book of garden-making, had already talked about stones as islands, mountains, and birds. It even mentioned triad stones. (See "Stone Formations" in the appendices.)

Stones have individual energy and character that make each one unique. Garden-makers of later generations after Soseki developed a great variety of symbolism and even further references to Zen teachings. Each garden has its own background, as we will see in the anecdotes in part two of this book.

When sufficient water is not available for water elements, an ocean, a lake, or a river is often represented in Zen gardens by sand, which is raked in circular lines around rocks and straight lines on flat areas. These marks, called *samon* (砂紋) or "sand patterns," represent the raker's mindscape. The viewer studying these traces can experience a sense of the raker's state of concentration.

Five Mountains

CHINA'S HIGHEST-RANKING Zen monasteries, referred to as the "Five Mountains," are situated in Zhejiang Province. This province had a port called Mingzhou (present-day Ningbo), sheltering the boats that sailed to and from Japan. As a result, monks from Japan studied mostly in this province. The Five Mountains that were developed in Japan are modeled after the Chinese ones.

Sadatoki Hōjō, the ninth regent of the Kamakura government, is regarded as the one who established the Japanese system of the Five Mountains in 1299, which included monasteries in Kamakura and Kyōto.

When political power shifted from Kamakura back to Kyōto in 1333, the ancient capital city became the center of the Rinzai School of Zen. Emperor Godaigo then reconstituted the Five Mountains, with the Nanzen-ji as well as the Daitoku-ji as the leading monasteries.

Later, in 1341, Takauji Ashikaga, the first *shōgun* of the Muromachi government, set the Five Mountains as:

1. Nanzen-ji, Kyōto, and Kenchō-ji, Kamakura
2. Tenryū-ji, Kyōto, and Engaku-ji, Kamakura
3. Jufuku-ji, Kamakura
4. Kennin-ji, Kyōto
5. Tōfuku-ji, Kyōto

(At the time of Takauji, the Kamakura Zen monasteries were still as important as those in Kyōto. That was why he mixed these ratings.) Later in 1346, Takauji made the Nanzen-ji above the Five Mountains and the Tenryū-ji at the top of the Five Mountains, as mentioned earlier.

Yoshimitsu Ashikaga (1358–1408), the third *shōgun* and grandson of Takauji, founded the Shōkoku-ji in 1382 in the northern vicinity of the imperial palace in Kyōto as the family temple of the Ashikaga clan, with the legendary Musō Soseki honored as a posthumous founder. Yoshimitsu built a seven-storied octagonal pagoda in the compound—the highest building in Japan at that time—and wanted the Shōkoku-ji to be a part of the Five Mountains.

With that in mind, in 1386 Yoshimitsu revised the Five Mountains system in Kyōto. The highest, above all others, came the Nanzen-ji. Then there followed:

1. Tenryū-ji
2. Shōkoku-ji
3. Kennin-ji
4. Tōfuku-ji
5. Manju-ji

This order of rank has been fixed ever since. (See "Zen Temples in Kyōto Selected" and "Map of Zen Temples in Kyōto" in the appendices.)

By this time, the Rinzai School had gained exclusive patronage of the ruling class and was, in turn, controlled by the rulers. Its monasteries were all officially or governmentally sanctioned, with abbots appointed by the emperors based on recommendations by the *shōguns*. Somehow, our master Musō Soseki lived right at the time of the Five Mountains reclassifications but stayed free of such political maneuvering.

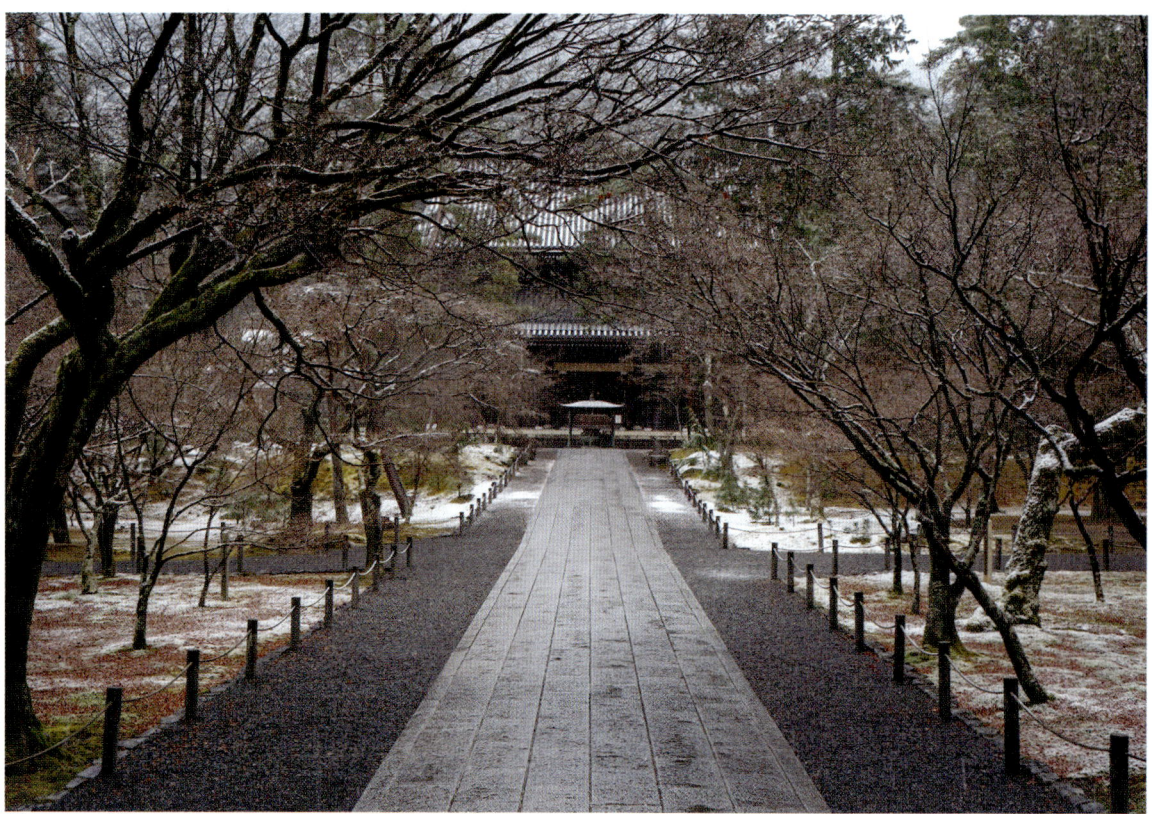

Fig. 7. Nanzen-ji

The Golden and Silver Pavilions

BUILDING AN IDEAL place to reside may be a dream for many, but few can turn it into reality. Yoshimitsu Ashikaga could, because he had accumulated great wealth through trade with Ming Dynasty China.

After his father Yoshiakira was assassinated, Yoshimitsu became the third *shōgun* of the Ashikaga clan at age ten in 1368. He received a dharma robe from Shun'oku Myōha (1312–1388), abbot of the Tenryū-ji, in the same year. He then studied Zen with Gidō Shūshin (1325–1388), a dharma heir of Soseki.

Yoshimitsu strengthened the power of the government and, in 1378, moved its headquarters to the Flower Palace on Muromachi Street at Imadegawa Street, northwest of the imperial palace, which was the exact center of Kyōto. In addition to having founded the Shōkoku-ji in 1382, as mentioned on page 29, he also established Rokuon'-in as its subtemple so that he could practice Zen there in the following year. He asked Zekkai Chūshin (1336–1405), also an heir of Soseki, to be the abbot of the Rokuon'-in and his teacher. (This temple is different from the later-built Rokuon-ji or the Golden Pavilion Temple.)

Yoshimitsu negotiated with the Southern Dynasty emperor and unified the imperial system in 1392. In 1394, at age thirty-seven, he was appointed prime minister, the highest position at court. In the same year, he retired and let his son Yoshimochi succeed to the position of *shōgun* at age nine. In 1395 Yoshimitsu became a Zen monk with the ordained name Dōgi.

Two years later, in 1397, Yoshimitsu purchased the Kitayama Tei (North Mountain Palace) for his residence and Zen practice. It had been the mountain villa of Kintsune Saionji (1171–1242), a courtier of the highest rank, who had served as regent. Though well known for its beauty, it had fallen into serious disrepair.

Yoshimitsu was fully involved in the design and construction of the palace, centering a pond surrounded by a circular path. This marked the beginning of what is now known as the Kinkaku-ji (Golden Pavilion Temple). Thus, it is unlike the earlier Zen architecture and gardens that had been constructed to support Zen monastic training.

The garden at this palace of splendor expresses the Pure Land in this world, merging the elegant taste of Heian Period court nobles and the Zen taste of the *samurai* clans of Yoshimitsu's time. His living quarters in the north and his wife Nariko's quarters in the south were built out in courtiers' living quarters style (*shinden zukuri* 寝殿造). The Golden Pavilion itself combines three styles—an Amitābha shrine with an aristocratic style on the first floor, a *samurai* residence style on the second, and a Zen-style relic shrine on the top. Outside, there is an actual waterfall with a large carp stone at its foot.

This was a time of great flourishing of the arts. With Yoshimitsu's patronage, Kan'ami Kiyotsugu (1333–1384) and his son Ze'ami Motokiyo (1363–1443) developed the art of the *Noh* play (能楽). *Suiboku-ga* (水墨画, or Chinese-style ink painting, also called *sumi-e*) became a practice of Zen monks, including Josetsu (dates unknown) and later his student Sesshū Tōyō (1420–1506?), who would be a celebrated painter and landscaper. They both trained at the Shōkoku-ji. Yoshimitsu's tenure cultivating a variety of arts and crafts is nowadays characterized as the Kitayama (North Mountain) culture.

In 1407, in preparation for a visit by Emperor Gokomatsu in the following year, Yoshimitsu started constructing thirteen buildings at the Kitayama Tei. The imperial abode would consist of eight buildings with golden dragons on top and sand of five colors on the ground. A tall seven-storied pagoda for that compound was completed that year.

Fɪɢ. 8.
Kinkaku-ji

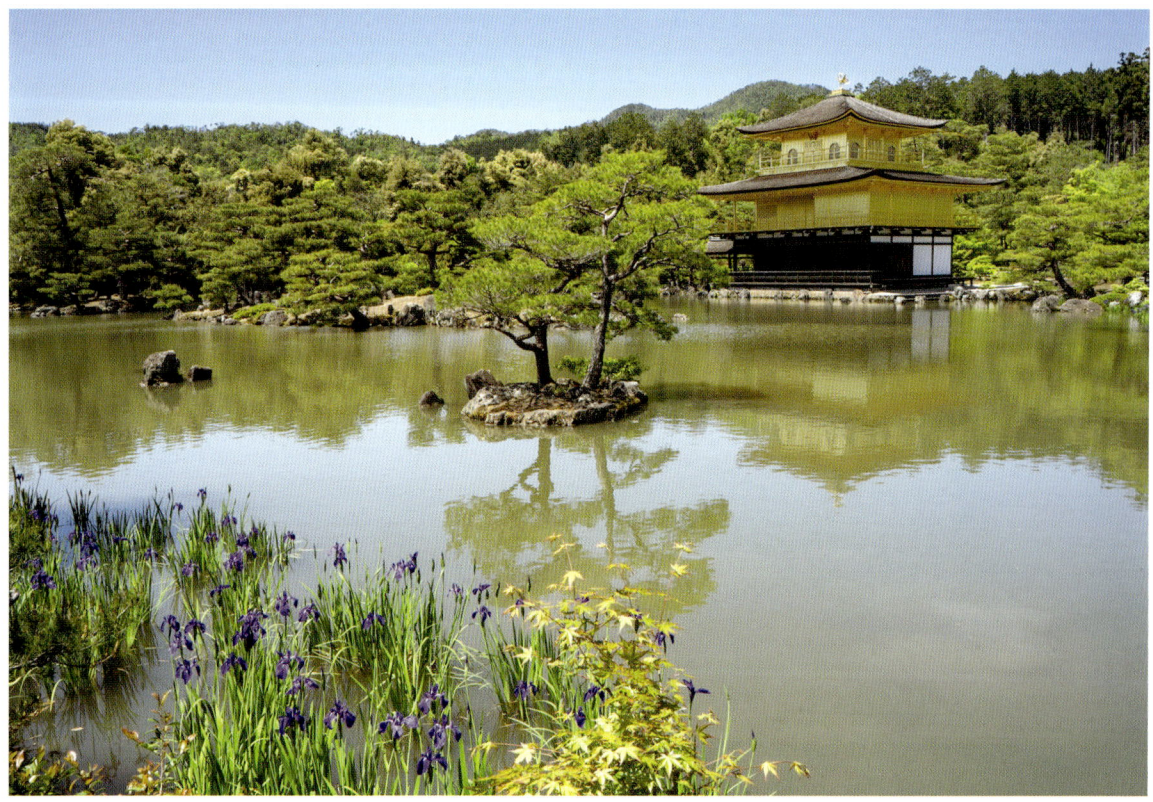

Yoshimitsu willed that after his death this palace become a Zen temple to be named Rokuon-ji (Deer Garden Temple), as a subtemple of the Shōkoku-ji. He died in 1408 at age fifty-one.

Over eighty years later, and mimicking his grandfather's Kitayama Tei with its Golden Pavilion on a pond, Yoshimasa Ashikaga (1436–1490), the eighth *shōgun*, intended to build an East Mountain Palace with a pavilion on a pond.

Yoshimasa assumed the position of *shōgun* in 1443 at age eight. He started his actual rule of the nation at age fourteen. There ensued a number of power struggles among the clans of provincial *samurai* lords (*daimyō* 大名). Yoshimasa intervened aggressively but gradually started losing his control. From 1459 on, a number of disasters occurred, including famines, epidemics, and fires. The most devastating was the famine of 1461, in which many thousands of people starved to death. The shores of the Kamo River running through Kyōto were filled with dead bodies to the point of damming the stream. Revolting farmers threatened the government.

In 1467, the War of Ōnin Era broke out between lords of the western side of Japan, including Kyōto, and those of the eastern side. In 1473, with the war ongoing, Yoshimasa retired from the *shōgun* position and installed his nine-year-old son Yoshihisa to succeed him. Yoshimasa retained his power and influence with the government, but the young Yoshihisa would not listen to him.

In 1476 many buildings in the capital city, including the government palace on Muromachi Street, burned down. *Ōnin Ki* (Journal of Ōnin Era) says, "How is it that the blooming capital has been run over by foxes and wolves? Both buddha's law and king's law are destroyed. All schools of Buddhism have perished." The former emperor Gohanazono and Emperor Gotsuchimikado were evacuated from their palaces and lived with Yoshimasa, partying nightly. Yoshimasa at times got drunk in front of them. The war continued, but finally with the leaders of both sides dead, the war ended in 1477.

From 1480 on, Yoshimasa visited the Rokuon-ji, the former North Mountain Palace, every year for several years. The compound had been largely destroyed, but the Golden Pavilion was still standing. In 1482 he started building his own palace, now known as the Ginkaku-ji or the Silver Pavilion Temple. The national economy was in peril, but he managed to collect onetime taxes on properties owned by courtiers, temples, and Shintō shrines. He also mobilized labor by pressing commoners into service. In 1483, Yoshimasa moved into the palace while it was still under construction. In 1485, he became a Zen monk, and in 1486, Tōgu-dō, his residential area, was completed.

The garden of the East Mountain, on the foot of one of the East Mountains of Kyōto, overlooks the capital city. A two-storied pavilion facing east on a pond enshrines a

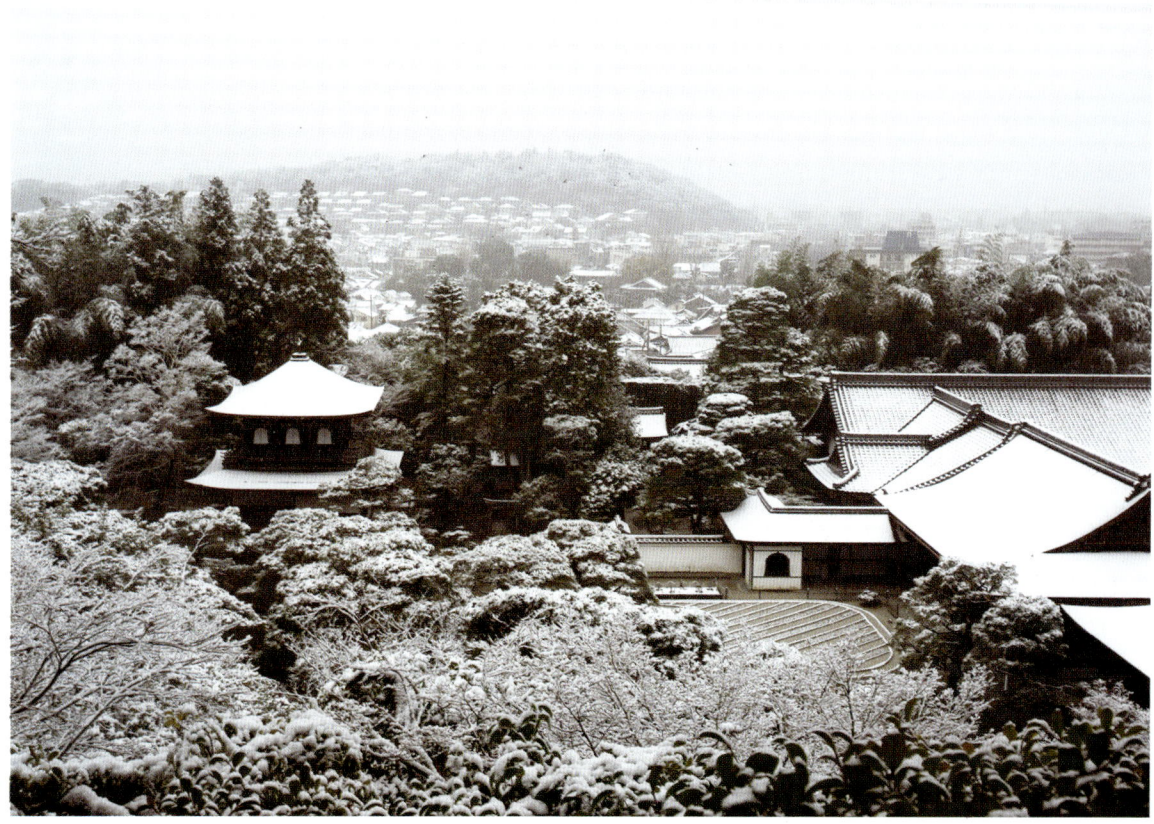

FIG. 9.
Ginkaku-ji

statue of Avalokiteshvara. (See "Garden Plan Example: The Ginkaku-ji" in the appendices.) A recent scientific study found that all sides were originally painted with black lacquer, but there is no trace of silver-leafing on the original pavilion. Nevertheless, people starting calling it the Silver Pavilion in the seventeenth century in comparison with the Golden Pavilion.

For the main buildings, Yoshimasa employed the *samurai*'s reception-room style (*shoin zukuri* 書院造). There were some additional pavilions, though the land is only one-seventh of the size of the plot for his grandfather's palace. The Tōgu-dō has four rooms, including Yoshimasa's personal Buddha hall (the size of eight mats), as well as his study (the size of four-and-a-half mats), which was to become a model for tea rooms in later times. We can see his preference for narrow space and subdued aesthetics, characterized as *wabi* (a simple, quiet, and austere quality).

Yoshimasa was surrounded by gifted lower-class art-stylist monks called *dōbōshū* 同朋衆 (literally meaning "equal companions"), who advised him on the selection of artworks for his huge collection. They also set up his rooms with scrolls and flowers, as well as served tea in a simple but exquisite manner. One of them, Zen'ami (1386?–

1482?), was known for his skills in designing gardens. Yoshimasa also sponsored Masanobu Kanō (1434–1506), founder of the Kanō School of painting. Although a total failure as a ruler and working with limited resources, Yoshimasa was able to pull together architectural and landscaping magic that has endured throughout time with his mastery in a variety of arts and his high taste.

The arts and crafts of the middle Muromachi Period are now characterized as constituting the Higashiyama (East Mountain) Culture, though not all artists associated with it had contact with Yoshimasa. For instance, Shukō Murata (1422–1502), a Pure Land School monk who was the original proponent of the *wabi* tea ceremony (*wabi cha* 侘茶), was active in Nara. Likewise, the Zen monk Sesshū Tōyō, who established a style of Japanese ink painting with much empty space (*yohaku* 余白), lived at this point in his life in the western end of the Main Island. Neither Shukō nor Sesshū had direct contact with the East Mountain Palace, center of the seasoned and subdued aesthetics (*kotanbi* 枯淡美), which ran through that time.

Donald Keene concludes his book *Yoshimasa and the Silver Pavilion: The Creation of the Soul of Japan* by saying:

> Yoshimasa may have been the worst shogun ever to rule Japan. . . . (But) we may even be tempted to conclude that no man in the history of Japan had a greater influence on the formation of Japanese taste. This was his sole, but very important, redeeming feature. The worst of the shoguns was the best, the only one to leave a lasting heritage for the entire Japanese people.

In 1489 Yoshimasa's successor and only son, Yoshihisa, died at age twenty-five. In 1490, Yoshimasa died at age fifty-five before the completion of his palace. Following his wishes, the East Mountain Palace was converted to the Zen Jishō-ji, a subtemple of the Shōkoku-ji, with Musō Soseki as an honorary posthumous founder.

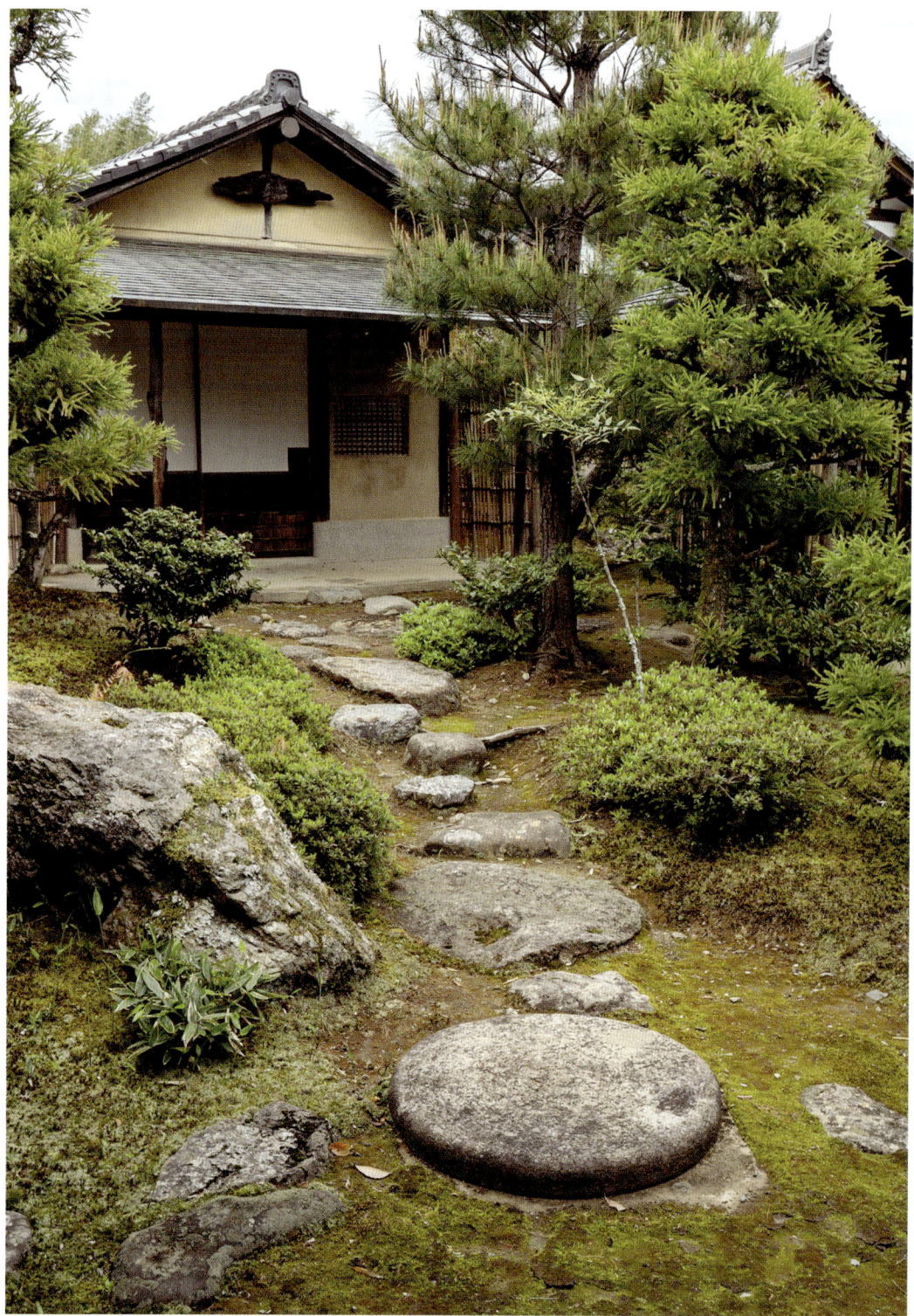

Fig. 10. Tenryū-ji

Condensed Space in Tea Ceremony

EMPEROR HANAZONO (1297–1348) preceded Godaigo. A legend has it that once, after he had abdicated his throne in 1318, he wanted to receive teachings from the renowned monk Shūhō Myōchō (1282–1337), who was living under the Gojō Bridge in Kyōto. Hanazono sent a messenger to look for him. The messenger, who knew Myōchō loved melons, showed one to a flock of beggars and said, "Come without a foot and get it." A beggar said, "Give it without a hand." The messenger identified him as Myōchō, dragged him to the palace, and brought him to Hanazono.

Hanazono said, "How auspicious—the Buddha's law meets the king's law." Myōchō said, "How auspicious—the king's law meets the Buddha's law." Hanazono was impressed and asked Myōchō to found the Daitoku-ji. Thus it is said, the Daitoku Monastery, established in 1325, became one of the most important Zen monasteries. Near the end of his life, in 1337, Myōchō recommended his successor Kanzan Egen (1277–1360) found another important training center, the Myōshin-ji.

At the Daitoku-ji, some subtemples developed inside the compound (*keidai tatchū* 境内塔頭). Now there are twenty-four subtemples, each with its own history. While the main buildings of the monastery are in the Chinese style, the buildings of these subtemples are in the Japanese style. As each subtemple at the Daitoku-ji was squeezed in, each compound had limited space so their gardens were designed to be viewed from inside the building, usually a small abbot's quarters. Thus, a style of small garden with a condensed landscape developed. You might see another Zen paradox here: the smaller the space, the vaster the scenery the gardener can create for viewers to enjoy.

Perhaps the individual most closely associated with the Daitoku-ji is Rikyū Sen (1522–1591). He lived there as a layperson during the Azuchi-Momoyama Period (1573–1600) after the collapse of the Muromachi government in 1573. This was still a time of warring states, but later when things had settled somewhat, Rikyū, who had the most influence on the practice of the *wabi* tea ceremony, served Hideyoshi Toyotomi (1537–1598), who unified Japan for a short time. As Rikyū was closely associated with the Daitoku-ji, this monastery became the center of tea ceremony. Some of the best-known tea rooms and tea gardens are found in the subtemples of the Daitoku-ji.

There are two major styles of tea rooms or tea houses: *shoin* style (as mentioned above, a *samurai* audience room style) and *sōan* (grass hut) style. A tea garden is called *roji* 露地, literally meaning "bare ground." The garden is meant to lead the guests to an egalitarian social gathering in elegant isolation. It typically has a fence, gate, plants, and stepping stones; a handwashing area, called *tsukubai* 蹲居, literally meaning "squatting," with a basin often made of stone and a wooden dipper ready to be used; a stone lantern; and a bench for waiting in a tiny space. In the past, there was a place to set swords down.

A tea room may have a small square entrance called a *nijiri guchi* 躙口, literally meaning a "bending over entrance." The room is simple and small—the size of four-and-a-half *tatami* mats is most common. Invited guests enter one by one, sit formally facing the central alcove called a *toko no ma* 床の間, literally meaning "(slightly higher) floor space." It holds a simple flower arrangement, and a scroll of calligraphy, usually by a Zen master, is installed in the center. The guests one by one bow to the scroll and appreciate the presence of the master, whether alive or not.

The first guest is seated closest to the *toko no ma*, and the next guests line up from there. Then, the host comes in from the *mizuya* 水屋, the preparation room, greets the guests, and starts making tea and then serving sweets and tea, again one by one. All the tea-whisking and serving movements are refined and ceremonial, which the guests enjoy watching. The first guest asks about the scroll, utensils, or flowers and leads a refined conversation. After everyone is served, the first guest asks the host to prepare to wrap up the gathering, which is also done ceremonially. The host finally thanks the guests and retires to the *mizuya*. The guests greet the scroll one by one again and exit the room.

The basic principles of tea ceremony are harmony, respect, purity, and serenity. A famous saying associated with the tea ceremony—*ichigo ichie* 一期一会, meaning "one lifetime, one meeting"—means to enjoy each moment of each gathering as something that only occurs once in a lifetime.

Seven Characteristics of Zen Art

ZEN GARDENS preceded a variety of Zen arts and helped shape them. In turn, by examining Zen arts, we can gain a deeper understanding of Zen gardens.

Ze'ami, who established the *Noh* play and was a great dramaturgist, spoke about *yūgen* 幽玄, meaning "subtle and profound." He emphasized silent and still space (*ma* 間) in the midst of music and dance. The stage he created for *Noh* was a plain wooden structure with a passageway called a *hashi gakari* 橋掛り, meaning "bridge way." In the center was a painting of an old pine tree, signifying anytime, anywhere, while the actor chants the location and the situation. *Noh* masks are simple but show different emotions according to the angle at which they are held. The actor's brocade robe is brilliant, yet works well in a quiet setting. Props are minimal.

Rikyū Sen was innovative in the tea ceremony, looking for something new and genuine all the time. For example, he took notice of a type of commonplace Korean bowl for eating rice called *ido jawan* 井戸茶碗 (Ido-type bowls), which was poorly produced with exterior cracks and some distorted shape. Recognizing in this innocent production the transcendence of perfection and imperfection, he put such bowls highest on the list of his utensil collection.

Bashō Matsuo (1644–1694) established the genre of poetry known as *haiku*, although he called it *hokku*. (The word *haiku* has been widely used since the late nineteenth century.) Bashō did not set down his own poetic theory, but his words were recorded and discussed by his students. He used such normally negative words as *lonely* (*wabi* 侘), *rusty* (*sabi* さび), *withering* (*shiori* 撓), *thin* (*hosomi* 細み), and *lightweight* (*karumi* 軽み) in a positive way. I would characterize *wabi* as a "simple, quiet, and austere quality," *sabi* as a "seasoned quality," *shiori* as a "fading quality," *hosomi* as a "fine-thread awareness," and *karumi* as an "artless and effortless quality."

Shin'ichi Hisamatsu, in his book *Zen to Bijutsu* (Zen and Fine Arts, 1976), speaks of Zen aesthetics with seven characteristics: asymmetry (*fukinsei* 不均斉), simplicity (*kanso* 簡素), loftiness (*kokō* 枯高), naturalness (*shizen* 自然), subtle profundity (*yūgen* 幽玄), unworldliness (*datsuzoku* 脱俗), and serenity (*seijaku* 静寂). These are all accurate, and this is a very helpful pioneering analysis. Hisamatsu says, "The fine arts of Zen must embody these seven characteristics fully harmonized as one."

I myself also wanted to explore seven characteristics with terms actually used by early Zen masters. I believe this is an authentic way to understand aspects of Zen art. The terms I landed on are direct (*tanteki* 端的), ordinary (*buji* 無事), vigorous (*kappatsu-patsu* 活潑々), gleaming (*jakushō* 寂照), pivotal (*daiyū* 大用), nondual (*funi* 不二), and inexhaustible (*mujinzō* 無盡蔵).

I see these as inner qualities of Zen aesthetics, manifestations of awakening. Awakening, as I suggested in my earlier book *Painting Peace*, is to realize the infinite value of each moment of your own life as well as of others (including things), then to continue to act accordingly.

Understanding these qualities may be helpful for the appreciation and creation of poetry, prose, and music, as well as visual and performing arts. It can also be applied to daily activities beyond art.

Part Two
Aesthetics and Stories

THE PHOTOGRAPHS on the right-hand pages hereafter show characteristics of Zen and its aesthetics. Although we have selected photographs that strongly demonstrate the concept profiled by each section, the scenes that follow embody all the seven characteristics of Zen art—upon examination, you can find any of them in any of the photos.

Zen terms for these characteristics have particular nuances and historical associations that often differ from their primary English-language connotations. So, in order to convey the richness of the words in the context of their Japanese and Chinese Zen literary background, at the beginning of each section I will present the romanized form of the Japanese word, its Japanese form, and a brief explanation of the word as well as some examples of Zen sayings that use it or point toward its aesthetics. These characteristics all contain ambiguity and paradoxes. That means that the opposite characterization is also true. For instance, when there is something direct, there is also something indirect, and the ordinary can be special.

The masters whose Zen sayings I am quoting will be briefly identified in the appendices (p. 129).

On each of the left-hand pages in this part of the book, you will see another photograph, accompanied by stories of the temple and gardens closely or remotely related to the right-hand detail.

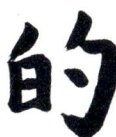

Direct
tanteki

IN ZEN, *direct* means there is nothing in between; nothing separates the viewer and the viewed. Intellectual analysis or explanations may not be helpful. Instead, just see whatever arises as it is and experience its essence intimately.

A monk asked Zhaozhou, "What is the meaning of Bodhidharma coming from India?"

The master replied, "The cypress tree in the garden."

—ZHAOZHOU

Not knowing is most intimate.

—DIZANG

When intimate language encounters an intimate person, the buddha eye sees the unseen. Intimate action is not known by self or other, but the intimate self alone knows it. Each intimate other goes beyond understanding. Since intimacy surrounds you, it is fully intimate, half intimate.

—DŌGEN

When you paint spring, do not paint willows, plums, peaches, or apricots—just paint spring. To paint willows, plums, peaches, or apricots is to paint willows, plums, peaches, or apricots. It is not yet painting spring.

—DŌGEN

1-1 *Shisen-dō*

This stone (→), surrounded by straight and circular patterns of sand, sits in solitude in the north garden of a temple with a unique name.

The Shisen-dō, or Poetic Sages Hall, is one of the rare Sōtō School temples in Kyōto. The majority of the Zen temples in the city belong to the Rinzai School, which flourished with the support of *shōguns* in the Muromachi Period. The official temple name is the Shisen-dō Jōzan-ji, named after its founder Jōzan Ishikawa (1583–1672). Jōzan was an aristocratic warrior who contributed to the establishment of Ieyasu Tokugawa's government in Edo. This temple was Jōzan's residence after he retired, and he lived here from age fifty-nine to age ninety. He originally called his house the Ōtotsu-ka (Uneven Nest), reflecting the ruggedness of this land in the northeast of Kyōto.

The larger view (↓) is a garden in front of the abbot's quarters. (See also 4-5.) The Poetic Sages Room of the temple displays a painting of thirty-six poet-sages selected by Jōzan and his literary associate Razan Hayashi. The painting is by Tan'yū Kanō of the Kanō style of painting. The calligraphy of the poems is by Jōzan himself in clerical script.

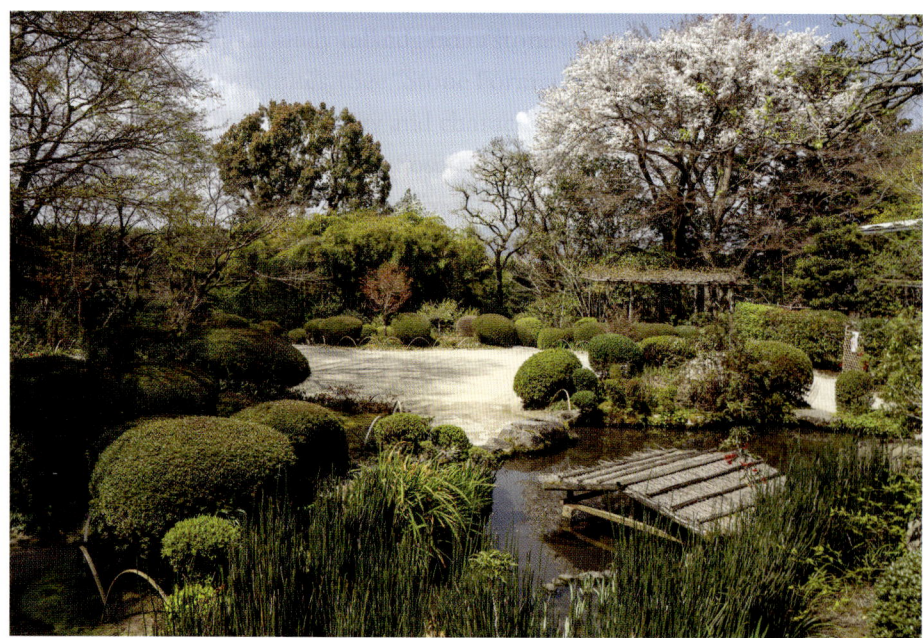

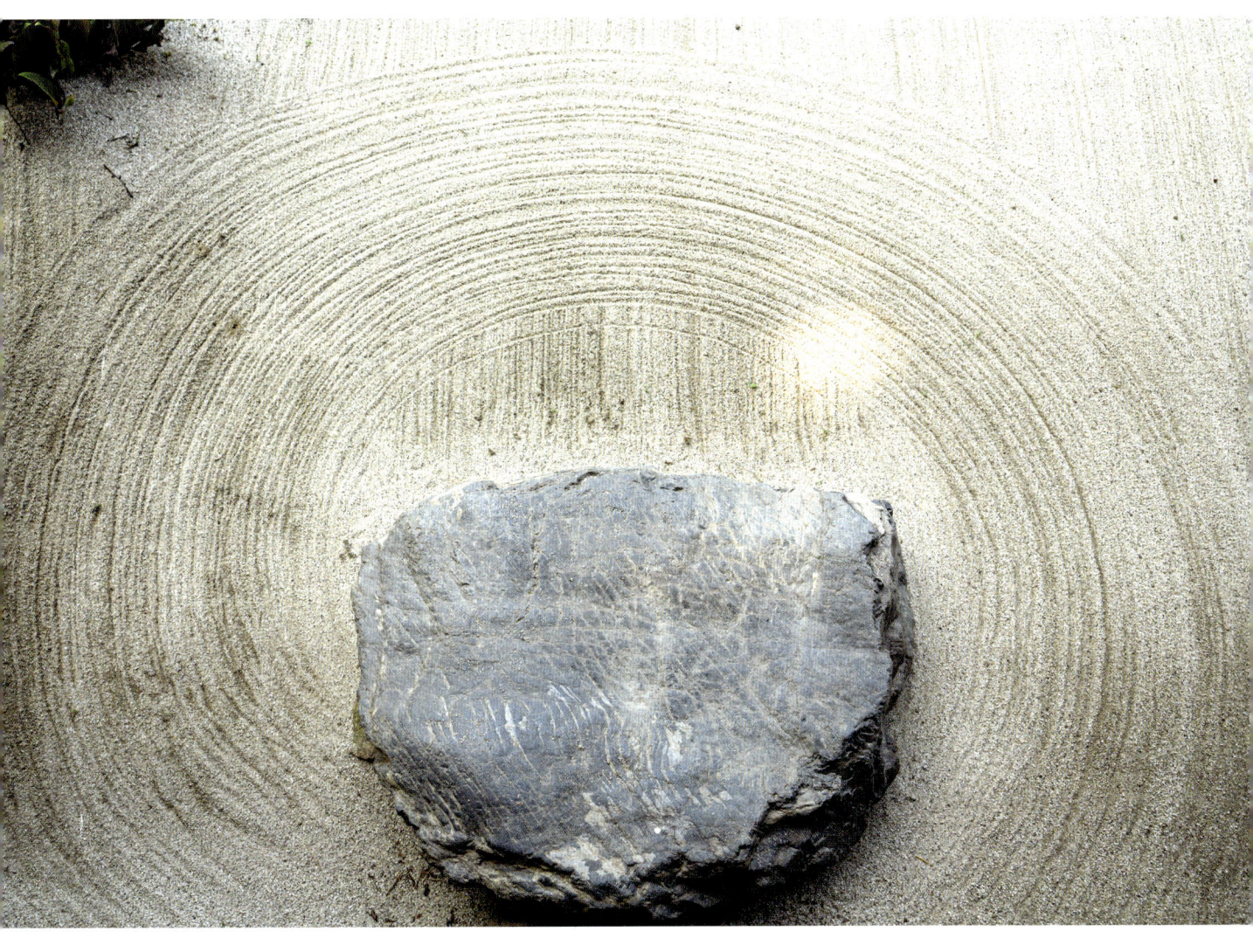

1-2 *Enkō-ji*

A wooden dipper sits on a bamboo holder, which is itself placed across a stone basin filled with clear water. (→) This basin is there for visitors to wash their hands in a garden called Suikin Tei (Water Harp Garden), near the entrance to the abbot's quarters at the Enkō-ji. This garden is indicative of the arts of the middle

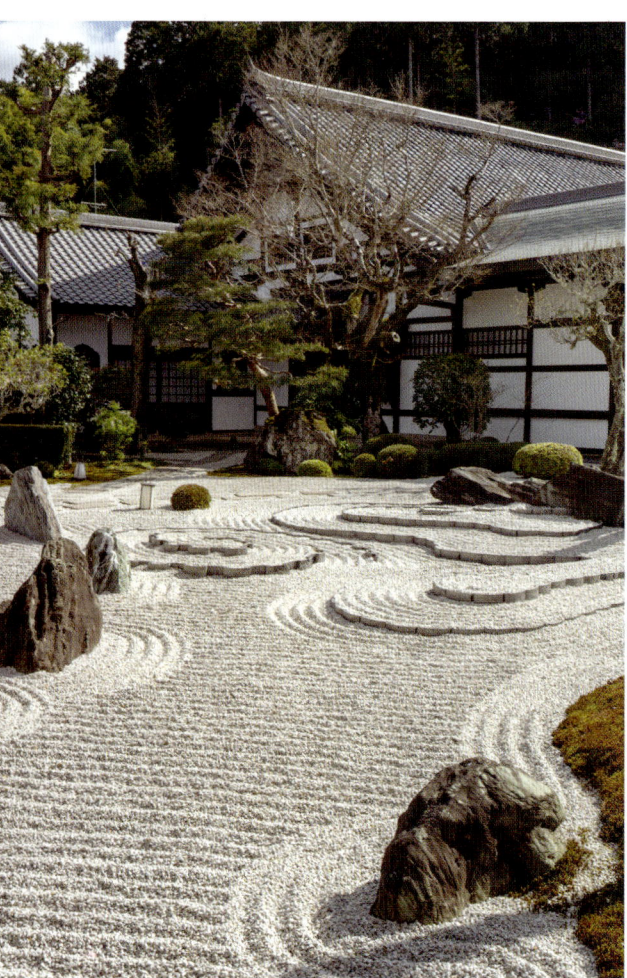

Muromachi Period, now characterized as constituting the Higashiyama or East Mountain Culture.

After entering the temple gate and passing down a straight walkway, visitors would also see (←) a dry landscape called Honryū Tei (Dashing Dragon Garden). The Enkō-ji is situated in the northeast of Kyōto, a few blocks away from the Shisen-dō. This temple was originally built as a school for monks and laity by Ieyasu Tokugawa in 1601 soon after he took power and shortly before he became the first *shōgun* of the Edo government. Ieyasu had reunified Japan in 1600 after winning a war with the Toyotomi family. He founded the Fushimi School Enkō-ji at the foot of Fushimi Castle in southern Kyōto. The Fushimi method of printing text, using the earliest wooden types, was produced there. More than 50,000 pieces of these types are still extant.

After the Meiji Restoration of 1868, the Enkō-ji became a training center for nuns of the Nanzen-ji Order of the Rinzai School. It is no longer a nunnery today.

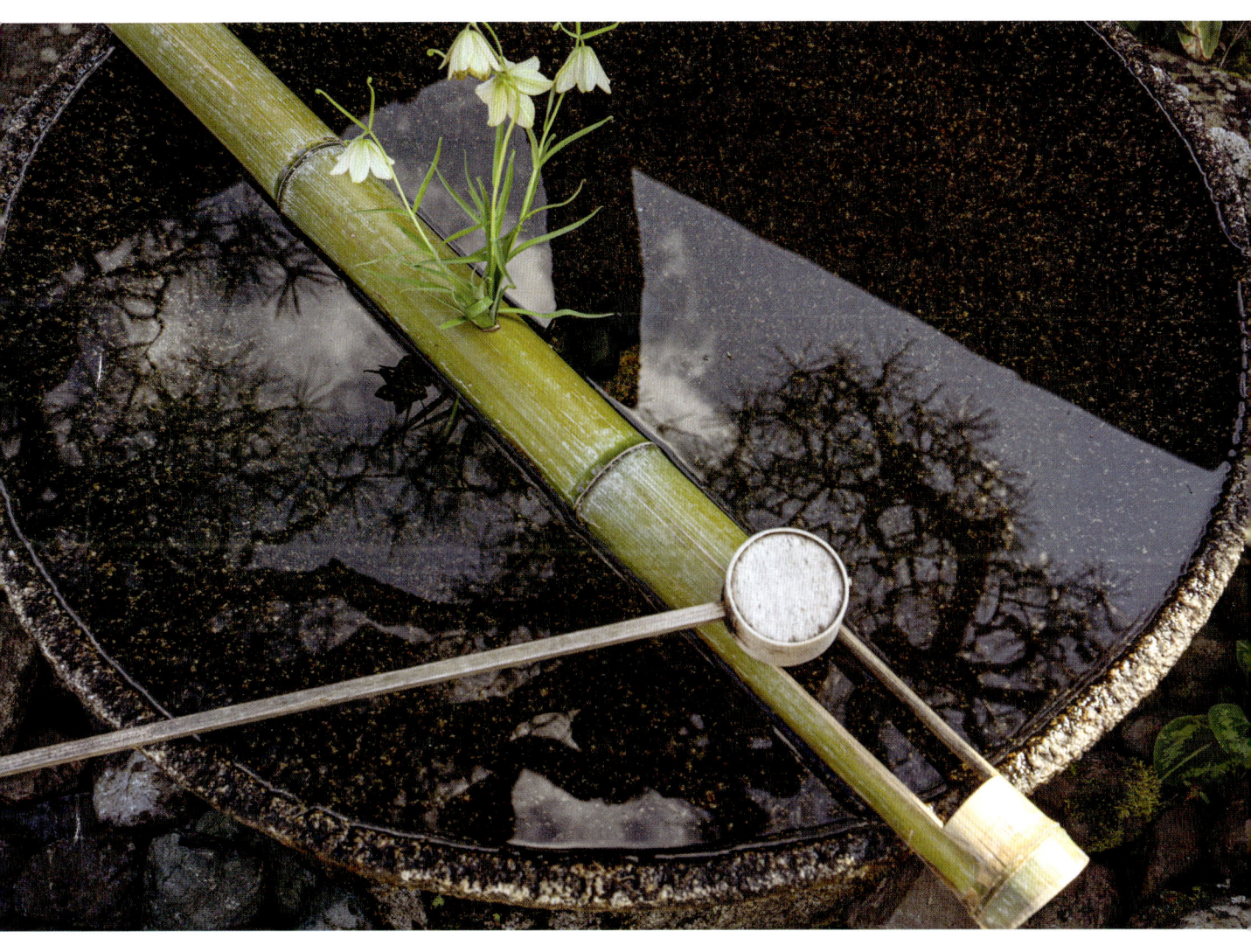

1-3 *Nanzen-ji*

Emperor Kameyama was on the throne from 1259 to 1274, from the ages of eleven to twenty-six. After he retired, this is the villa where Kameyama resided. Soon thereafter, Mongolian troops made two attempts to invade the southern island of Kyūshū by ships, but both times fierce storms destroyed their fleets.

In 1289 Kameyama was ordained as a monk. He became what was known as a dharma emperor—someone who retained power while also a Buddhist priest. During this time, ghosts began appearing in the palace. He asked various Buddhist priests to hold exorcisms, but nothing worked. Then, he asked Zen master Mukan Fumon to help. Fumon stayed at the villa with his monks in training and conducted scheduled formal practice, eating simple food. He invited Kameyama

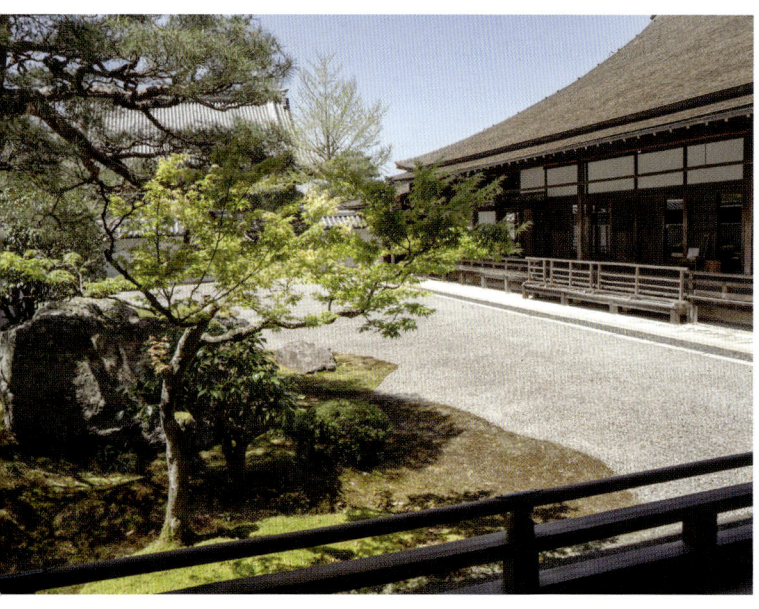

and his staff to join them, and after that, the ghosts stopped appearing. Kameyama was impressed and in 1292 asked Mukan to turn the villa into a Zen temple. This was the beginning of the Nanzen-ji. As it was an imperial monastery, it has been regarded as the highest-ranking Rinzai monastery in Japan.

Kameyama passed away in 1305 at age fifty-seven and was buried at the Kameyama Villa west to Kyōto.

The Nanzen-ji's abbot's quarters (←), rebuilt in 1703, are a Japanese national treasure.

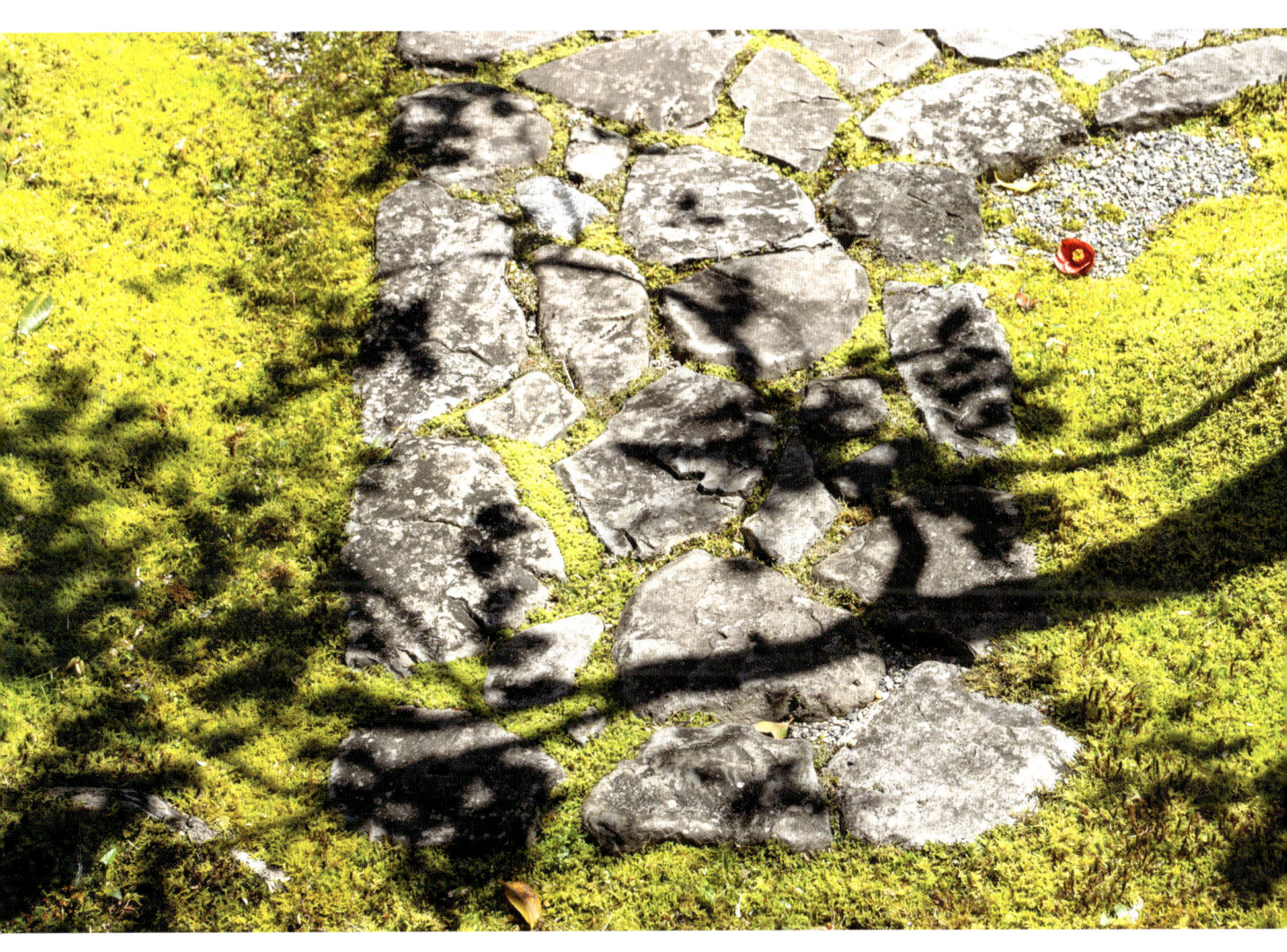

1-4 *Tenryū-ji*

At the edge of a pond under early autumn trees, stones partly covered with moss and lichens stand timelessly (→). Their arrangement seems artless and natural, perhaps hinting at a cliff, mountains, and islands. This is a portion of the Sōgen Pond at the Tenryū-ji. In the water there is a faint image of *koi* or carp, which are revered in Zen. Legend tells, as mentioned earlier, that if a carp can swim over a waterfall, it will become a dragon—a metaphor for a common meditation practitioner turning into an outstanding one. The opposite view (↓) shows the great abbot's quarters.

The Tenryū-ji, completed in 1345, was the life's work of Musō Soseki, a great Zen teacher as well as the most distinguished landscaper in the history of Japanese Zen gardens. The fact that Takauji Ashikaga, all-powerful first *shōgun* of the Muromachi government, resumed trade with China in order to secure funds to build the temple and garden reveals their historical significance.

The Tenryū-ji (Heavenly Dragon Temple) is situated to the west of central Kyōto, close to the Togetsu (Moon Crossing) Bridge on the Katsura (Laurel) River. (See also 4-4, 6-4.)

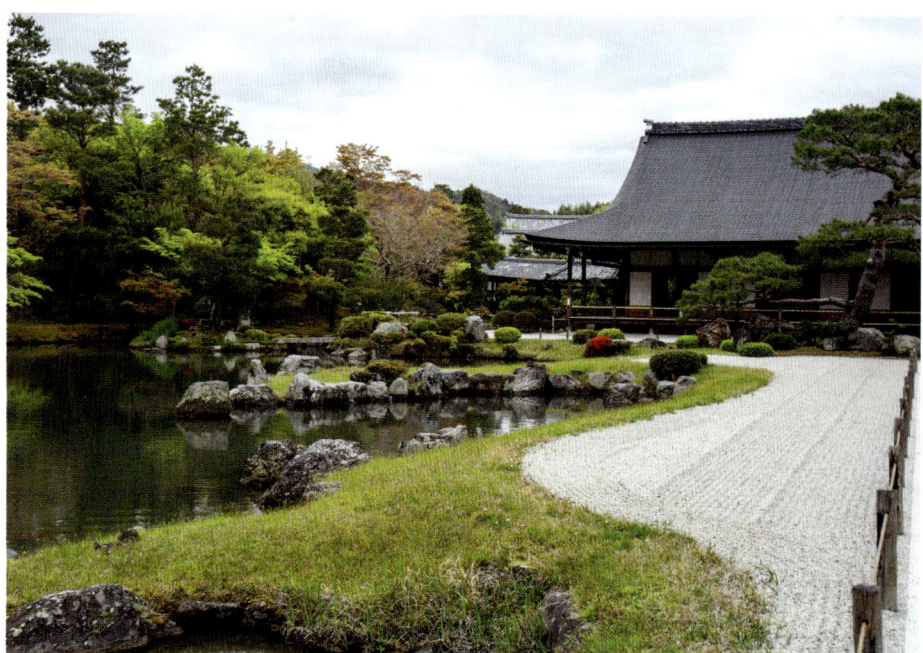

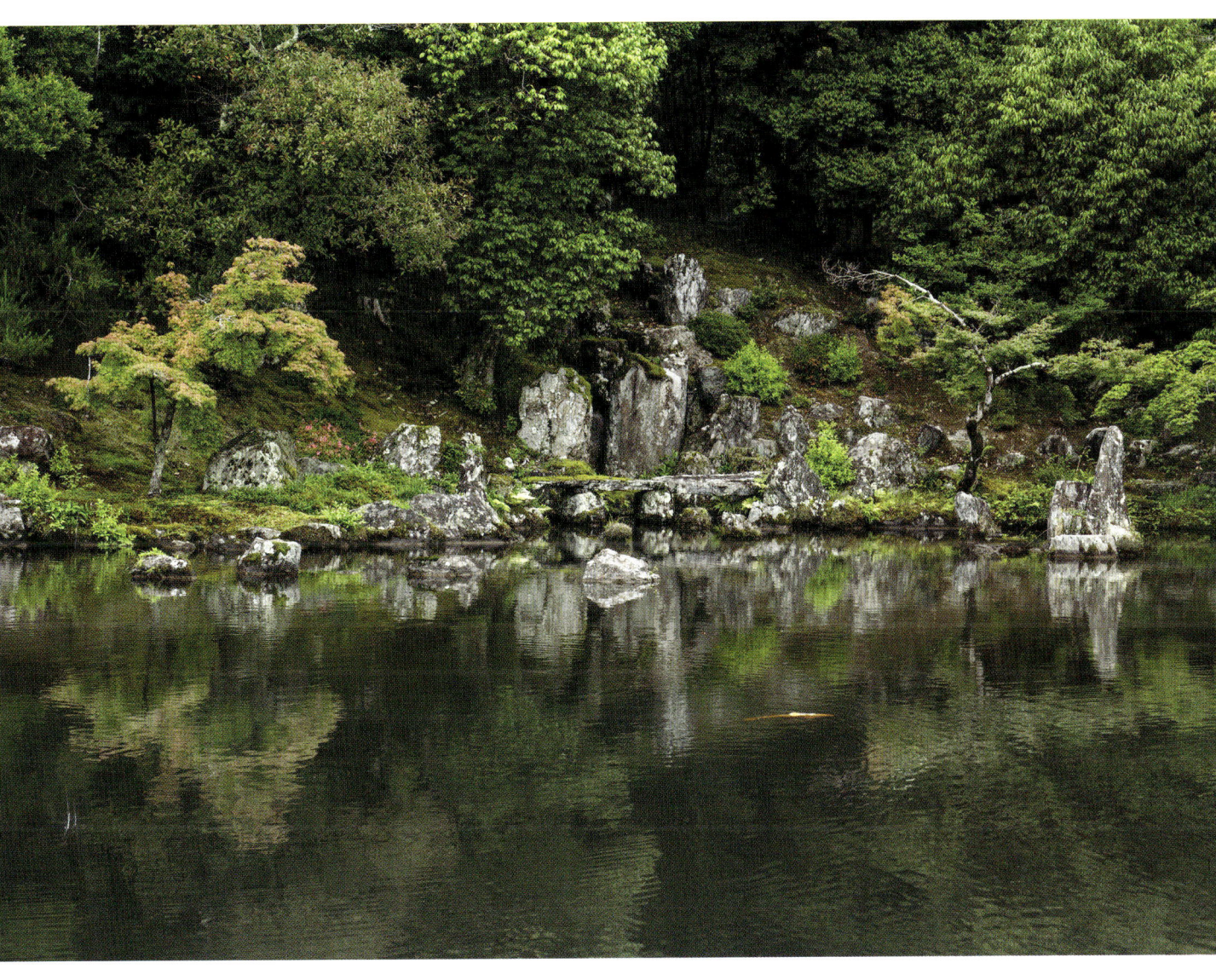

1-5 *Saihō-ji*

Known as the Koke Dera (Moss Temple), the Saihō-ji is situated to the west of central Kyōto, slightly south of the Tenryū-ji, but on the western side of the Katsura River. When Musō Soseki built this garden in 1339, prior to that of the Tenryū-ji, it was not covered with the various mosses you see in the photos.

These two photos were taken in the lower part of the garden. The standing rock (→) is wrapped with *shime nawa* 注連縄 (lengths of hemp rope with hanging cut and folded white paper), a Shintō rope signifying a sacred area. This rock is called a *yōgō seki* 影向石, meaning "manifestation stone." It indicates that the deity of the Matsuo Shrine—an earlier form of this compound—once descended on this stone. The other photograph (↓) shows the nearby Gold Pond.

Although this was not Soseki's original intention, much of the temple garden is now covered with over one hundred types of moss. Moss usually favors a humid, shady, and well-drained area. It takes a great deal of effort to maintain so much moss. Visitors at this Zen temple garden may notice workers weeding and cleaning the ground covered with its varied greenery.

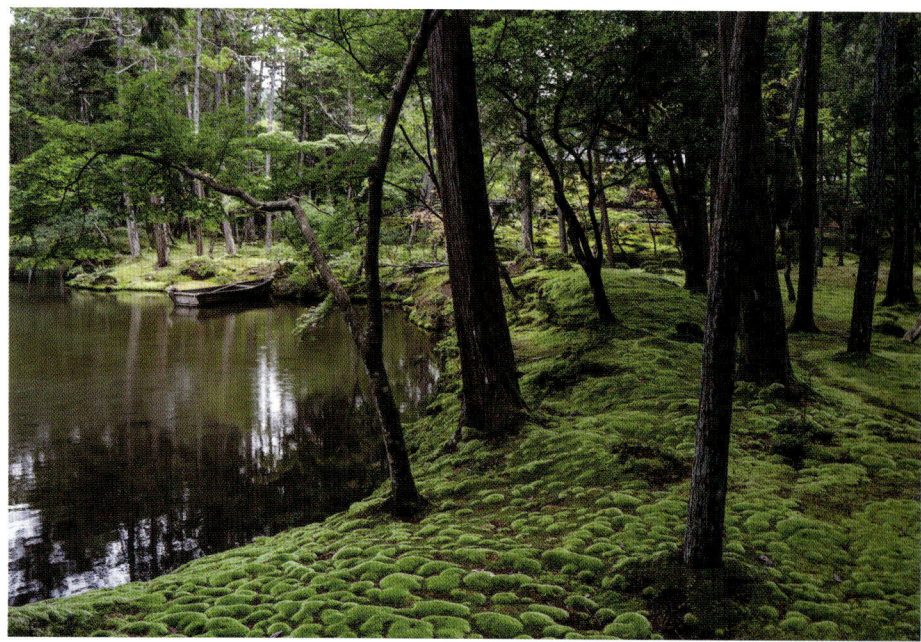

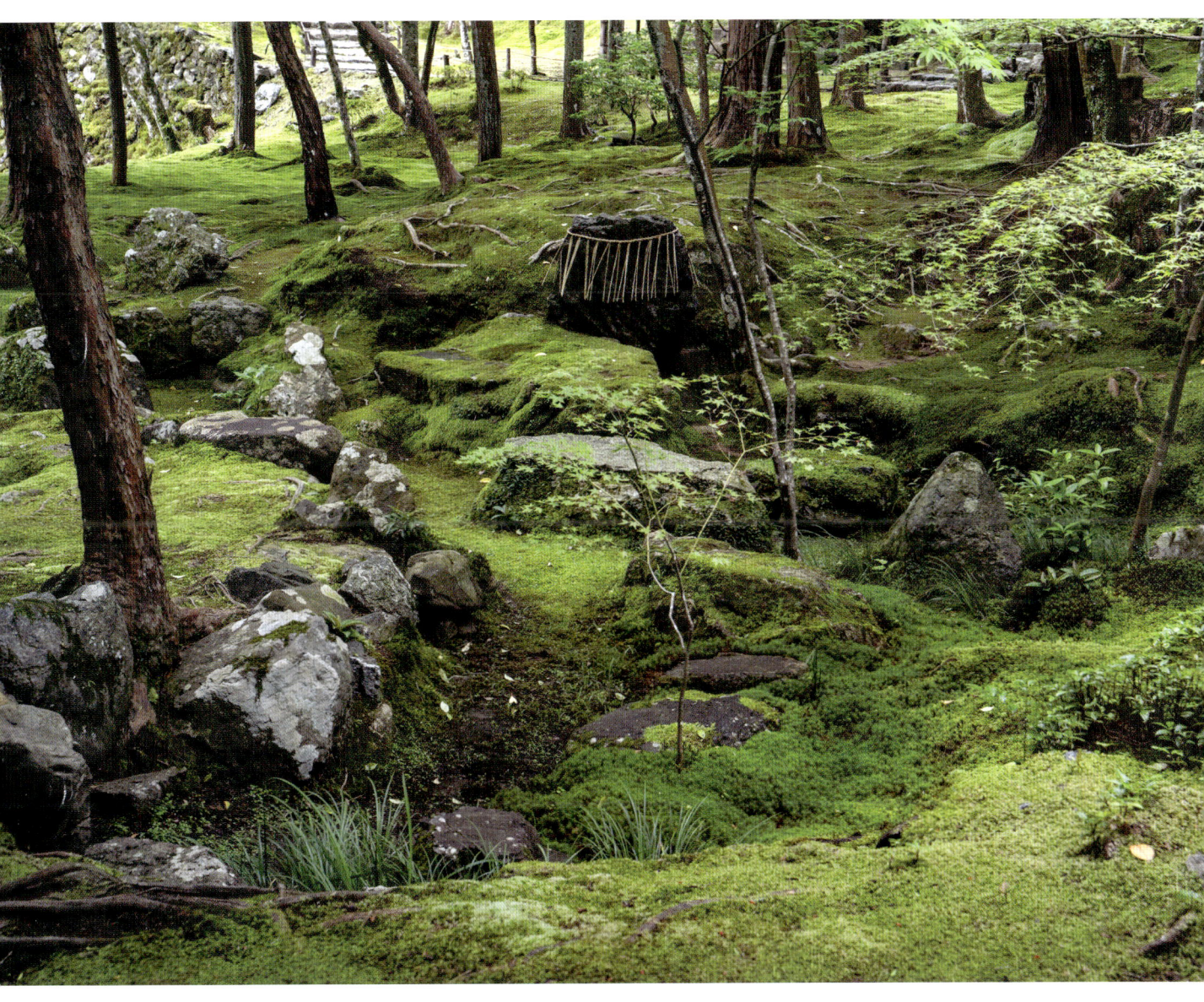

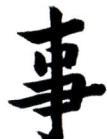

Ordinary
buji

FROM A Zen perspective, *ordinary* means nothing particular, nothing outstanding. A worn-out wooden dipper set on a garden's stone basin may not draw your attention at first. But once you notice it, waiting to be picked up by visitors for rinsing their hands, it is obvious that it's there. It's just an ordinary utensil for everyday use, yet its shape, its age, its history, its beauty may be timeless.

A wooden dipper is a miracle. A stone basin is a miracle. Water in the basin is a miracle. Everything is unique and precious. Everyone is unique and precious. Every moment is unique and precious.

The emphasis in Zen on the uniqueness of each moment calls for becoming free from an effort to be different, stand out, and be impressive. The ordinary is just as it is. Just maintain an everyday mind, be an everyday being.

One who embodies nothing particular is a precious person.

—LINJI

Plainness is the extreme end of brilliance.

—SU DONGPO

Everyday mind is enlightenment.

—NANQUAN

A verse can have *karumi* (literally meaning "lightness," indicating effortless and artless).

—BASHŌ

2-1 *Tōji-in, Tenryū-ji*

This is one of two strolling ponds at the Tōji-in, one of the ten subtemples of the Tenryū Monastery. As mentioned, this monastery was created by Zen master Musō Soseki at the request of Takauji Ashikaga, the first *shōgun* of the Muromachi government, to console the spirit of Emperor Godaigo around 1346.

While the main monastery was being constructed, Takauji built a temple nearby for his family in 1341, naming it *bodai-ji* 菩提寺. *Bodai* means "enlightenment" and *ji* "temple." It is a temple to hold prayer rites to wish enlightenment for the ancestors who are deceased and enshrined there. Takauji made this temple an annex of the Tōji Zen Monastery in the central part of Kyōto, and he asked Musō to be the founder. After Takauji's death, it became his tomb site and was renamed Tōji-in.

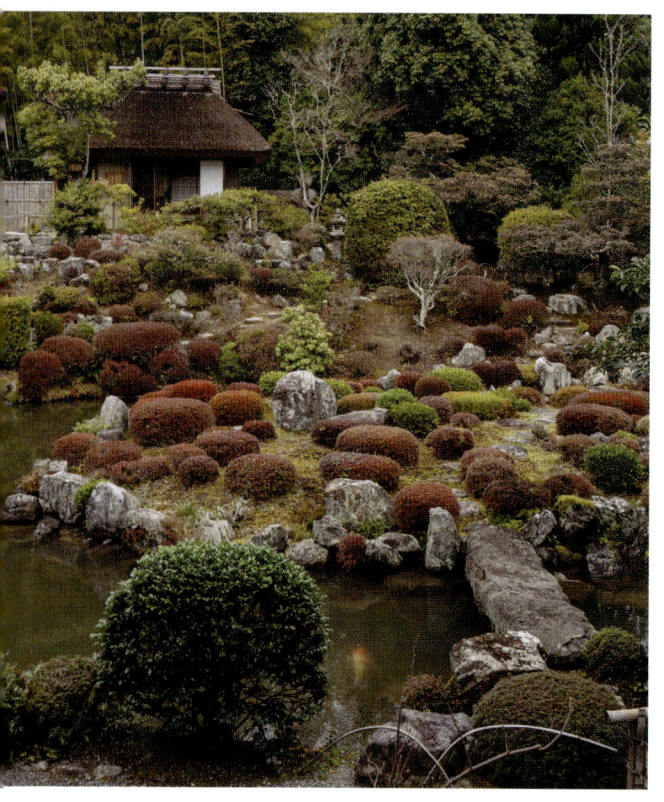

This photograph (→) of a white heron flying over the Fuyō (Cotton Rose) Pond was taken in the month of February. A pine tree is reflected on the pond. The other photo (←) shows the pond from another angle, with a view of a great many roundly pruned bushes and a thatch-roofed hut at the foot of a bamboo grove.

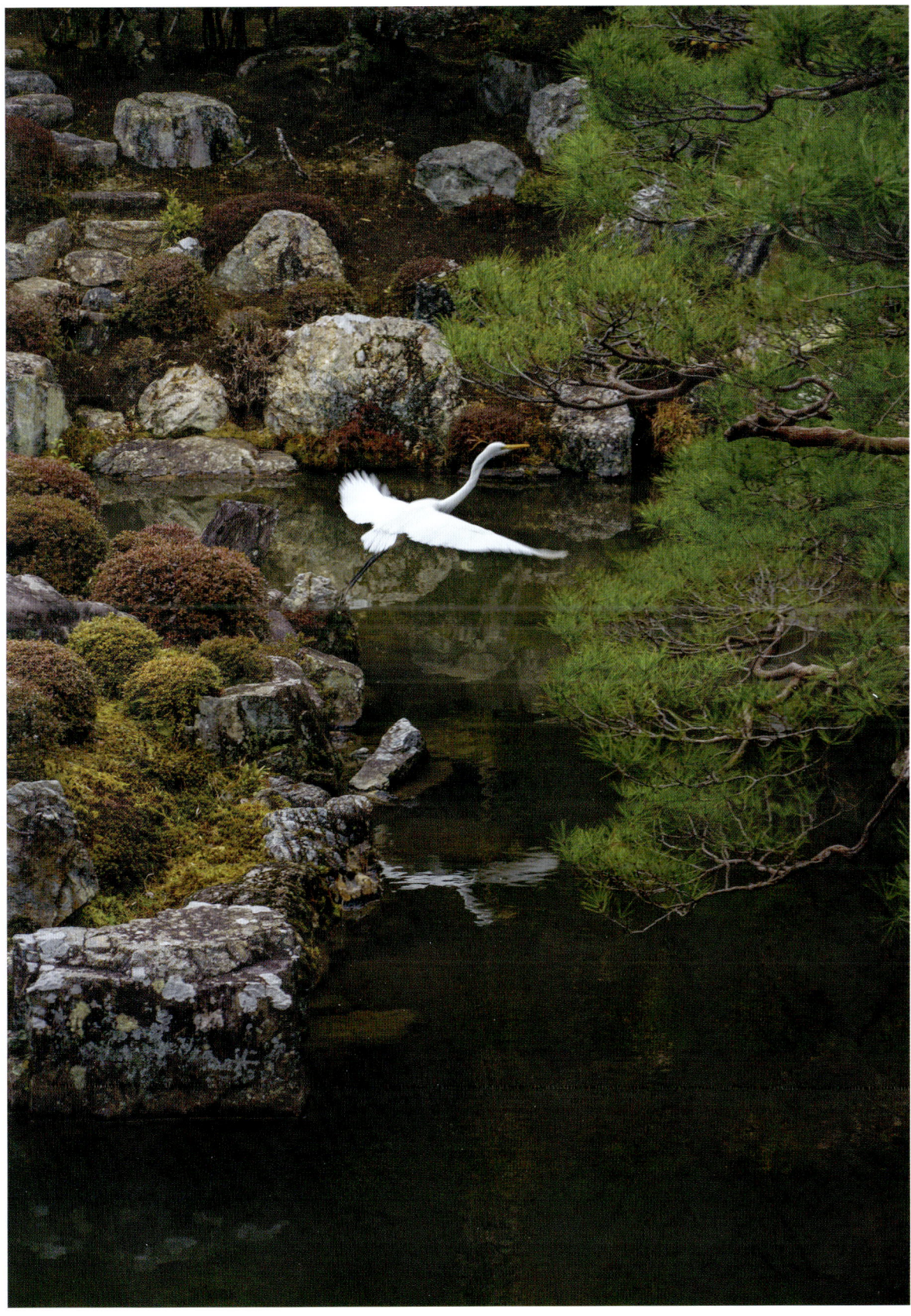

2-2 *Tōrin'-in, Myōshin-ji*

During the Muromachi Period (1336–1573), monasteries that were controlled by the government, including the Five Mountains, were called *zenrin* (Zen forests), and those that were not were called *rinka* (forests below). The Myōshin-ji was a leading *rinka* center fully focused on training. Thus, nowadays, out of the 5,650 Rinzai temples, 3,350 belong to the Myōshin-ji Order. The monastery is surrounded by forty-two subtemples.

The Tōrin'-in, to the east of the main campus, is famous for its three-hundred-year-old small *natsu tsubaki* (summer camellia) trees. This plant is better known as *shara sōju*. *Shara* comes from the Sanskrit *shāla*, which is this type of tree. *Sōju* means "a pair of trees." There is a legend that when Shākyamuni Buddha passed away, the four pairs of *shāla* trees around his deathbed grieved, and one of each pair withered and turned white. Thus, they are also called white crane trees. In the center of the photo (→) you see a pair of trees, looking like a single tree, in the garden in front of the abbot's quarters.

The other photograph (↓) shows a dry landscape, behind which sits a pond with a slightly arched stone bridge and a pagoda. The dry landscape and pond are located in the back of the temple compound.

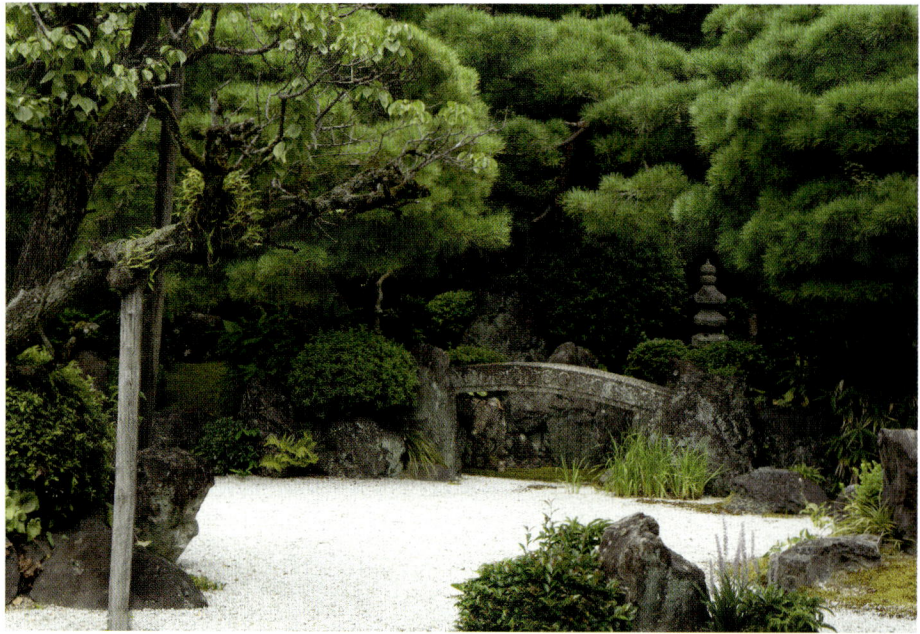

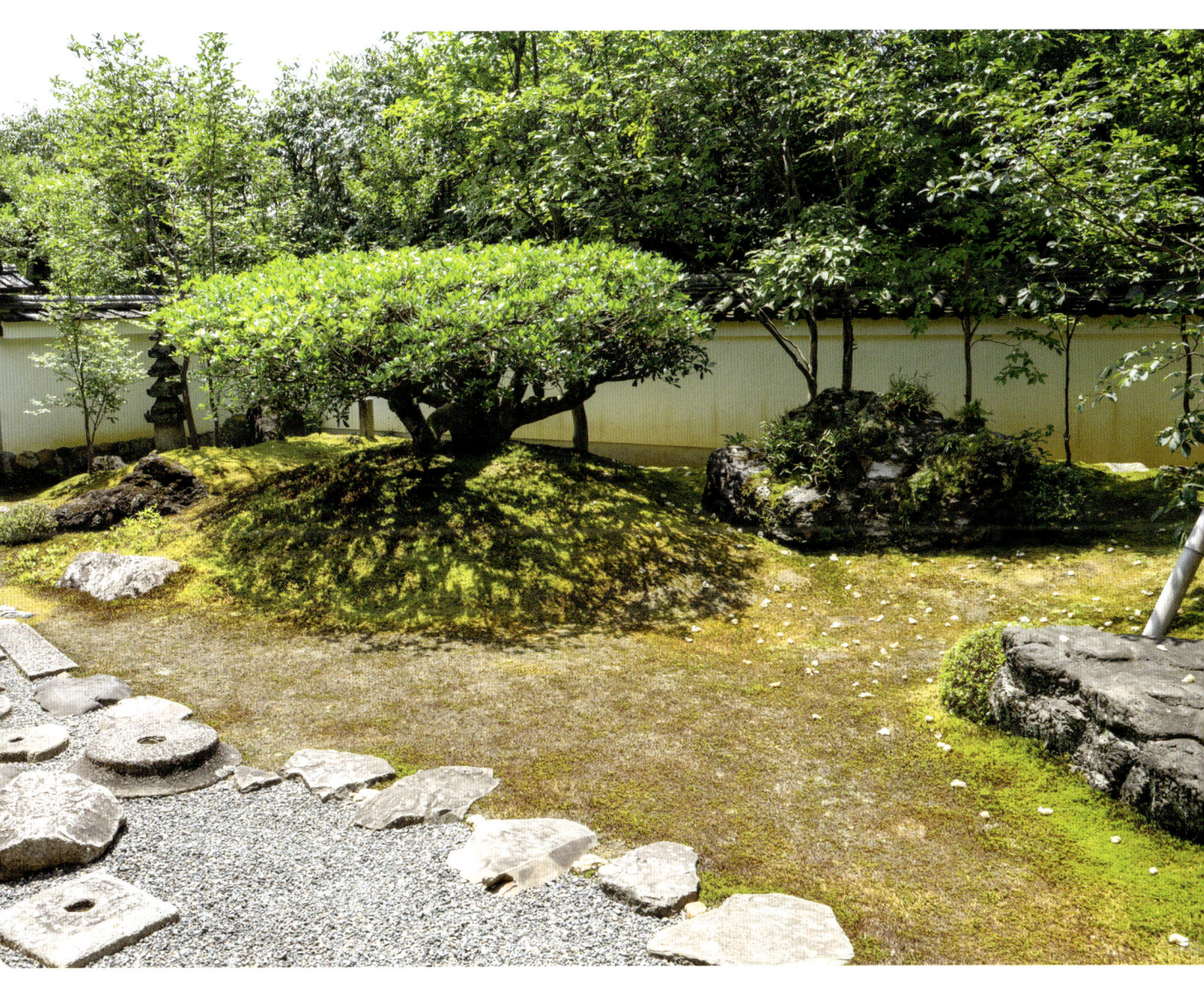

2-3 *Nanzen'-in, Nanzen-ji*

The Nanzen'-in is situated directly south of the abbot's quarters of the Nanzen Monastery as its closest subtemple. In fact, it is the original monastery as established by Dharma Emperor Kameyama in 1289. It is the only Zen garden from the Kamakura Period (1185–1333) to have survived to this day.

The garden to the south of the main building retains its original form—a landscape in the strolling style (*kaiyūshiki teien*) on two ponds backed by a dense forest. The dragon-shaped upper pond has a Daoist image of the immortals' land (*penglai* 蓬萊 in Chinese) in the center. The lower pond has an island in the shape of the cursive script of the ideograph for *heart*—心.

By the way, when you look for accommodations in the city, you might like to try a *shukubō*, or temple for lodging, with refined temple-style meals and an opportunity to join morning services with the abbot. Rooms may be divided by thin sliding doors with little privacy. Of course, a *ryokan* with personalized service or a hotel would be more comfortable. In between these extremes is a *kaikan* or monastery guest house. It's like a noncommercial hotel with a monastic atmosphere. I recommend the Nanzen-ji Kaikan and (Myōshin-ji's) Hanazono Kaikan.

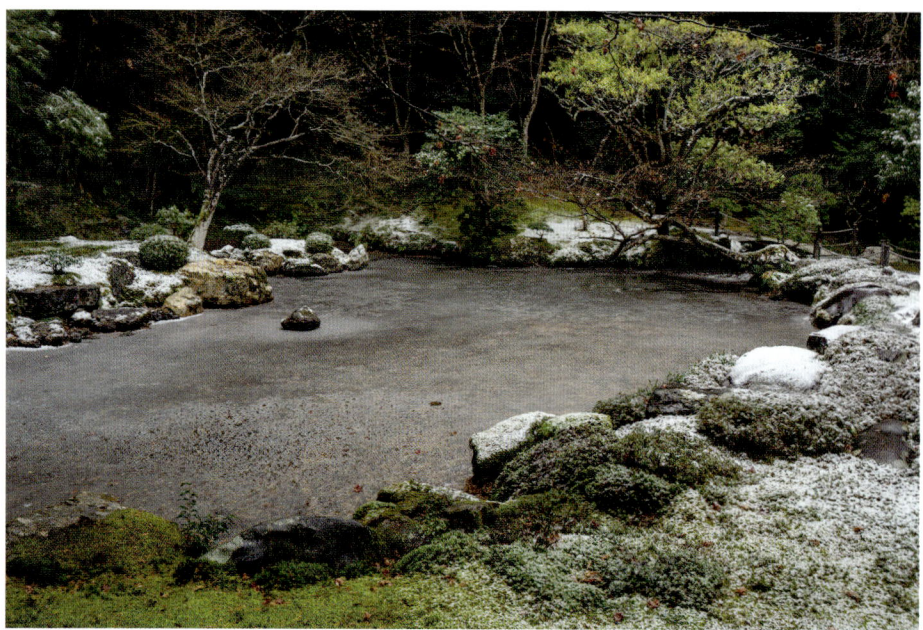

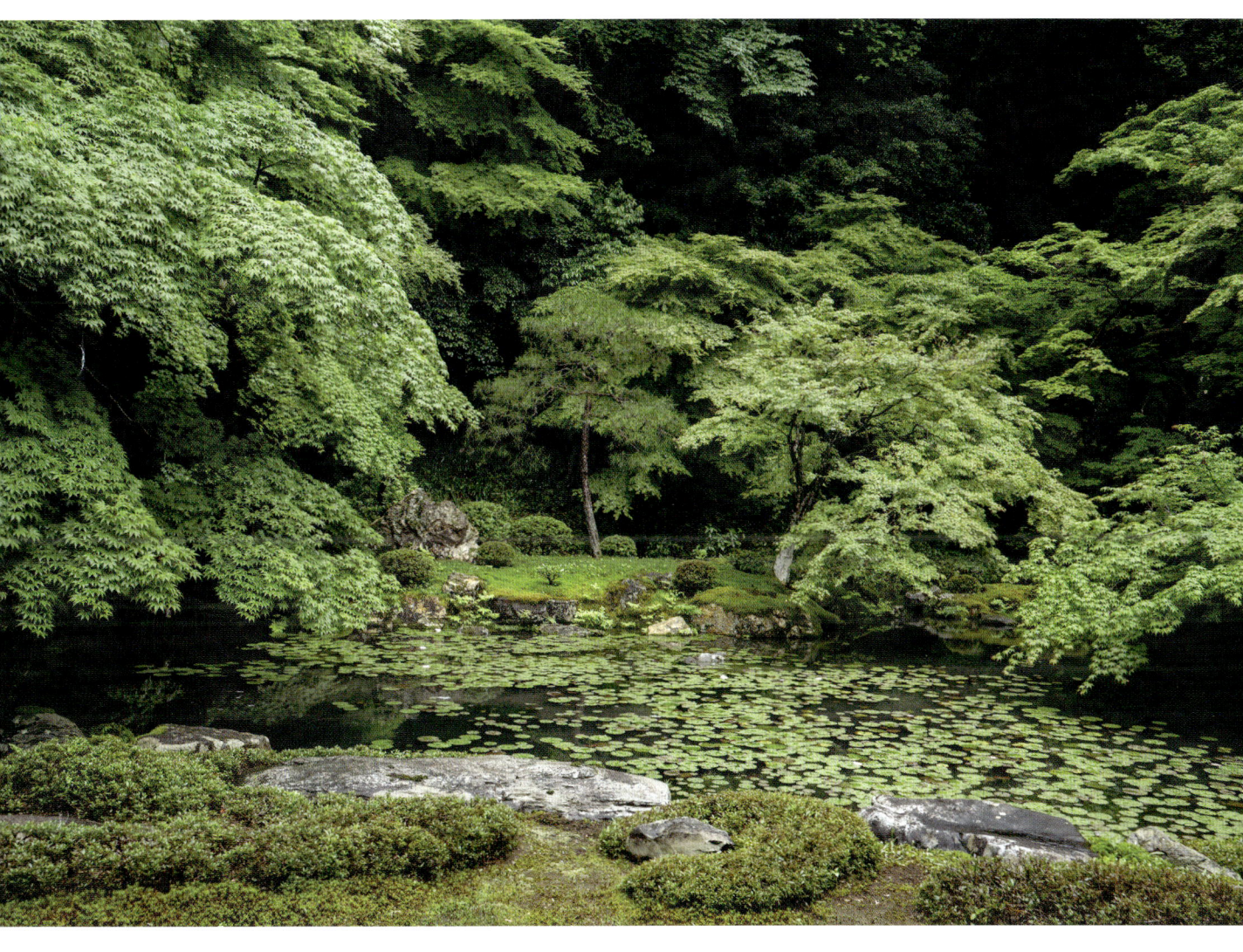

2-4 *Zuihō-in, Daitoku-ji*

This subtemple of the Daitoku Monastery was created by Sōrin Ōtomo, a *samurai* aristocrat, between 1553 and 1555. Sōrin was a Christian—as this was before Christianity was banned in Japan starting in 1587—though he also practiced Zen. Sōrin asked his Zen master Tesshū Sōkyū to be the founder of this temple. The name Zuihō is Sōrin's dharma name. A Christian *samurai* who built a Zen garden with a Buddhist name: Wasn't he eclectic?

The stepping stones on the mossy ground in the photo (→) lead to a tea house called Yokei An (Extra Auspicious Hut), which is behind the photographer. The flat round stone with a black cross tied on it is called *tome ishi* 留石, meaning a "blocking stone," and signifies no entry. You can see another blocking stone in the other photo (↓). This garden is called Kammin Tei (Leisurely Nap Garden).

Hosts and guests at small gatherings have walked on these stones for over four hundred years. Dressed in fine *kimonos*, they walk mindfully in their *setta*—leather-soled sandals—enjoying the view of the garden just swept and sprinkled for welcoming the guests—reserved, solitary, and quiet. People with refined taste would have appreciated the excellence of the calligraphy on the hanging scroll and blossoms in a tiny vase, refined conversation enhancing the joy of all those present.

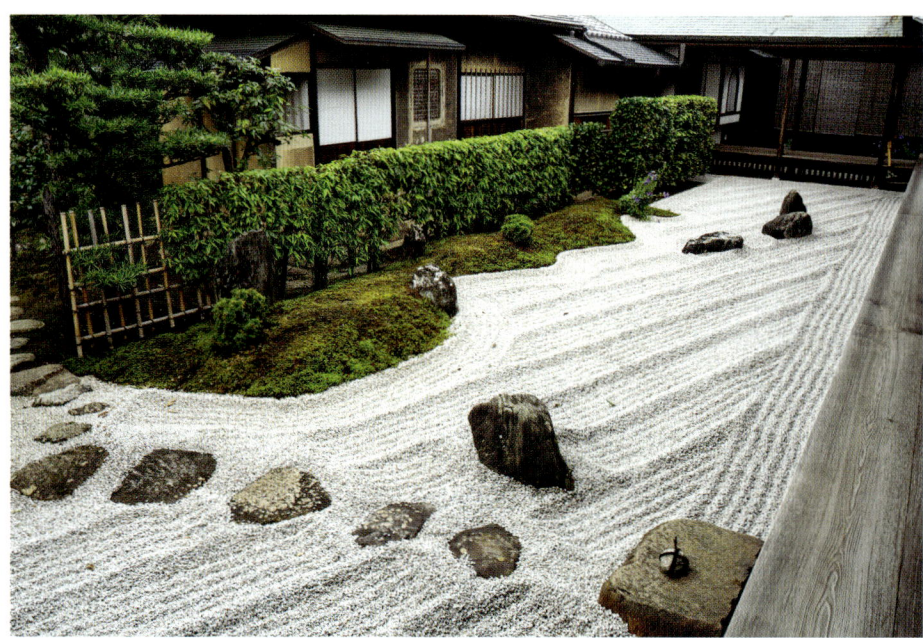

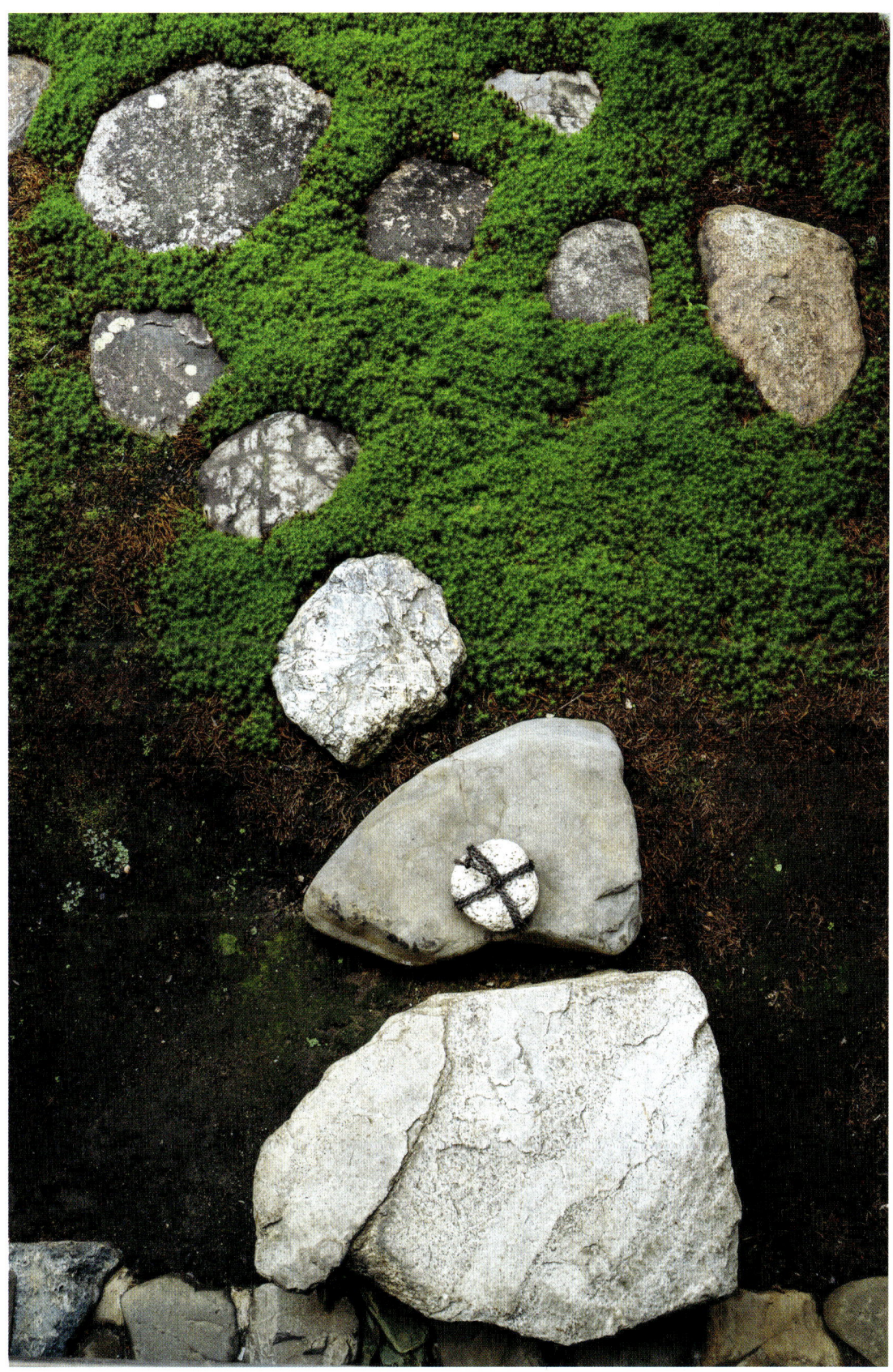

2-5 *Tenju-an, Nanzen-ji*

Autumn is in its prime, viewed here from a *shoin* or audience hall (→). The photo below (↓) shows maple leaves in orange, red, and yellow over the entrance to the abbot's quarters of the Tenju-an, one of the fifteen *tatchū* or subtemples of the Nanzen Monastery.

As mentioned, Dharma Emperor Kameyama turned this palace into a Zen temple and asked Zen master Mukan Fumon to be its founder in 1291. This became the first imperial Zen monastery. (See 1-3.) The Tenju-an was founded as a *stūpa* temple for Mukan by Zen master Kokan Shiren in 1339.

If you visit Kyōto in November, you will find maple leaves in a variety of colors all over the city. It's a great time to be there. The other ideal time is late March to April when cherry blossoms take over the city. Kyōto is known for its humidity; walking a few blocks under the scorching sun makes your shirt damp with sweat. If you hurry into a freezingly air-conditioned coffeehouse, you might catch a cold. So a summer vacation in this city may not work so well—unless you bring a sweater.

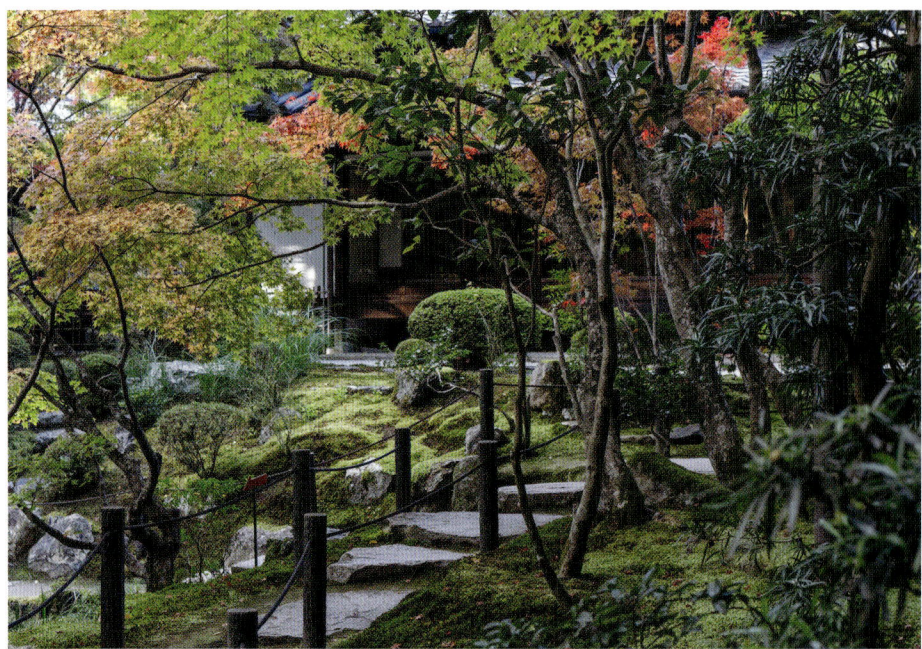

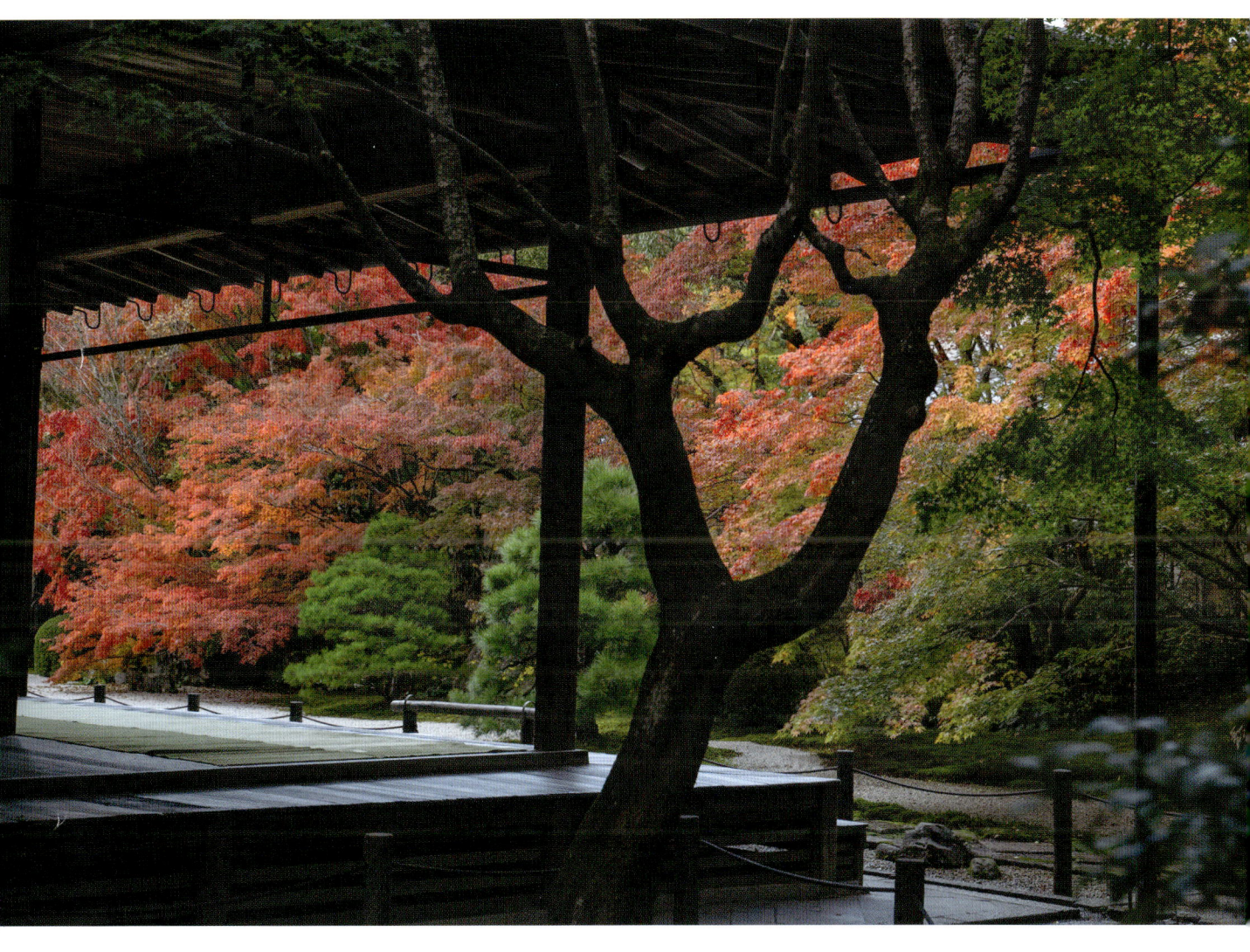

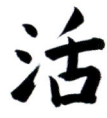
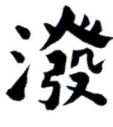

Vigorous
kappatsupatsu

IN ZEN, *vigorous* indicates vital—fully active, just like a flipping fish. There is stillness in motion and motion in stillness. Sitting silently and solidly in meditation can be a fresh, vigorous, and dynamic experience.

There is life in each object, music in each moment, realization in each scene. There are glances between trees, between clouds, between mountains. There is conversation among grasses. There is a dance among stones.

The East Mountain travels on water.

—YUNMEN

Because mountains are high and broad, their way of riding the clouds always extends from the mountains; their wondrous power of soaring in the wind comes freely from the mountains.

—DŌGEN

Concentration in the midst of activity excels concentration in stillness by a hundred, a thousand, or even a hundred million times.

—HAKUIN

Valley sounds are the long broad tongue.
Mountain colors are no other than the unconditioned body.
Eighty-four thousand verses are heard through the night.
What can I say about this in the future?

—SU DONGPO

3-1 *Tōfuku-ji*

The gardens at the huge abbot's quarters of the Tōfuku Monastery fully surround the building. The older version of this building was lost to fire in 1881 and was rebuilt in 1890. The garden was completed in 1939 by Mirei Shigemori, a renowned garden designer. Previously, Shigemori had documented over five thousand gardens, which he published as *Nihon Teien-shi Zukan* (Illustrated History of Japanese Gardens), in twenty-six volumes, in 1938. His intention for creating this garden was to capture the solemn style of the Kamakura Period gardens while also imbuing it with a contemporary sensitivity.

These gardens are named the Eight-stage Gardens after the eight-stage attainment of the way of Shākyamuni Buddha, starting with his descent from the Tushita Heaven. The main garden in the south consists of the "Oceanic Continent," "Mountain of Immortals," "Gourd," "Abbot's Quarters," and "Five Mountains." (A dried gourd as a drinking vessel symbolizes ease and comfort.) The small east garden holds the "Great Dipper in the Milky Way." The small west garden and the medium-size north garden share checkered patterns: the western (↓) with equally large squarely trimmed bushes on sand signifying rice fields, the northern (→) with square moss greens among white flat stones. Using such patterns was novel for gardens at the time of creation.

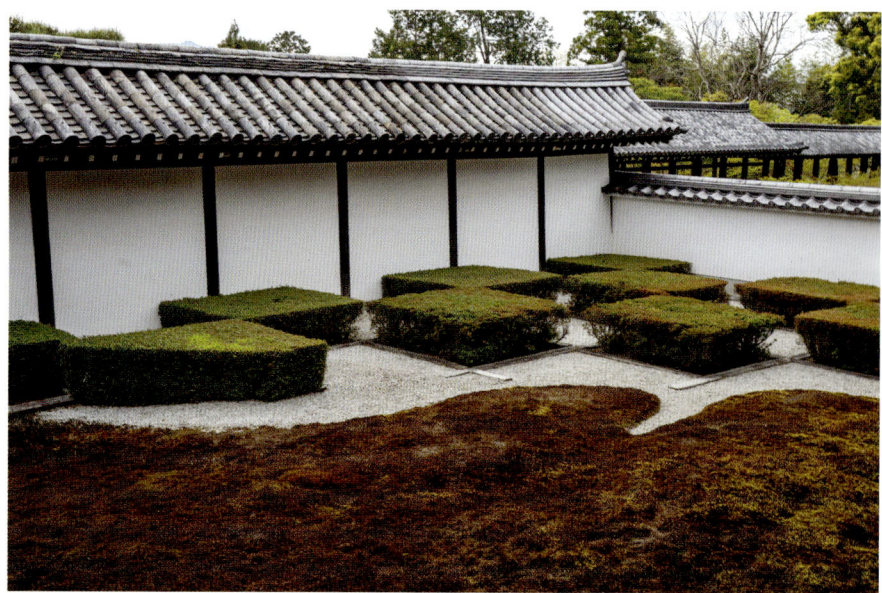

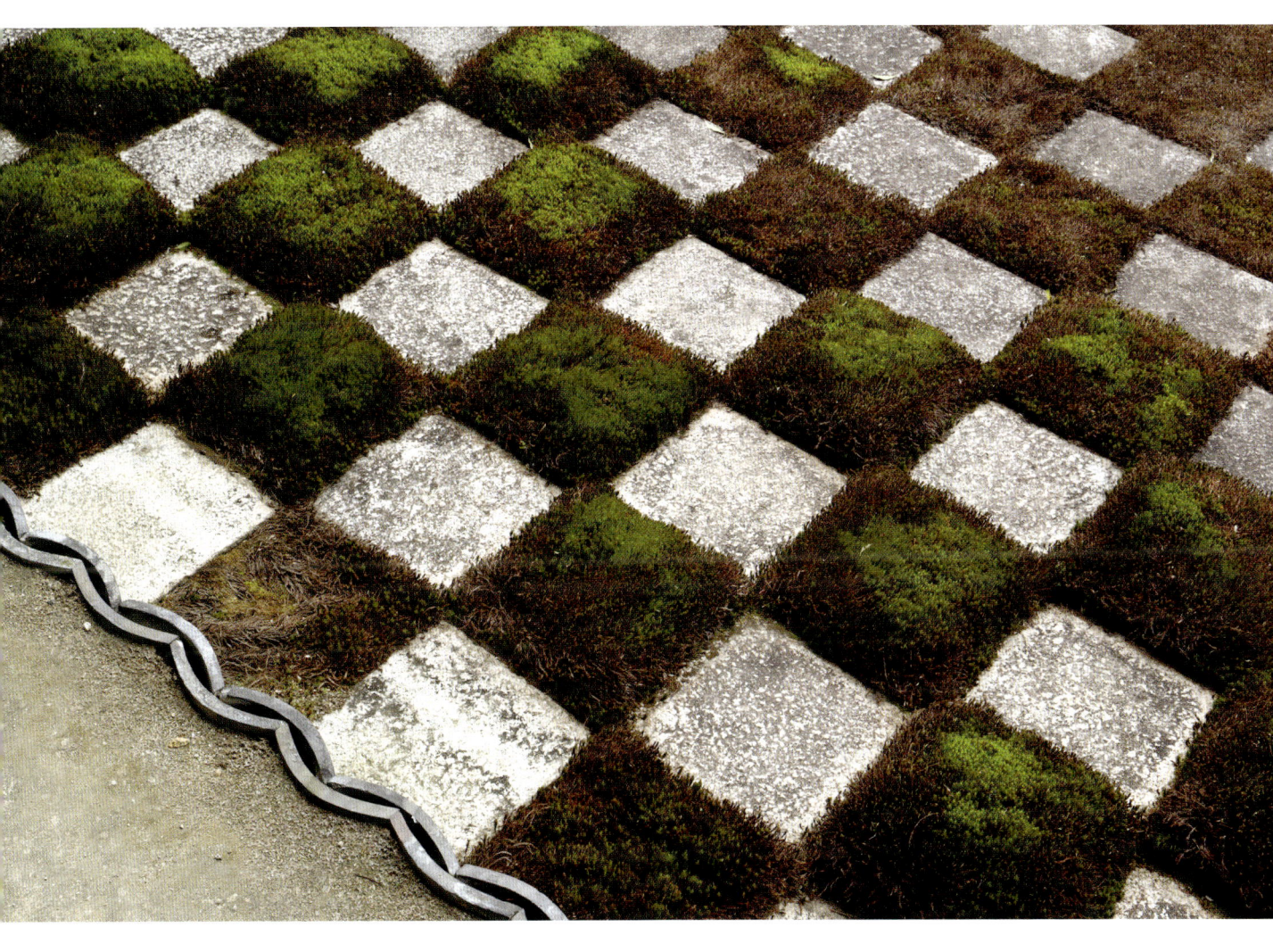

3-2 *Ginkaku-ji*

The ancient capital city of Kyōto lies in the northeastern part of the Kyōto Basin. While the Kinkaku-ji (Golden Pavilion Temple) stands on the northwestern end of the basin, the Ginkaku-ji (Silver Pavilion Temple) is situated in the northeastern part of Kyōto. It represents the Higashiyama Bunka or East Mountain Culture, a fifteenth-century movement of deeply refined and subdued aesthetics that became the basis of Japanese art and crafts.

As mentioned earlier, the name Ginkaku or "Silver Pavilion" is in contrast with the Kinkaku or "Golden Pavilion." The word *silver*, however, is purely symbolic; as discussed, silver leaf foil was not used to cover the surface of the pavilion called the Avalokiteshvara Hall. (See p. 32.)

A large platform of white sand from the nearby Shira Kawa (White River) is raked flat in stripes, with a thin border line extending southeast in front of the Avalokiteshvara Hall. This is called Ginsha Dan or the Silvery Sand Bank. It and another sand structure, an upside-down cone shape with a flat top called Kōgetsu Dai (Facing the Moon Platform) not shown here, were created by an unknown landscaper in the Edo Period. (See 6-2, "Garden Plan Example: The Ginkaku-ji," in the appendices.)

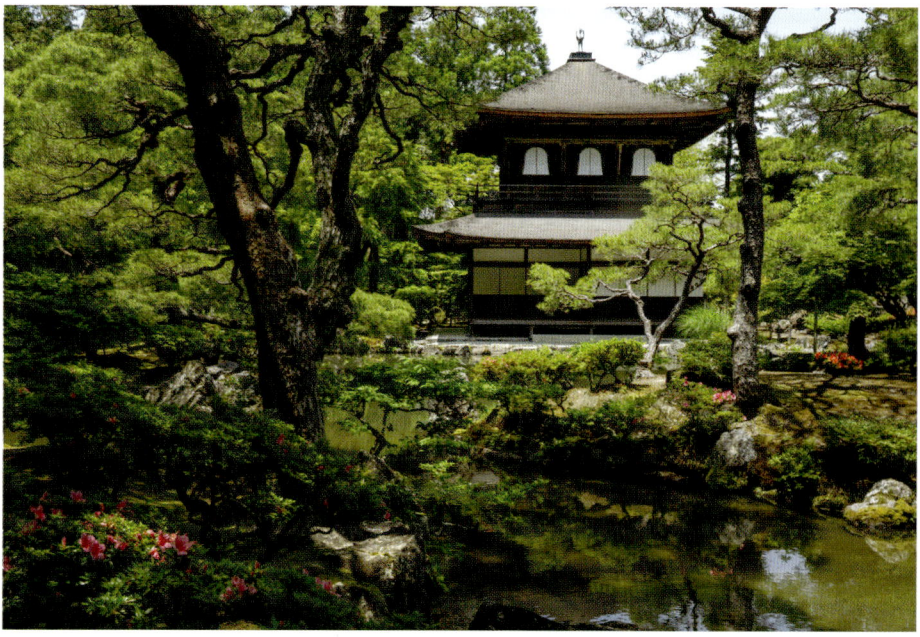

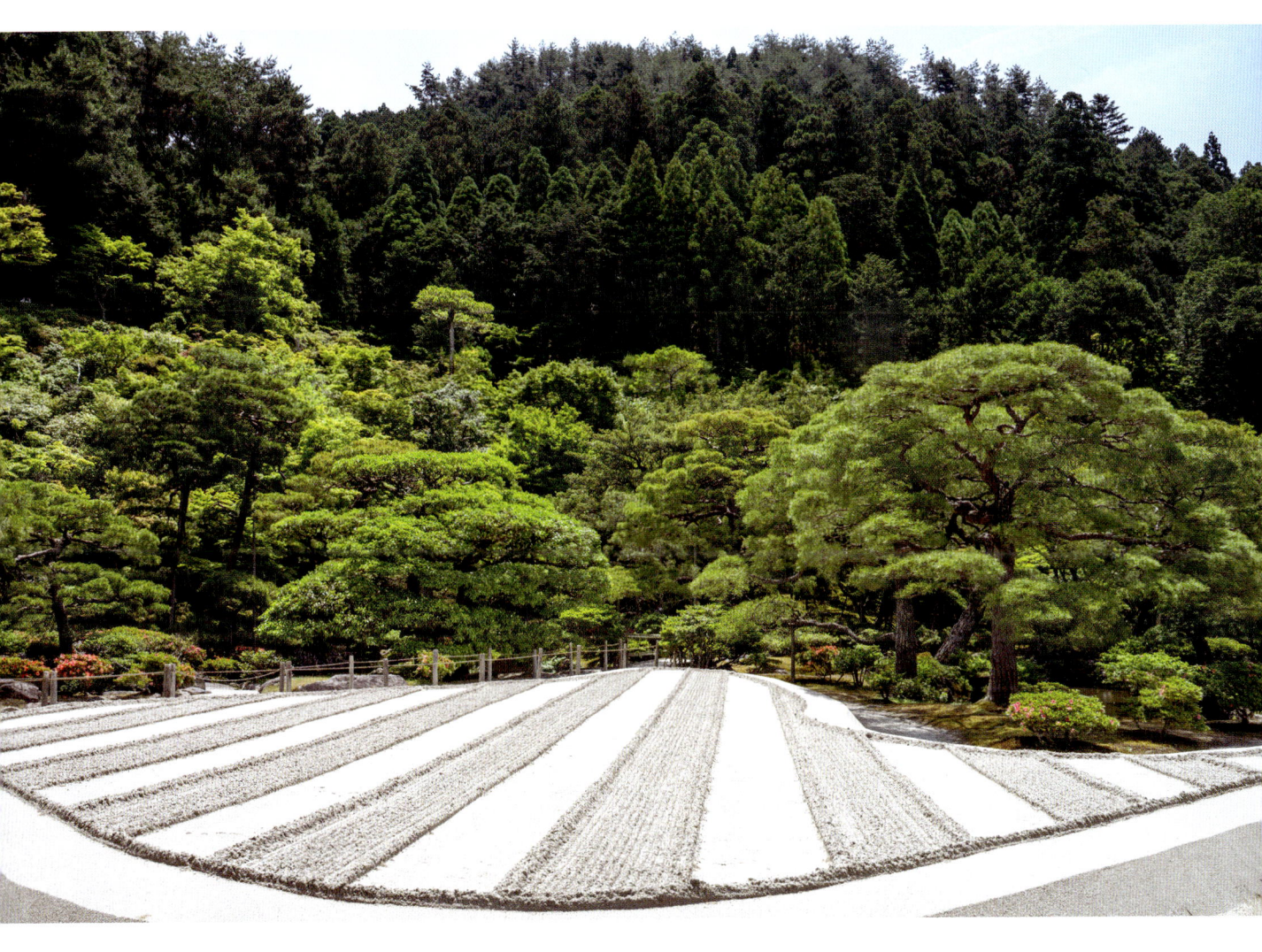

3-3 Hōgon'-in, Tenryū-ji

The Tenryū Monastery, the foremost of the Five Mountains, has an array of sub-temples to its east and south. The Hōgon'-in is situated directly south of the great abbot's quarters of the monastery.

This garden, with the flamboyant name of Lion's Roar, was created by a diplomat—Zen master Sakugen Shūryō (1504–1579), who led a trading fleet to the Ming Dynasty China. At that time, China only allowed the entry of a Japanese fleet every ten years, and such fleets were the only diplomatic connection between China and Japan. Shūryō was the vice ambassador on the first mission and the ambassador on the second.

"Lion's Roar" is an epithet for the Buddha's teaching. As the designer and producer of this garden, which features a strolling path and Mount Arashi as a borrowed landscape in the background, Shūryō must have wanted to enhance a viewer's awareness of the sound of the wind and the chirping of birds as expressions of profound buddha dharma.

These photos (→) (↓) show an unusual area of sand and dark pebbles at the southwestern end of the Lion's Roar Garden called Kukai or Ocean of Suffering. The rocks represent animals who are on their way to hear the Buddha's discourse.

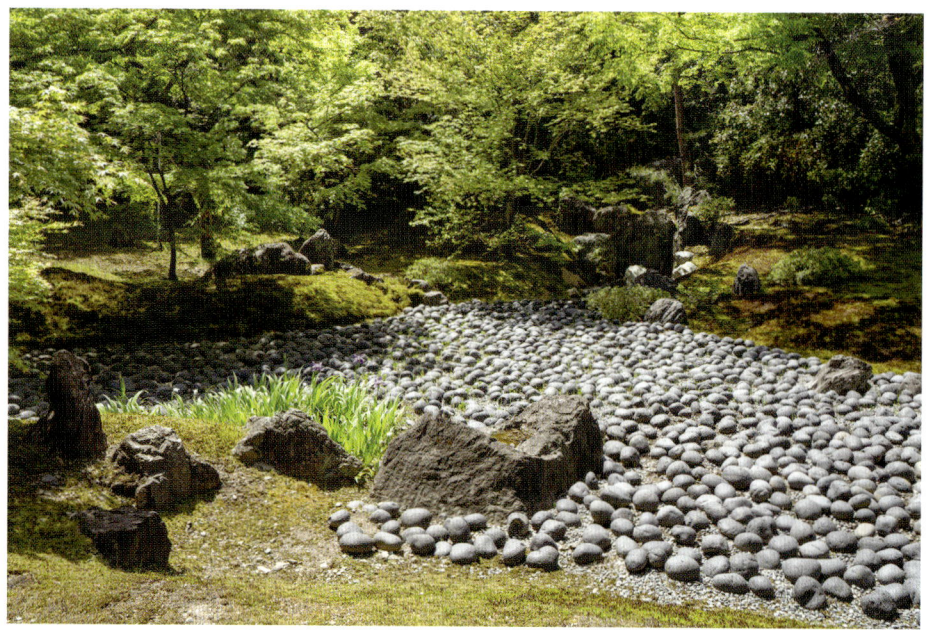

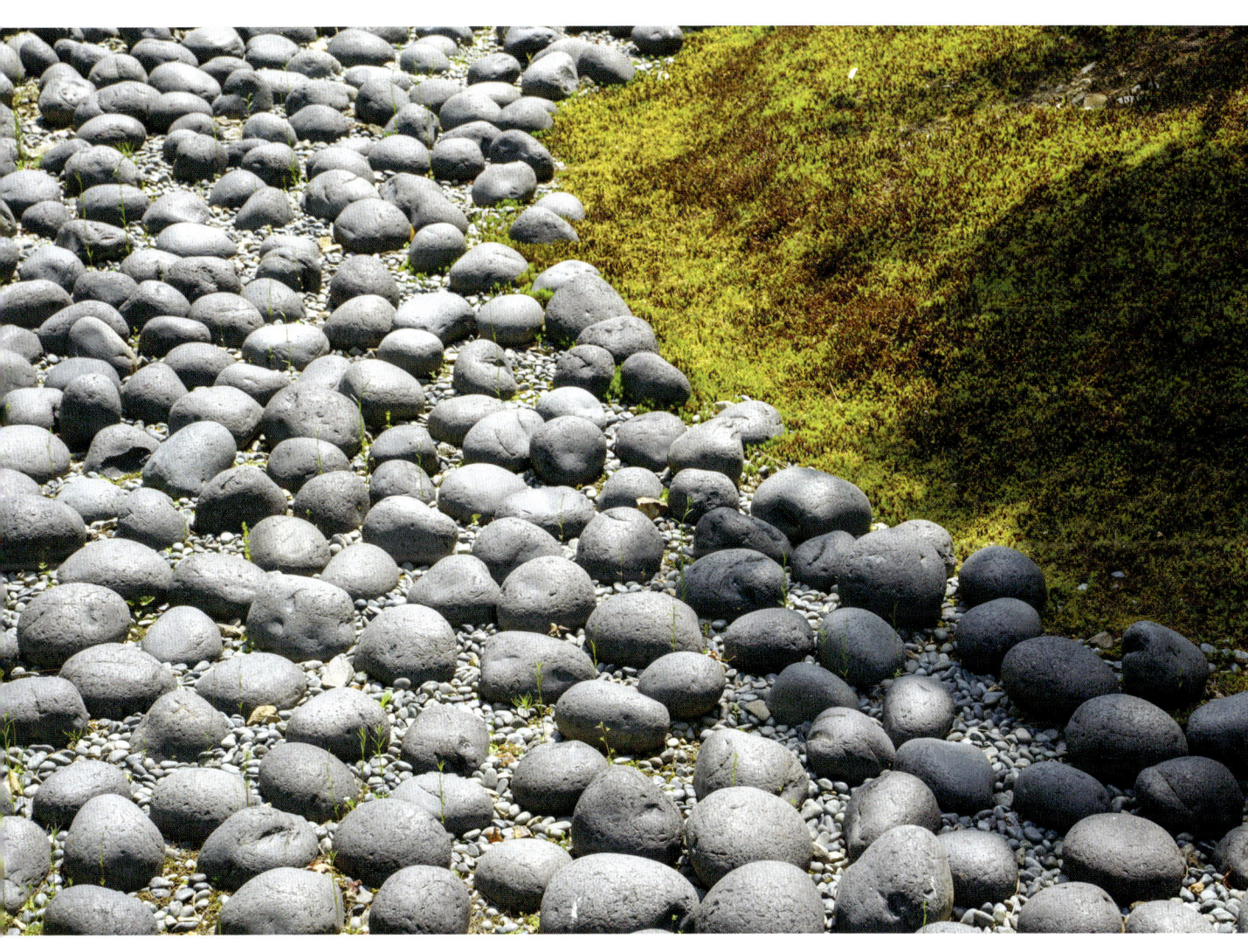

3-4 *Kinkaku-ji*

In the back of the Golden Pavilion, there are three water sources from the rear mountain: Ginga Sen (Milky Way Fountain), Ganka Sui (Water under the Boulder), and Ryōmon Ryū (Dragon Gate Waterfall). This photo (→) is a waterfall splashing onto the prominent carp stone. (See p. 22.)

The other photo (↓) shows the main pond of this compound. Called Kyōko Ike (Mirror Lake Pond), it reflects the pavilion, although the golden structure is invisible on the right in this particular case. From a position on the shore where irises are blooming, we see Ashihara Jima (Reed Field Island) where two pine trees are standing.

You may have read the Ivan Morris translation of the novel *The Temple of the Golden Pavilion* by Yukio Mishima. This story is based on an instance of arson at the pavilion carried out by a twenty-one-year-old novice monk in 1950. The novice, who stammered, had an obsession with beauty and desire for its destruction. Mishima, who had been a stammerer himself, studied the novice's eccentric psychological makeup and developed a fictional character. The narration takes the form of his confession.

Reconstruction took place between 1952 and 1955, but the Golden Pavilion did not regain the national treasure status that was removed when it burned down.

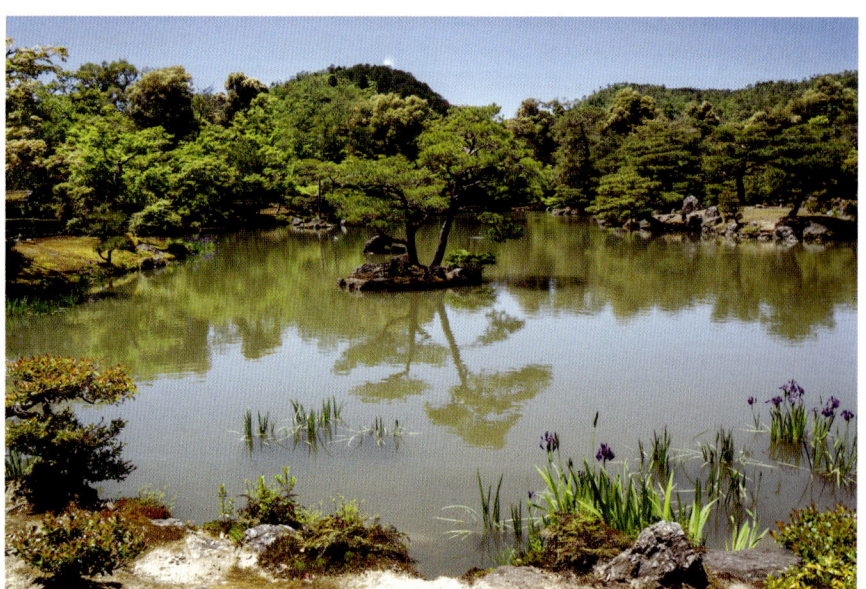

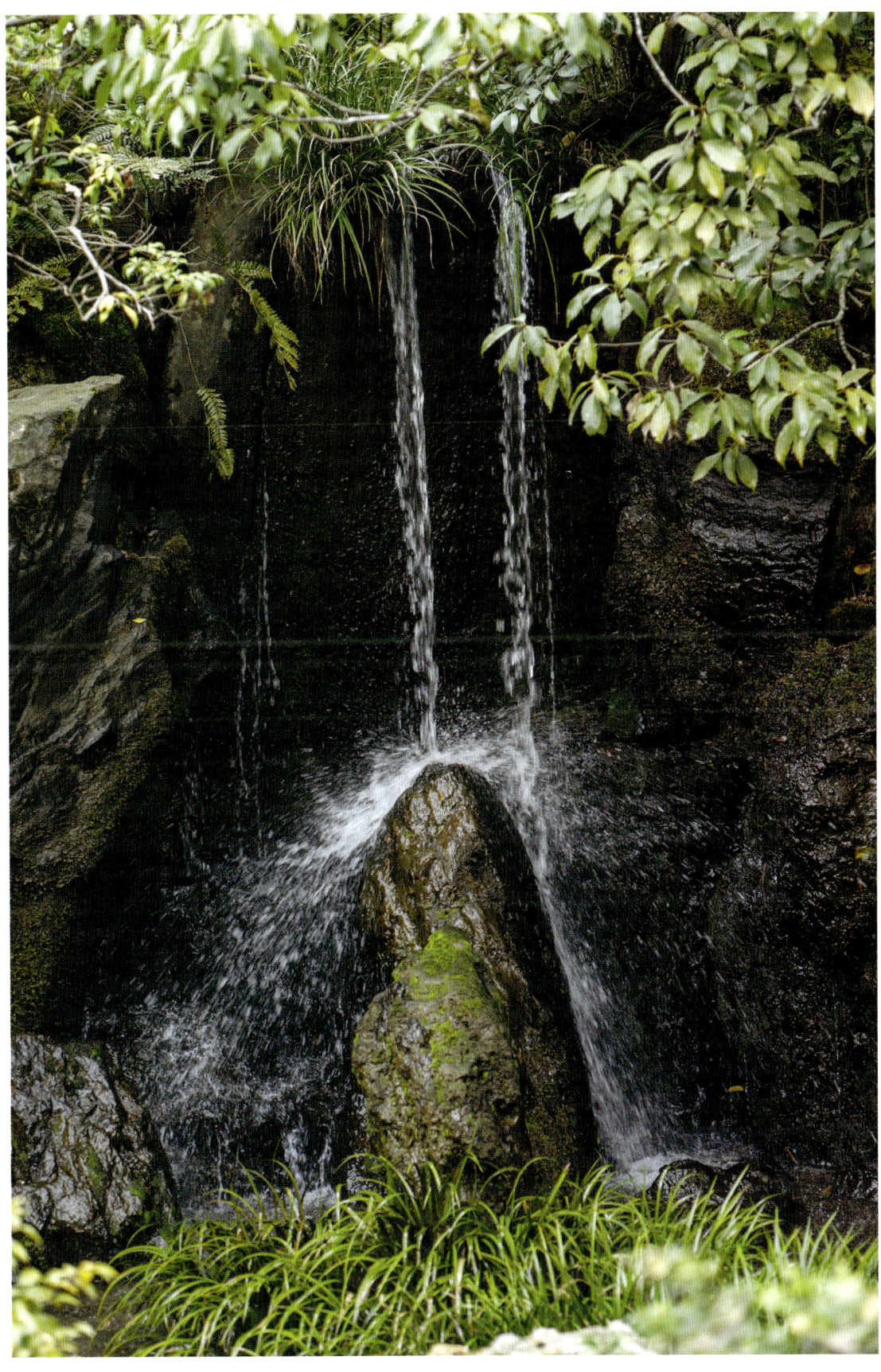

3-5 *Kennin-ji*

Myōan Eisai was the first monk to bring Zen teachings from China to Japan, doing so in the early thirteenth century. Kyōto was then under the strong influence of the headquarters of the establishment Tendai School of Mount Hiei, northeast of the city. Tendai centers offered a comprehensive practice of Buddhism focused on scriptural studies, meditation, Mahāyāna precepts, and Vajrayāna rituals. During that time, a new trend of Kamakura Period Buddhism advocating a single practice of chanting Amitābha Buddha was threatening the establishment. So Eisai taught an inclusive practice of both Vajrayāna and Zen to avoid confrontation.

Lanxi Daolong from China (Japanese name Rankei Dōryū) became the abbot of the Kennin-ji in 1259 and established a pure Zen practice. The monastery compound was afterward destroyed by war three times, but it was restored in the late sixteenth century.

In its huge, dry landscape (→) with white sand representing an ocean, three groups of stone formations consisting of lucky-numbered (seven, five, and three) "islands" have discs of moss representing land, while the stones themselves symbolize mountains.

The gate here (↓) is called *chokushi mon* 勅使門, meaning "the gate for the imperial messenger," which is obviously not for daily use. Behind it is the dharma hall. (See also 5-2.)

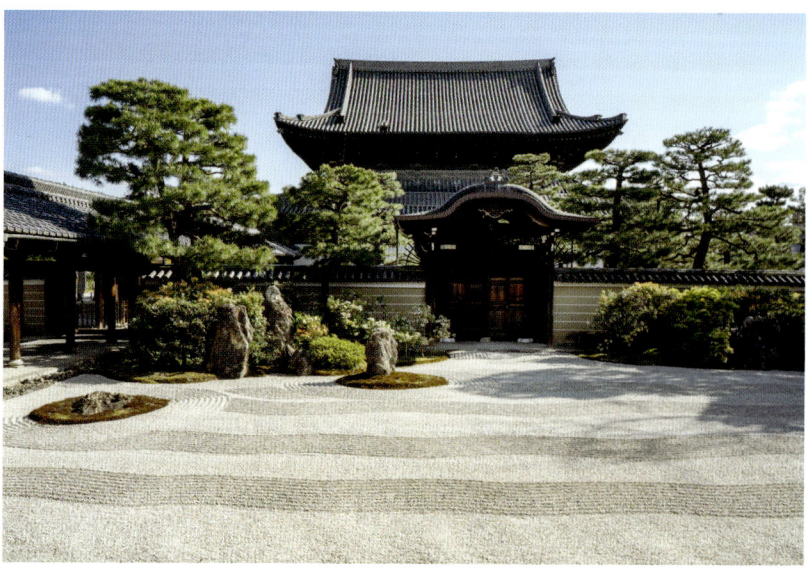

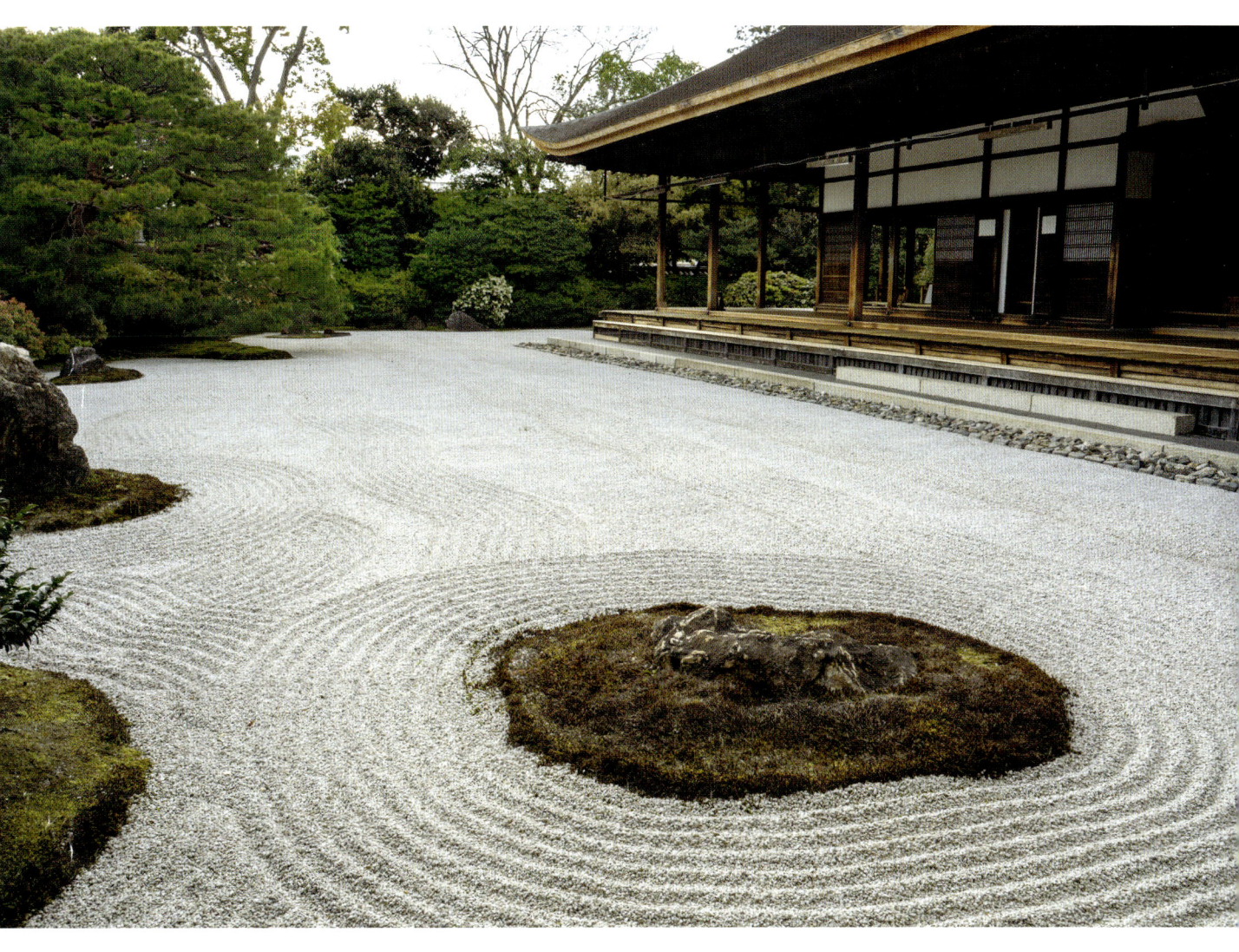

Gleaming
jakushō

寂
照

I<small>N</small> Z<small>EN</small> aesthetics, *gleaming* or subdued light represents quietness, serenity, and *nirvāna*—in this case indicating freedom from desire. An austere room quieted with dim light is suitable for contemplation and seeing through the true nature of things as they are. Thus, it's customary to avoid bright light in meditation halls and tea rooms. Shade provides a setting for spiritual awakening in accordance with the teaching of "turning light to shine within."

By being serene and aware, we leave behind a mind restrained by superficial characteristics of things and settings. Gleaming also connects to the famed Japanese sense of *wabi* and *sabi*. We may feel in an object in nature a universal loneliness, which may be characterized as *wabi*. We may feel in an object or in poetry a refined solitude caused by aging and decay, which may be characterized as *sabi*.

Shiori (wilting) does not indicate a pathetic verse. *Hosomi* (thinness) does not mean a fragile verse. *Shiori* (also interpreted as fading quality) exists in the feature of a poem. *Hosomi* (interpreted as fine-thread awareness) exists in the heart of the poem.

—K<small>YORAI</small>

Those who have mastered blossoming (in *Noh* performance) know about wilting. Thus, wilting is above blossoming.

—Z<small>E'AMI</small>

From the position of no mind, conceal your own mind to yourself and fill the moment between motions.

—Z<small>E'AMI</small>

4-1 *Ryōan-ji*

Behind the abbot's quarters, there is a tea house (→) called Zōroku An (Hiding Six Hut). You might also call it "Turtle Hut," as a turtle hides its head, tail, and four legs inside its shell. It may imply that it fits six people.

In the back garden (↓) sits a stone lantern and a stone basin with water held in a square pool. The ideographs carved on the four sides are: 吾, 唯, 知, and 足 (in the order of top, right, left, and bottom). The rectangular part in each character, 口, meaning "mouth," is represented by the square watery expanse in the center. The meanings of the symbols are, respectively, "I," "only," "know," "satisfaction."

Tea ceremony involves detailed procedures and movements, for which people spend their lifetimes learning a great variety of rules. Nevertheless, whether the practitioner is masterful or innocent, the guests' responsibility is just to enjoy. For example: A grand tea master once invited Hollywood star Ingrid Bergman to a full course ceremony with a meal. Bergman at one point said, "Grand master, when are you going to serve tea?" He said, "I already did. The green stuff in a small bowl." Bergman said, "Oh, I thought it was spinach soup!"

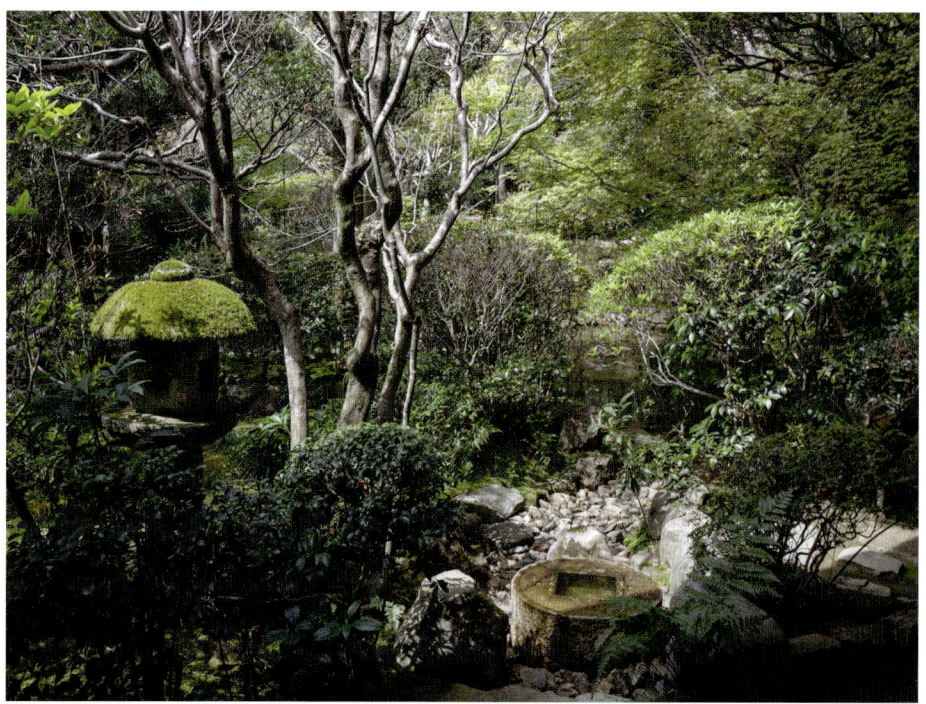

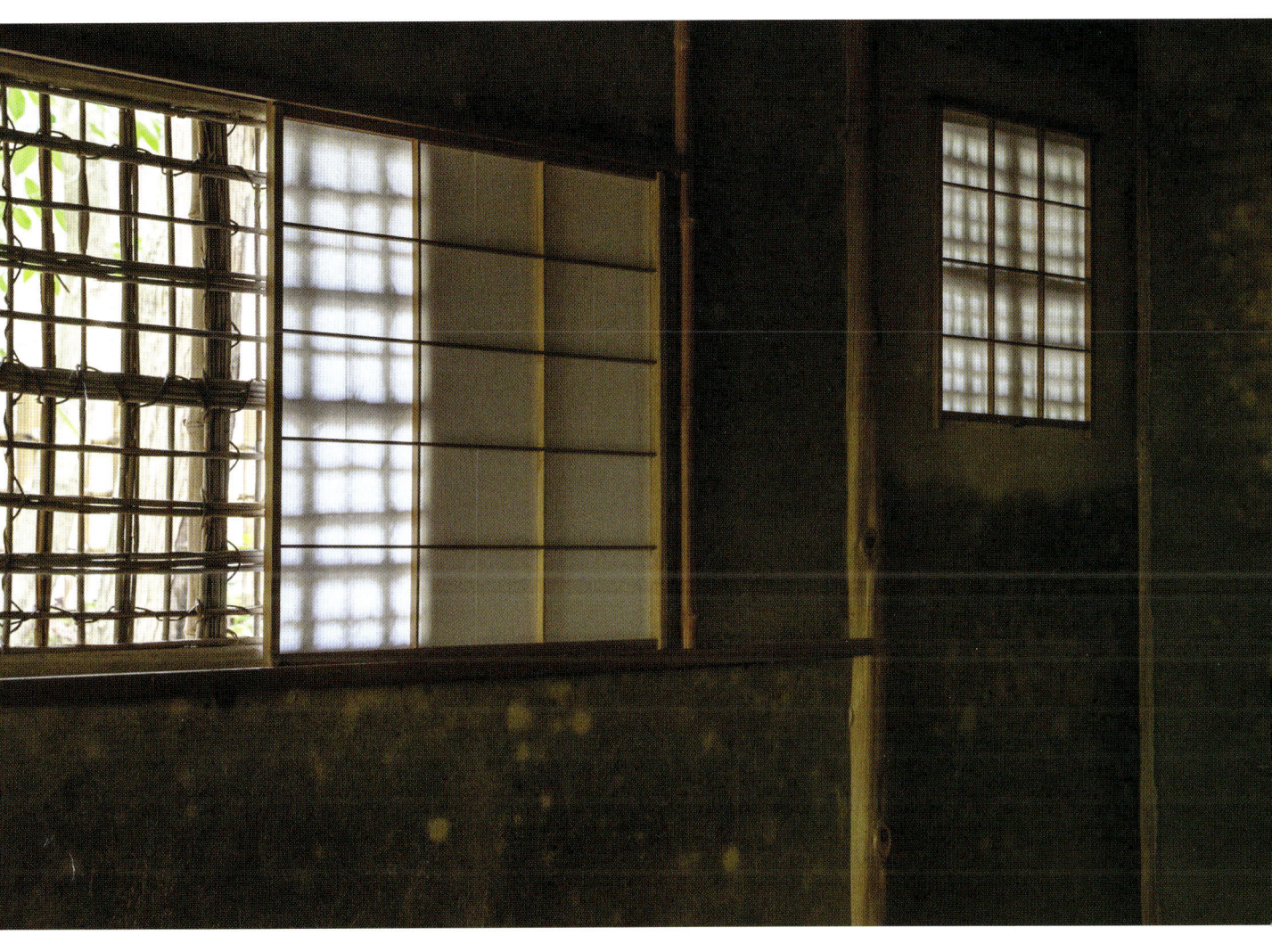

4-2 *Kōrin'-in, Daitoku-ji*

Rikyū Sen, who established the *wabi* (austere) style of tea ceremony, resided at a subtemple of the Daitoku Monastery and was active as a lay Zen practitioner. That's why the Daitoku-ji has the highest concentration of outstanding tea huts and tea gardens.

Most of its twenty-four subtemples were founded during the fourteenth to sixteenth centuries. To the south of the main compound of the monastery, the Kōrin'-in is nested tightly with other subtemples, including the Zuihō-in (2-4), the Ryōgen'-in (5-1), and the Ōbai-in (5-4). The Kōrin'-in was built around 1533, and its tea house in 1928.

The round stepping stones for crossing over the pond (→) are an offering to guests for intimate tea ceremony gatherings. The stones have the shape of mill-stones for husking beans and grains. They have rotary querns with six sections of grooving. For milling by hand, a round top stone and bottom stones of similar sizes are placed around a wooden hub in the center. The top stone has a vertical handle on top near the edge and holes to put grains or beans through and push them out.

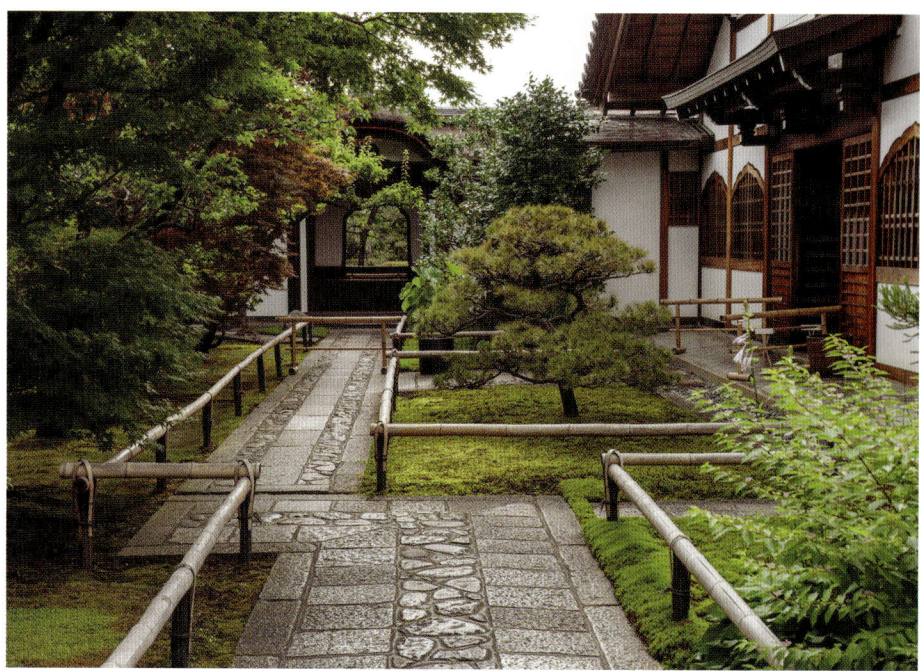

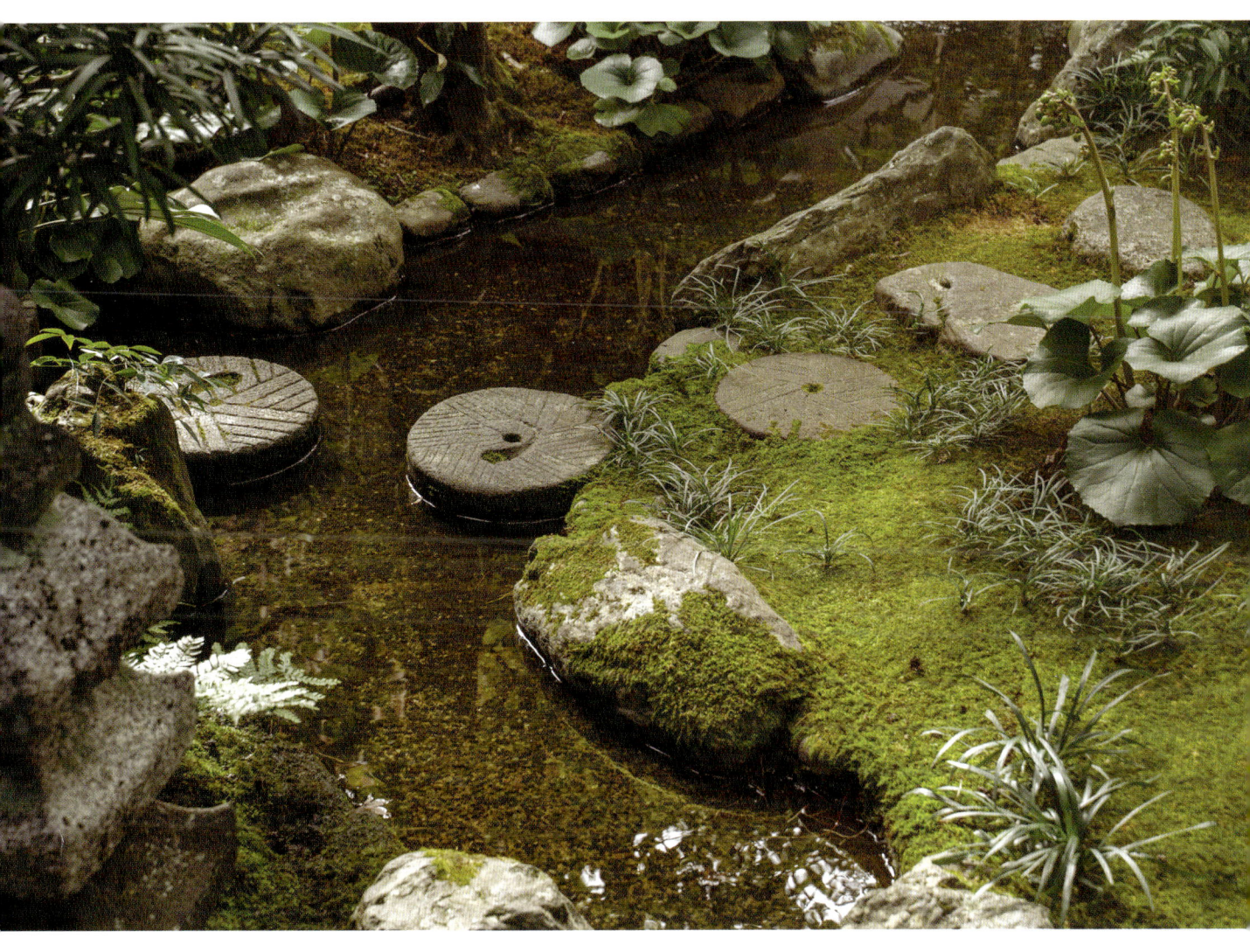

4-3 *Konchi-in, Nanzen-ji*

Konchi-in, a subtemple of the Nanzen Monastery, was established by Ishin Sūden in 1605. Sūden was a trusted advisor on lawmaking and diplomacy to Ieyasu Tokugawa, who established a tight feudal system as the founding *shōgun* of the Edo government. Sūden, who was nicknamed "Black-robed Prime Minister," had the authority to appoint the abbots of the Five Mountains and the Ten Important Temples in Kyōto.

As befitting an all-powerful ruler, Ieyasu was to be enshrined in the Tōshō (East Illuminating) Shrine upon his death. This Shintō sanctuary was built in Nikkō, north of Edo, and a branch of the Tōshō Shrine was built in the northwestern part of the Konchi-in in Kyōto. Ieyasu was given the title of Tōshō Gongen (Tōshō Avatar). Throughout Japanese history until modern times, Buddhism and Shintōism were mixed, with the belief that Shintō deities are avatars or incarnations of Buddhist deities.

Here you see a stone lantern (→) standing in the garden at the side of a passage to the Tōshō Shrine in the northwestern part of the Konchi-in compound.

The other photo (↓) shows the garden in front of the abbot's quarters. (See "Stone Formations" in the appendices.)

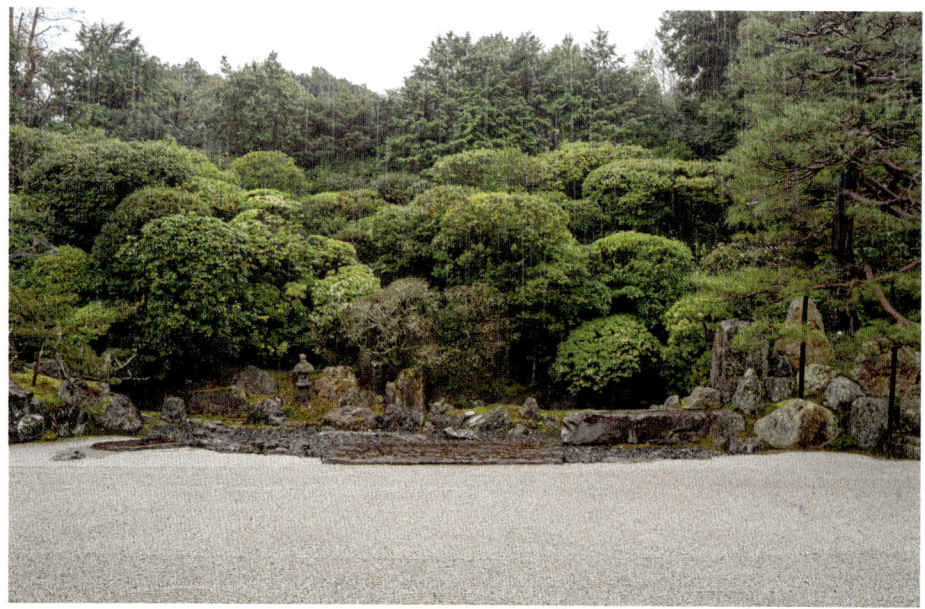

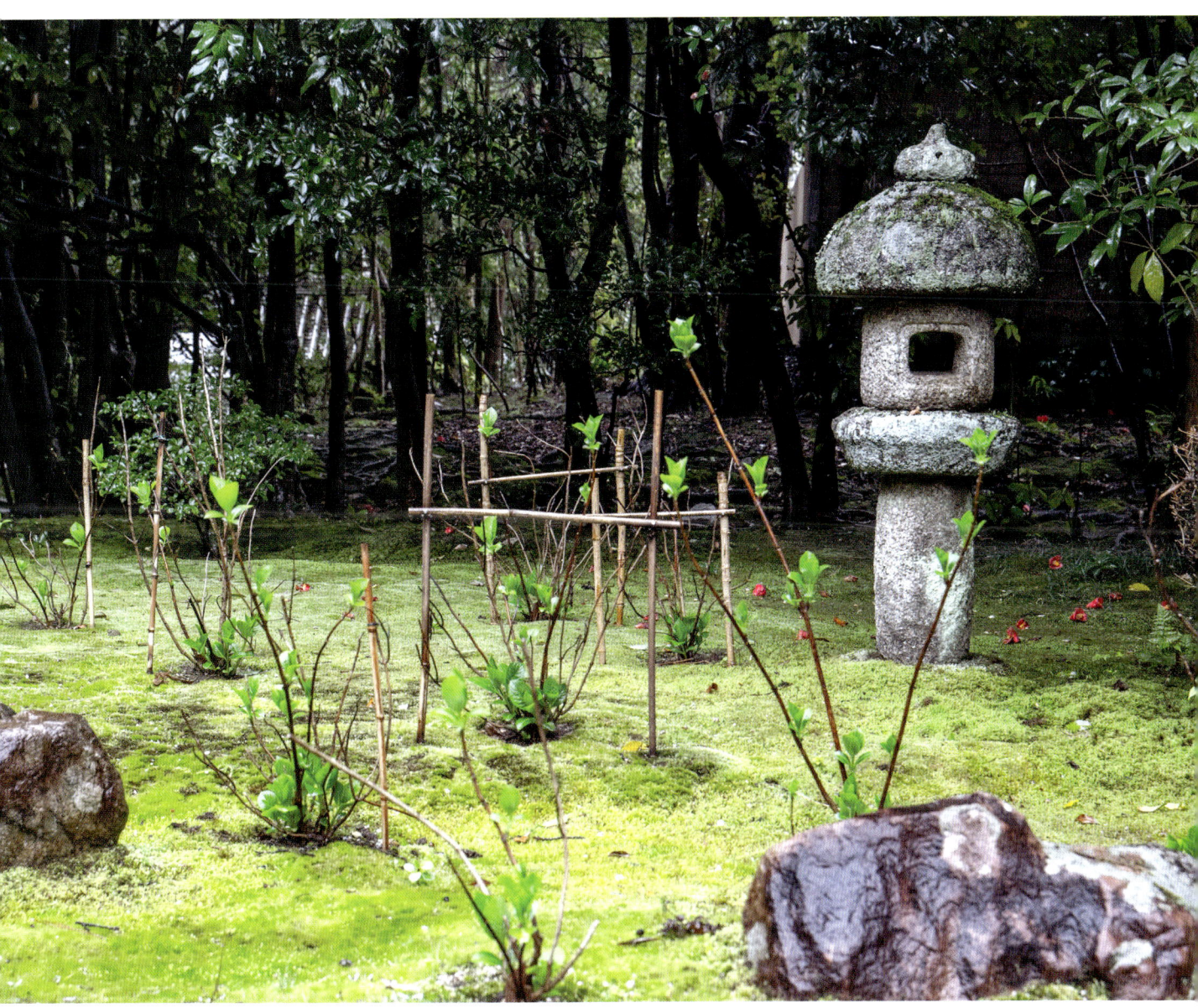

4-4 *Tenryū-ji*

From the abbot's quarters of the Tenryū Monastery, there is a view of the Sōgen (Caoxi Source) Pond and beyond (↓). Caoxi, in the Shao Region (present-day Guandong Province) of China, is where the Sixth Ancestor Huineng lived and taught. Huineng is highly revered as the founder of the Sudden Enlightenment School, which eventually dominated Zen thought in China. His influence still seems present right in this garden.

Deeper in the forest beyond the pond (→), a somewhat wild-looking bamboo grove hosts rhododendron blossoms in bloom. (See also 1-4, 6-4.)

Zen gardening is often associated with sand, rocks, well-pruned trees, and ponds. But sometimes such gardens have untamed woods as a backdrop—real wilderness.

While enjoying trees from the past, are we doing something positive for the next generations? Christiana Figueres and Tom Rivett-Carnac write in *The Future We Choose: The Stubborn Optimist's Guide to the Climate Crisis*, "Plant trees. As many as

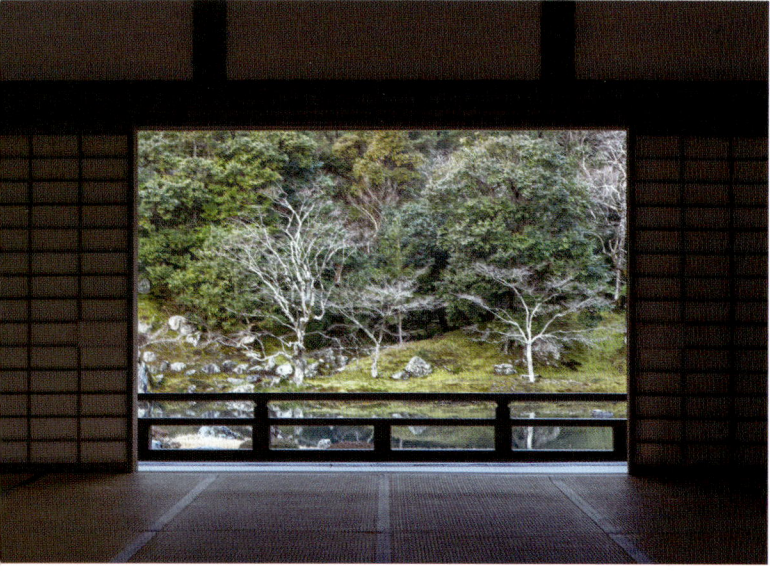

you can."[*] This is their encouragement for direct action to reverse climate change. If each one of us resolved to help plant one hundred or more trees in our community, yard, or anywhere in the world, it would be a good beginning of a great turning.

[*]Christiana Figueres and Tom Rivett-Carnac, *The Future We Choose: The Stubborn Optimist's Guide to the Climate Crisis* (New York: Vintage Books, 2021), 168.

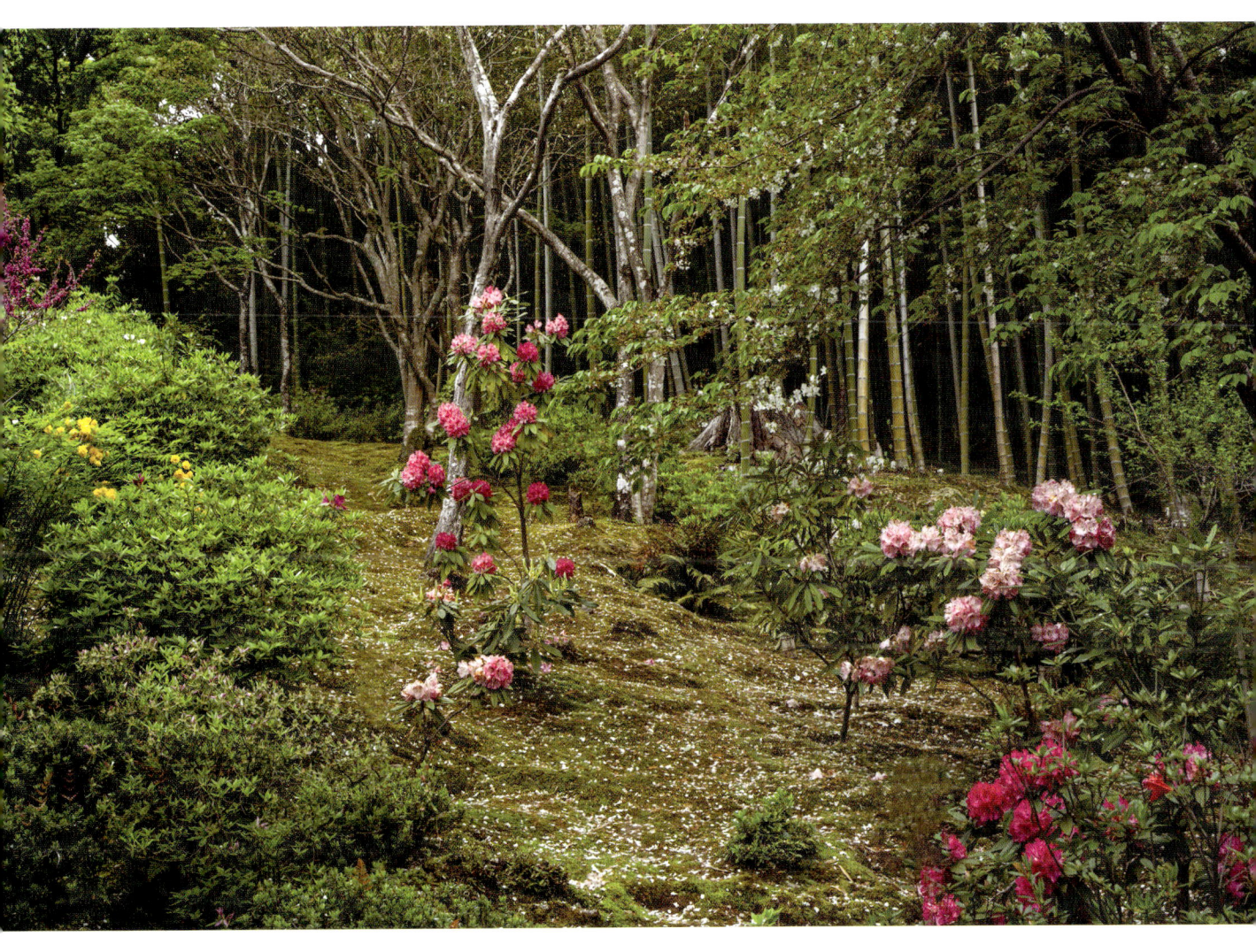

4-5 *Shisen-dō*

This is again the Shisen-dō (Poetic Sages Hall), situated in far northeastern Kyōto at the side of the East Mountain range. As mentioned earlier, this was originally a residence of a retired *samurai* aristocrat. So the entire building is rather humble in the *shoin* style of a *samurai's* audience hall. (See also 1-1.) The straight roof of the abbot's quarters is slated, while the center of the building has a thatched roof.

From an entrance leading by a flat-stone path on the sanded ground to the abbot's quarters (→), the dry landscape garden is glimpsed through a small window. (The horizontal bamboo poles here signify no entry.)

The garden in front of the abbot's quarters (↓) has a stripe-raked sand field with an array of roundly trimmed azalea brushes. Pruning is essential for maintaining the overall shape of the landscape. A dense shape-making style of pruning— whether round or square—is called *karikomi* 刈込, literally meaning "cut to push down." You see such bushes in many Zen gardens. It is an artificially controlled aspect of gardening. A natural forest behind such tightly pruned bushes makes a good contrast.

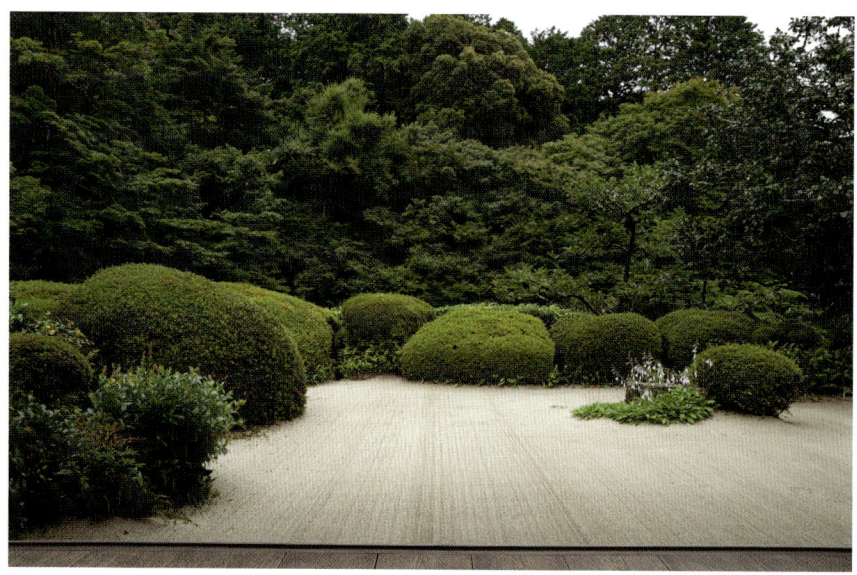

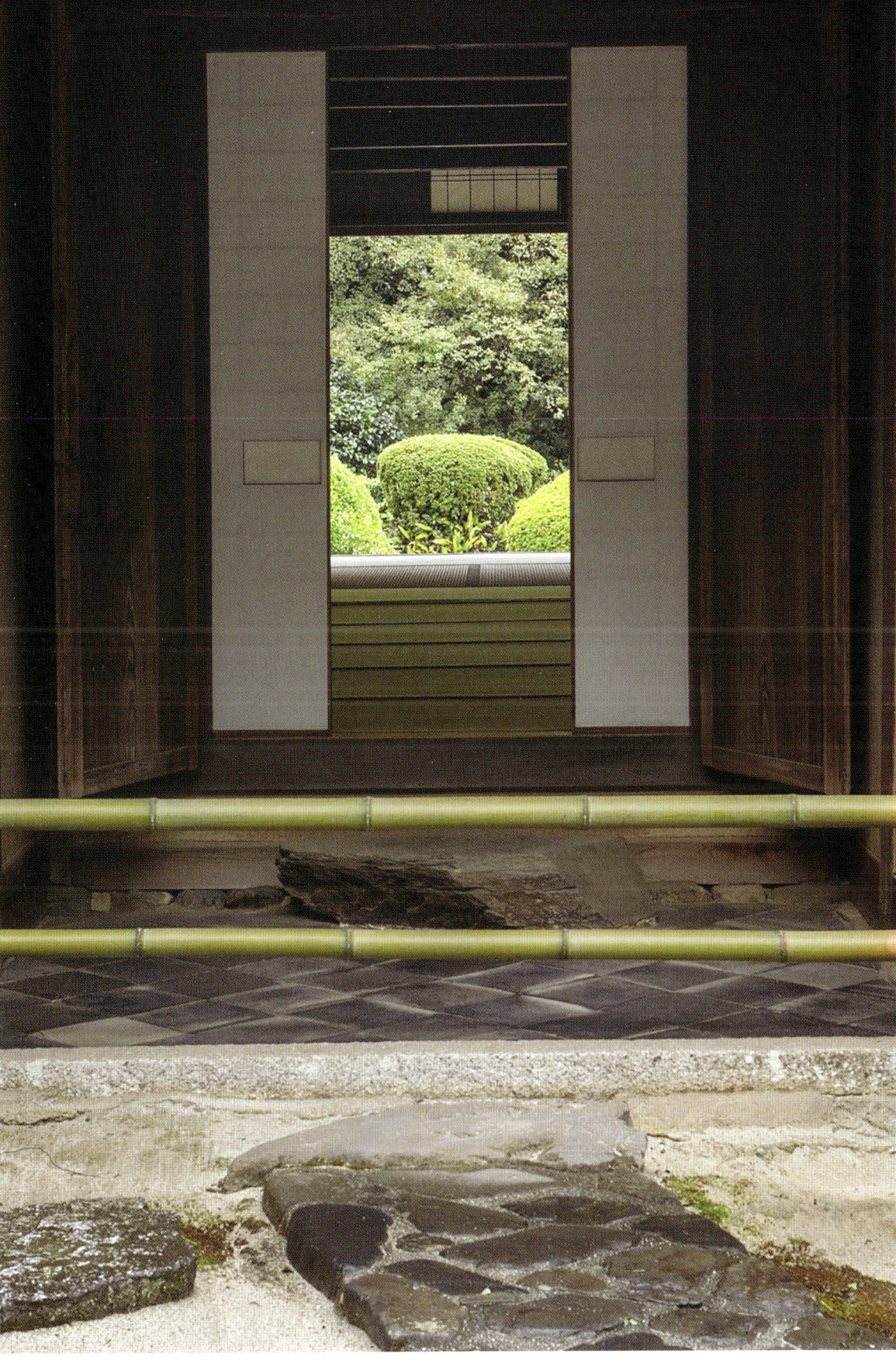

Pivotal

daiyū

PIVOTAL IN Zen indicates with great function, meaning something unpretentious, surprising, or seemingly worthless that can change someone's life. A broken brush line in a landscape painting, a low tone of *shakuhachi* flute, the subtle cracks of a tea bowl—any of these may be enough to help awaken you to something profound and genuine. This is pivotal.

Something precious could work as well. Take, for example, a scroll of a masterful work of calligraphy elegantly displayed in a tea room's alcove. What is written on it may be a well-known poetic phrase. But the true function of such a scroll in a tea room is to allow the guests to witness the presence of the calligrapher, usually a Zen master, who may or may not be alive. The depth of the master's spiritual practice and vastness of personality evident in the artwork may help awaken the guests. This is great function.

Are mountain colors and valley sounds one phrase or half a phrase of dharma?

—DŌGEN

A great function is revealed right now, free of all rules.

—YUANWU

All awakened ones throughout space and time, honored ones, great beings who help all to awaken, together may we realize wisdom beyond wisdom!

—ZEN CHANT DEDICATION

Miracles are nothing other than fetching water and carrying firewood.

—LAYMAN PANG

5-1 *Ryōgen'-in, Daitoku-ji*

The Ryōgen'-in, established around 1502 by some *samurai* provincial governors, is the oldest of the twenty-four existing subtemples of the Daitoku Monastery. The space seen in the photo (→) is called Tōteki Ko (East Waterdrop Pot), created by Gakushō Nabeshima in 1960. Located between the abbot's quarters and the kitchen, this is a *tsubo niwa* 壺庭, literally a "pot garden," indicating an indoor garden. This phrase is associated with the saying *kochū tenchi* 壺中天地, "a world inside a pot." It comes from an ancient Chinese legend that two men went inside an earthen medicine pot through its neck and enjoyed the life of sorcerers inside it. It is thought that this *tsubo niwa* is the smallest Zen garden in Japan.

The garden in front of the abbot's quarters (↓), created in 1980 by the then abbot, is called Isshi Dan (One Branch Platform). The turtle island in an oval mossy spot of land with standing rocks has a geometric shape and a naturally rugged center.

The Ryōgen'-in is right in the south of the fairly space-restricted main compound of the Daitoku-ji. It is tightly surrounded by other subtemples whose roofs are visible (→).

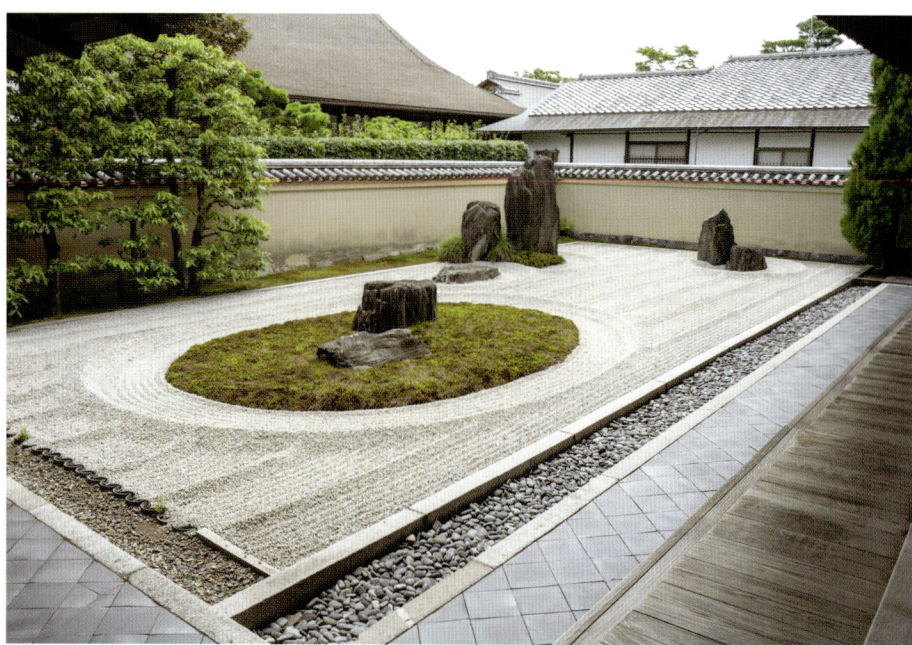

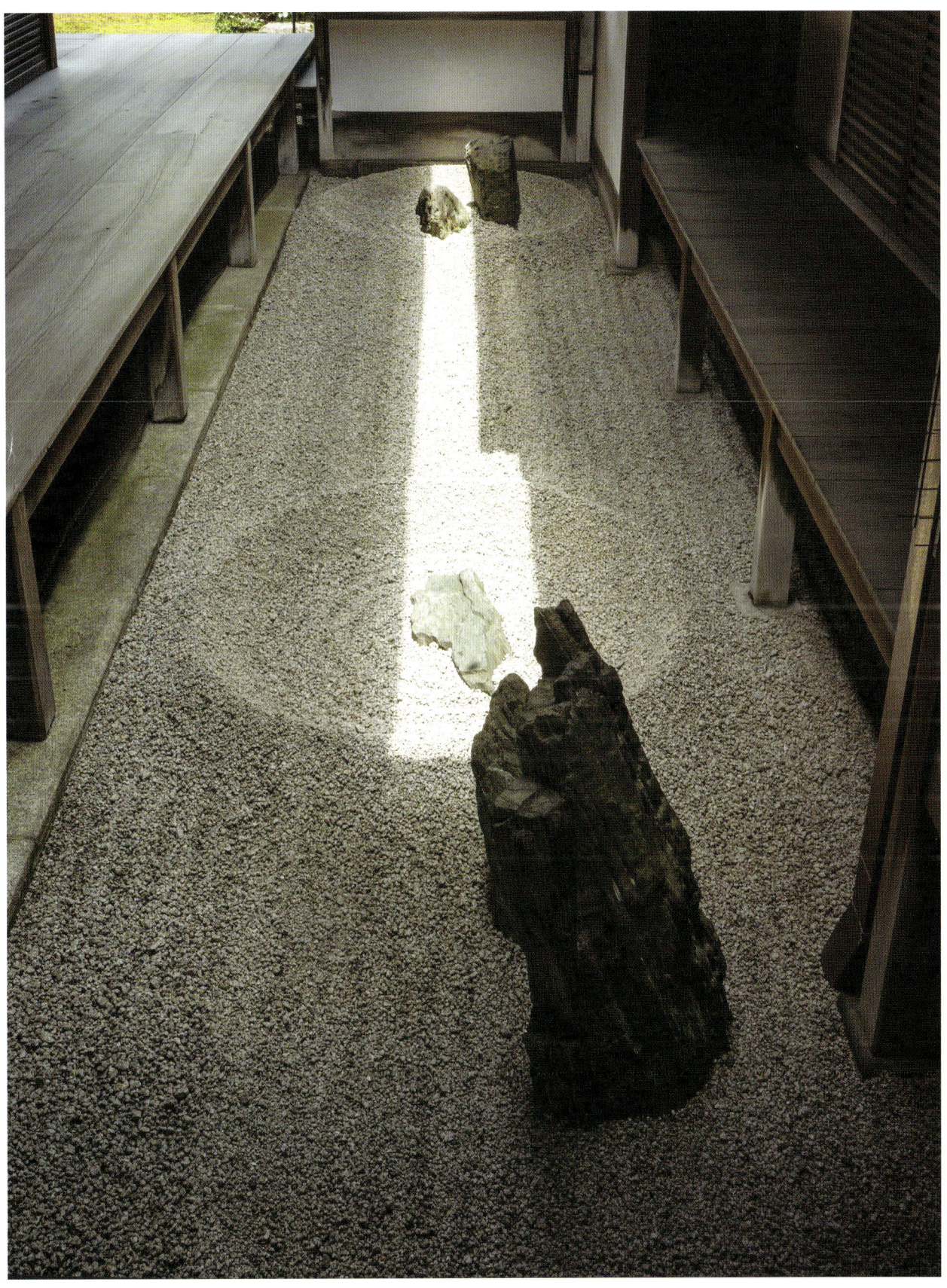

5-2 *Kennin-ji*

The garden here (→), called Chō'on Tei (Sound of Tide Garden), is located between the large *shoin*, a *samurai*-style drawing room as seen in this photo, and a small *shoin* behind the photographer. These buildings are in the back of the abbot's quarters of this monastery.

The garden to the south in front of the abbot's quarters (↓) is the Daiō-en (Great Hero Garden). "Great Hero" is another name for the Buddha, meaning the one who wins against the temptations of demons. In Chinese Zen monasteries, you sometimes see horizontal signs across the front of the buildings saying "Great Hero Hall" at the Buddha halls. This garden was designed and constructed in 1940 by Kumakichi Katō, a third-generation landscaper. (See also 3-5.)

One of the most prominent stone sculptors and landscape designers in the Western world is Isamu Noguchi (1904–1988). He was inspired by traditional Japanese Zen gardens and crafted his own Zen-style gardens to match contemporary architecture. As an artist, I myself have had occasion to design dry landscape gardens for homes in Northern California. Where the conservation of water is crucial, gardens with sand and rocks are ideal. Free from any need to plant, weed, or prune, their maintenance costs are minimal.

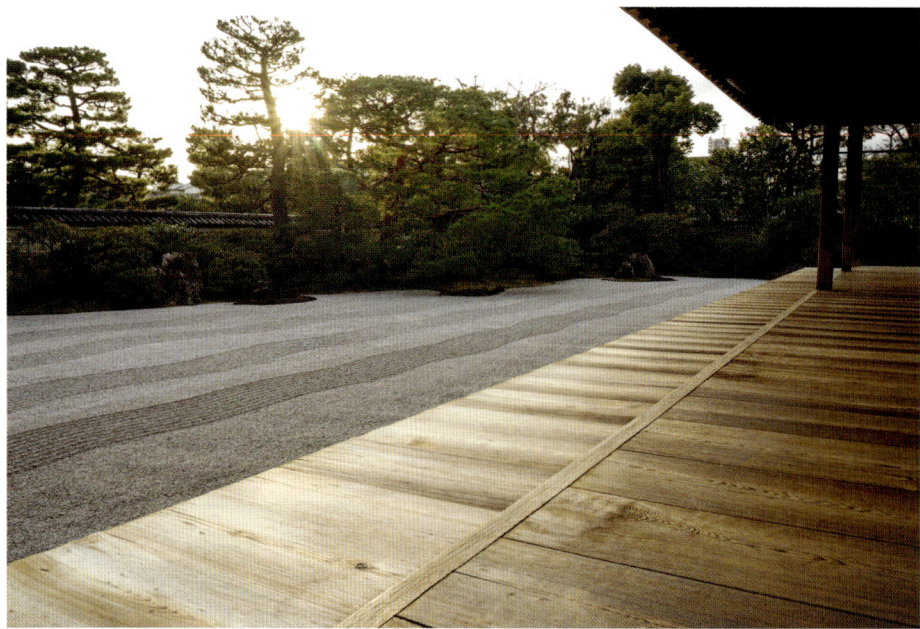

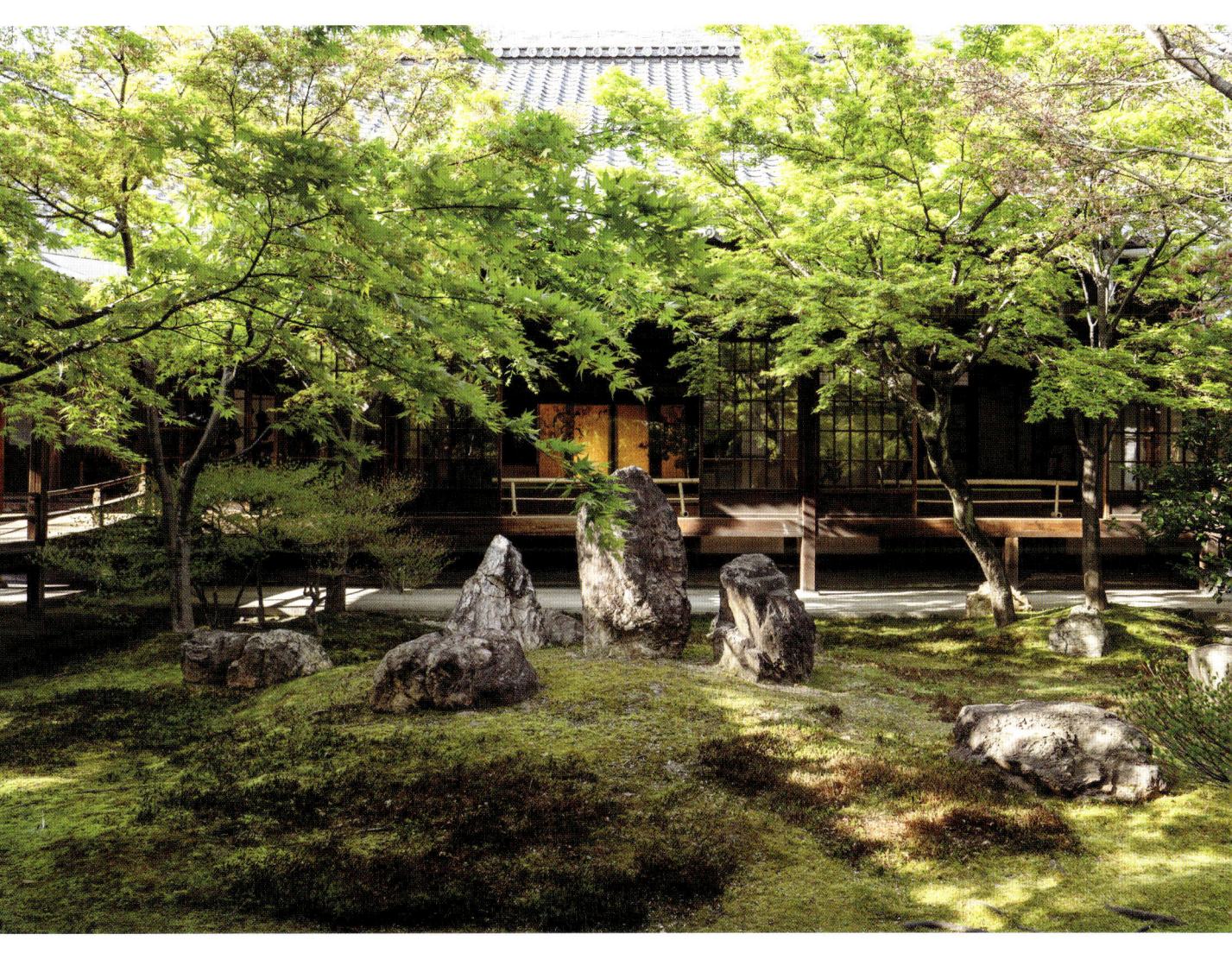

5-3 *Kōmyō-in, Tōfuku-ji*

The Kōmyō-in, one of the twenty-five subtemples of the Tōfuku Monastery, was founded in 1391 by Kinzan Myōshō, the seventieth abbot of the monastery.

Its main garden, called Hashin Tei (Heart of the Waves Garden) (↓), was created in 1939 by Mirei Shigemori at about the same time as he was building gardens around the abbot's quarters of the Tōfuku-ji. (See 3-1.) His aim was to create "a garden that is alive." Right after passing the gate and stepping into the entrance hall, visitors see the front garden through a rare circular window installed in the center of a pair of *shōji* or sliding doors with rice paper pasted on rectangularly divided spaces.

The name of the main garden comes from a verse: "There is no cloud rising on a mountain peak. There is a moon falling on the heart of waves." Multiple standing rocks with pointed crests line up on the white-sand beach and on the plot of moss around it. In the higher mossy area, triad stones symbolizing three Buddhist deities backed by large roundly sculpted azalea bushes look down on the landscape.

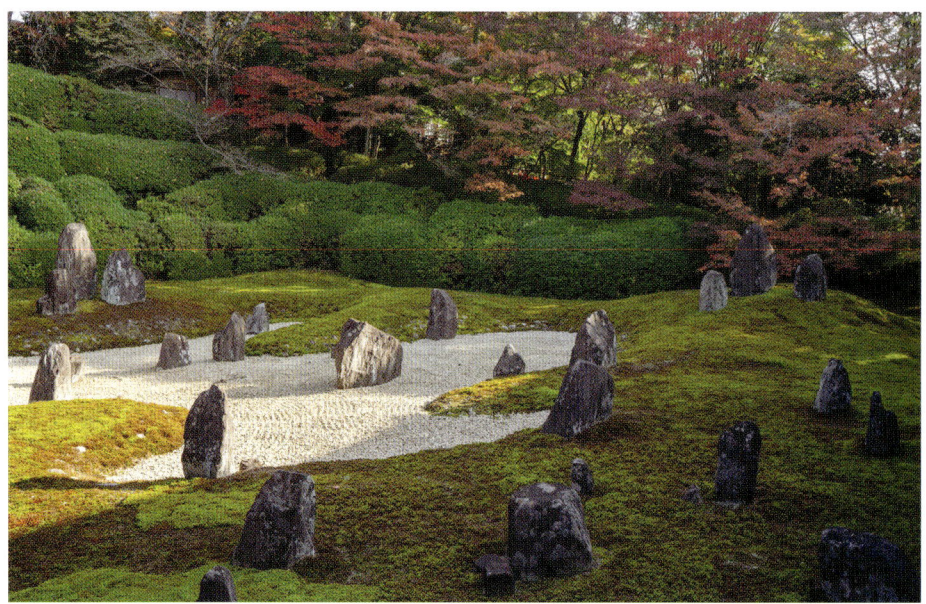

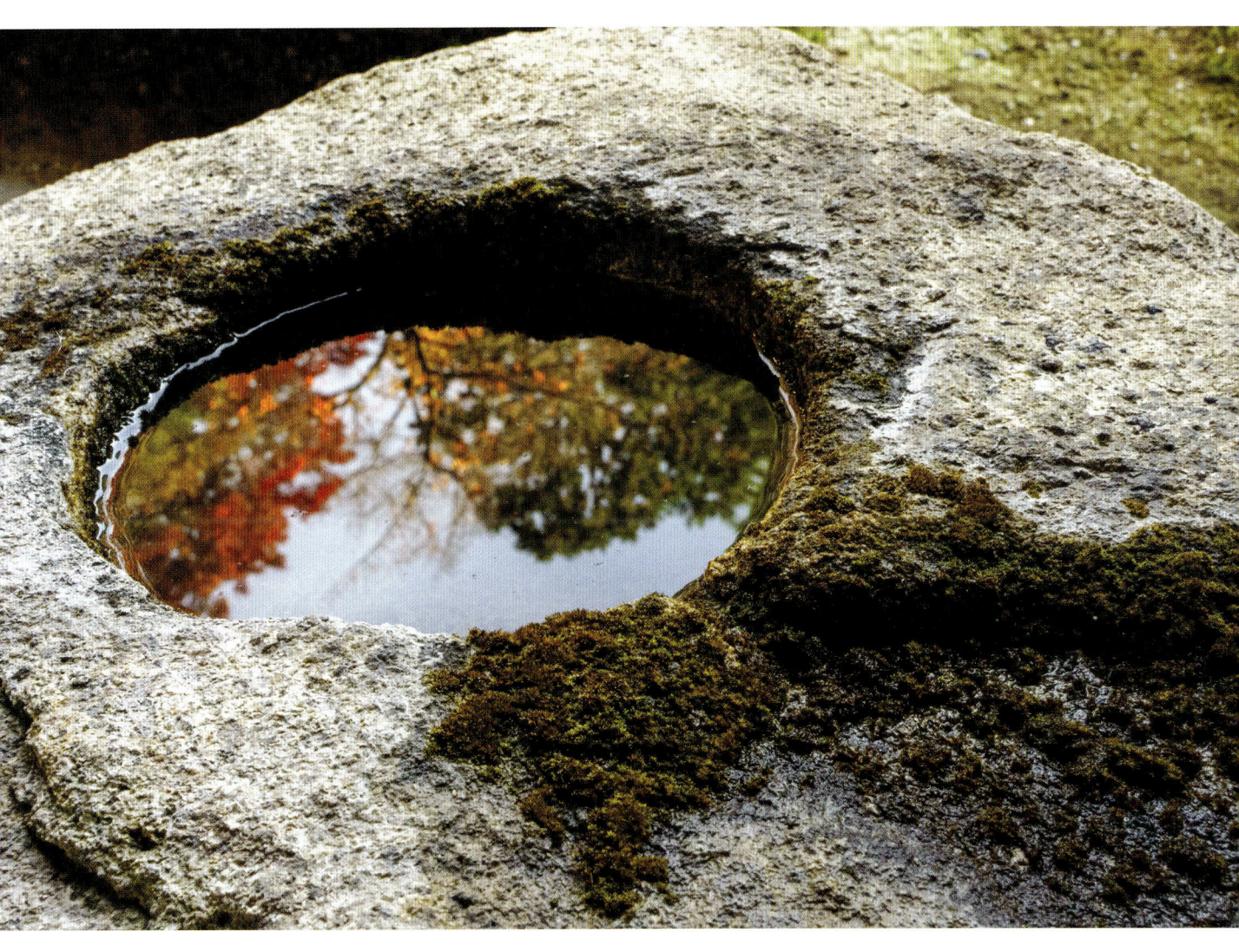

5-4 Ōbai-in, Daitoku-ji

The garden in front of the abbot's quarters here (↓) has a strange and rather disturbing name: Hatō Tei (Cracked Head Garden). It comes from its Chinese counterpart Potou, a mountain in the Huangmei Region (Hebei Province), where Daoxin, the Fourth Ancestor of Chinese Zen, lived for thirty years in the seventh century. Mount Potou's pointed peak looks cracked in the center. Daoxin later renamed it Shuangfeng (Dual Peak) Mountain. This temple name of "Ōbai" is the Japanese way of pronouncing Huangmei, meaning "Apricot." The two standing pointed rocks in the Cracked Head Garden (↓) seem to represent Mount Putou.

The other photo (→) shows another garden with a mossy ground. It is called Jikichū Tei (Directly Hitting Garden), and its design is attributed to Rikyū Sen, who established the *wabi*-style tea ceremony and was tea master to the regent Hideyoshi Toyotomi. In 1582, Hideyoshi, who was about to reunify Japan after 120 years of the Warring Period, held a grand-scale funeral at the Daitoku-ji for his liege lord Nobunaga Oda. Nobunaga, who also endeavored to unify the country, had been ambushed and forced to kill himself before he could achieve this goal. Hideyoshi expanded the Ōbai-in as Nobunaga's *stūpa* site.

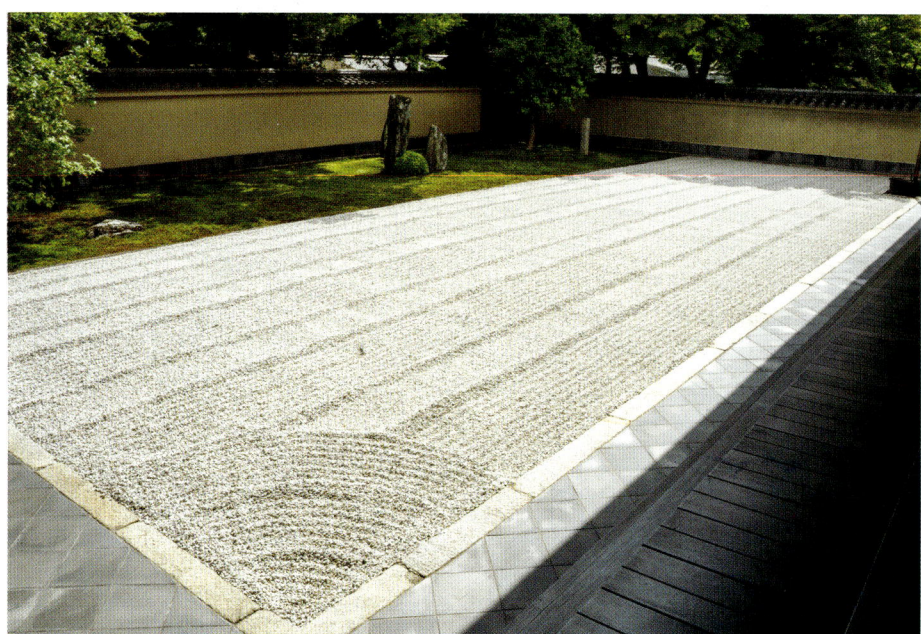

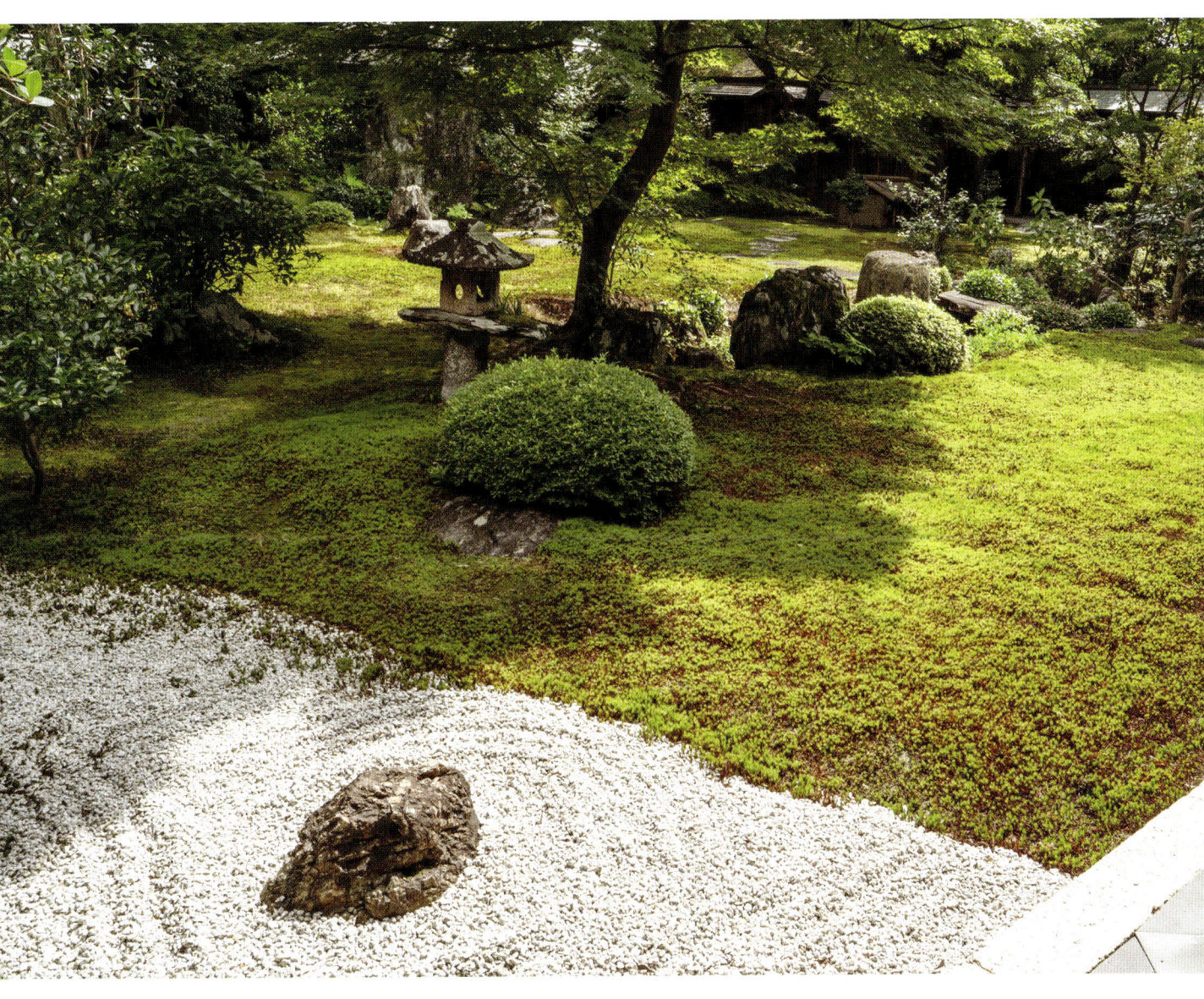

5-5 *Ryōan-ji*

Blooming cherry blossoms, with their short-lived subtle colors and fragrances, are people's favorite to the point of obsession in Japan. From late March till sometime in April, the news media reports daily on the percentage of blooming trees in various locations, showing how the full-bloom tides are inching northward. Cherry blossoms are so central to the culture that in traditional thirty-one-syllable *waka* poetry, the word *hana* (flower) on its own means cherry blossoms.

Here (→), the flowers are reflected on the large Kyōyō Chi (Mirror Containing Pond) in the broad Ryōan-ji compound. When visiting this temple, guests get a ticket at the front gate and walk along the northern side of this pond, which contains Sarasvatī Island. Then, they go into the main campus with its celebrated garden in front of the abbot's quarters. (See 4-1.)

The walk back on the southern side of the pond overlooks the subtemple called the Daiju-in in the distance (↓). This photo of the pond with water lily leaves floating on the surface and azaleas in bloom on the bank was taken slightly after the cherry blossom season.

The Ryōan-ji is one mile southwest of the Kinkaku-ji (Golden Pavilion Temple). This area is known as Rakusei (Western Kyōto).

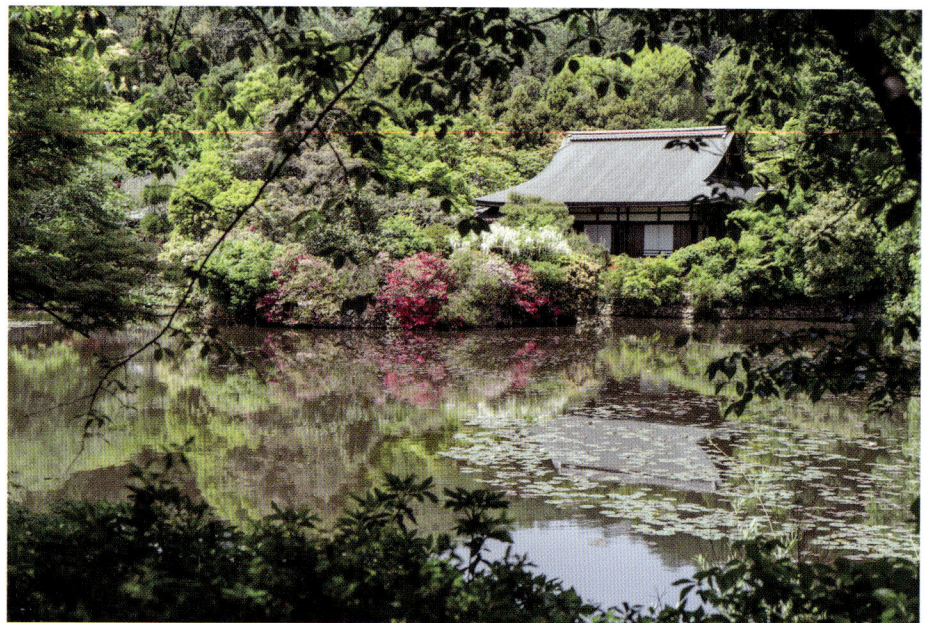

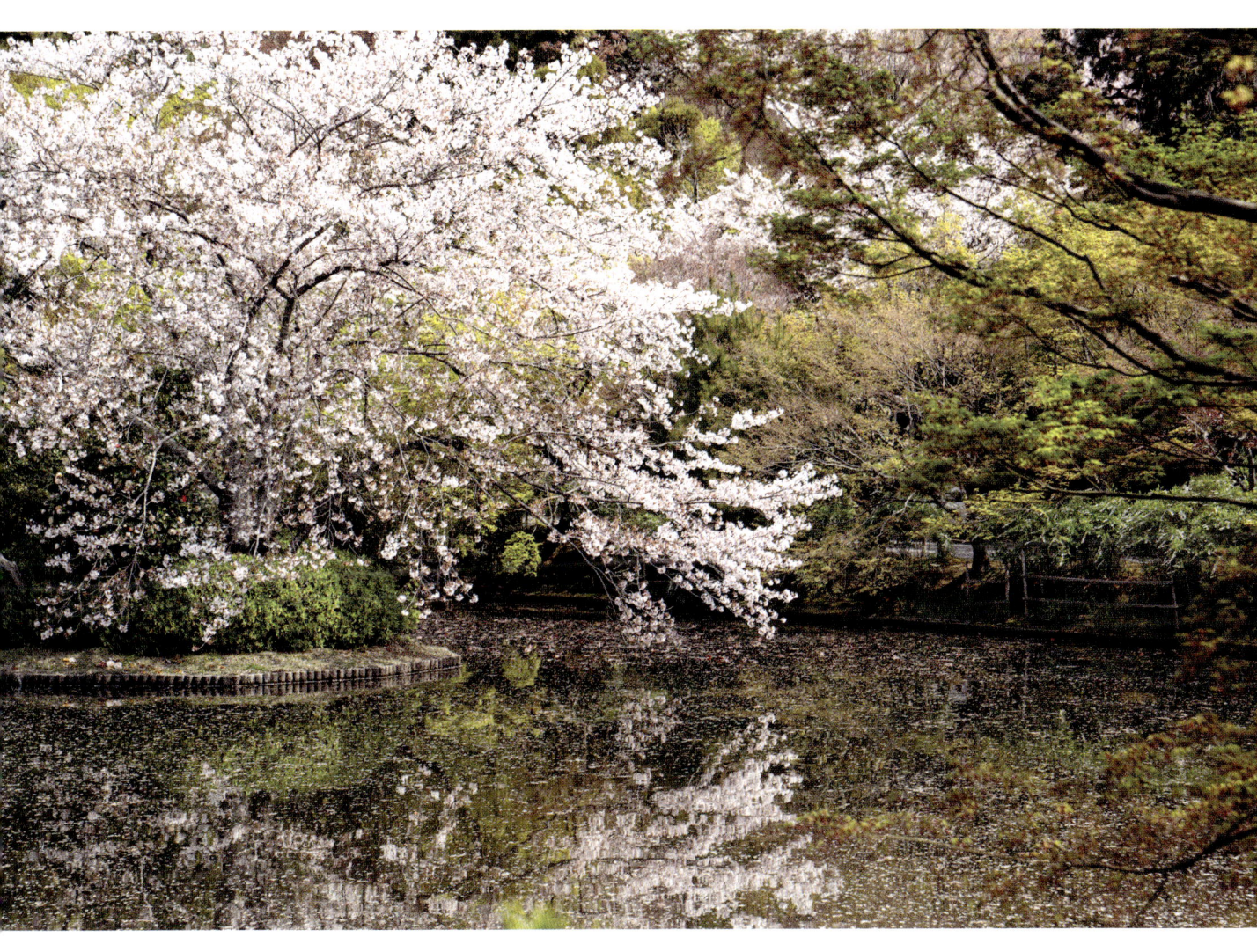

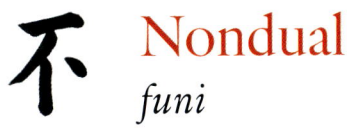

Nondual
funi

THE CONCEPT of "not two" includes "not many." Nondualism sees all things as diverse, yet one. It is both acknowledgment of and freedom from differences and particularities. A brush-drawn circle by a Zen practitioner is beyond perfect and imperfect. It is whole and complete. It is inclusive of a solid section and broken parts, of circular and crushed. It symbolizes the selfless experience of reality in meditation.

Emptiness functions as a decoding word for the practice and art of Zen. It does not mean that things don't exist or that things are hollow. Rather, it means there are no distinct boundaries among things. Nothing is completely independent from other things, and nothing is permanent. All things are connected and can be experienced as one, as *nondual*. In meditation, things are diverse but at the same time singular. Symmetry and asymmetry, simple and complex, fleeting and timeless are all there in front of us.

Form is boundlessness. Boundlessness is form.

—*HEART SŪTRA*

An ancient buddha said, "Mountains are mountains, waters are waters." These words do not mean mountains are mountains; they mean mountains are mountains.

—DŌGEN

In darkness, all words are one. In brightness, phrases are murky or clear.

—SHITOU

Wondrously within nonduality, drumming and singing go together.

—DONGSHAN

At the moment of attaining the way, green mountains and white snow are painted on countless scrolls. Motion and stillness are nothing but a painting. Our endeavor at the moment is brought forth entirely from a painting.

—DŌGEN

6-1 *Rinsen-ji, Tenryū-ji*

Shikō Itō, an internationally known abstract *suiboku-ga* (black ink painting) artist born in 1936, was commissioned by the then-head of the Tenryū-ji Order to design a garden at the Rinsen-ji. She created this powerful grand-scale dry landscape, consisting of only sand and rocks, in 1974. Standing in the center (↓) are rocks representing the trinity of bodhisattvas—Maitreya, Mañjushrī, and Samantabhadra. Around them at varying distances are flat stones for the Sixteen Arhats, disciples of the Buddha.

Musō Soseki, the founding chief priest of the Rinsen-ji, was based here a few times and passed away here. The Rinsen-ji (meaning "Facing the River Temple") is on the Katsura River, west of the center of Kyōto. As it is the Soin (Ancestral Temple) of the Tenryū Monastery, the Founder's Hall is here, enshrining a portrait statue of Soseki. (See p. 24.) The master is buried under the so-called lotus stone beneath the floor.

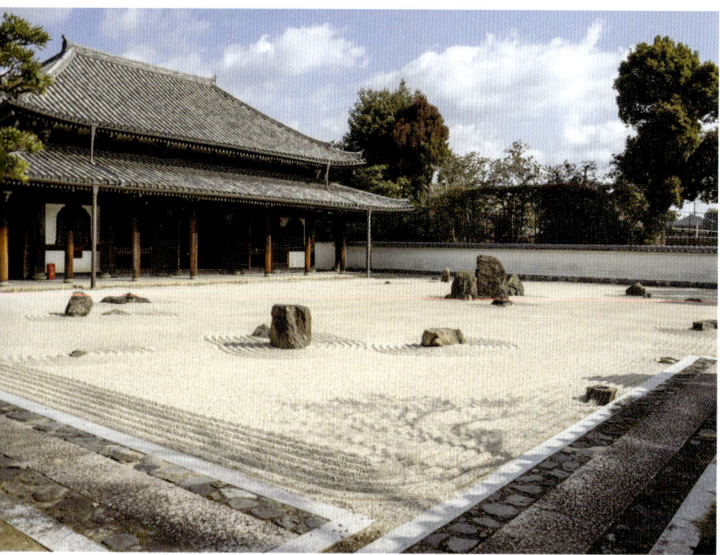

The Rinsen-ji is a subtemple of the Tenryū-ji, located less than a mile away to its southeast. Seen here (→) is the southern facade of the Sanne-in Hall, enshrining Maitreya Bodhisattva. The "Three Meetings" conveyed by the word *Sanne* represent Maitreya Bodhisattva's three "Dragon Blossom" assemblies of expounding dharma to save all sentient beings, which is believed to occur 5,670,000,000 years after the passing of Shākyamuni Buddha. The garden is named Three Dragon Blossom Assemblies Garden.

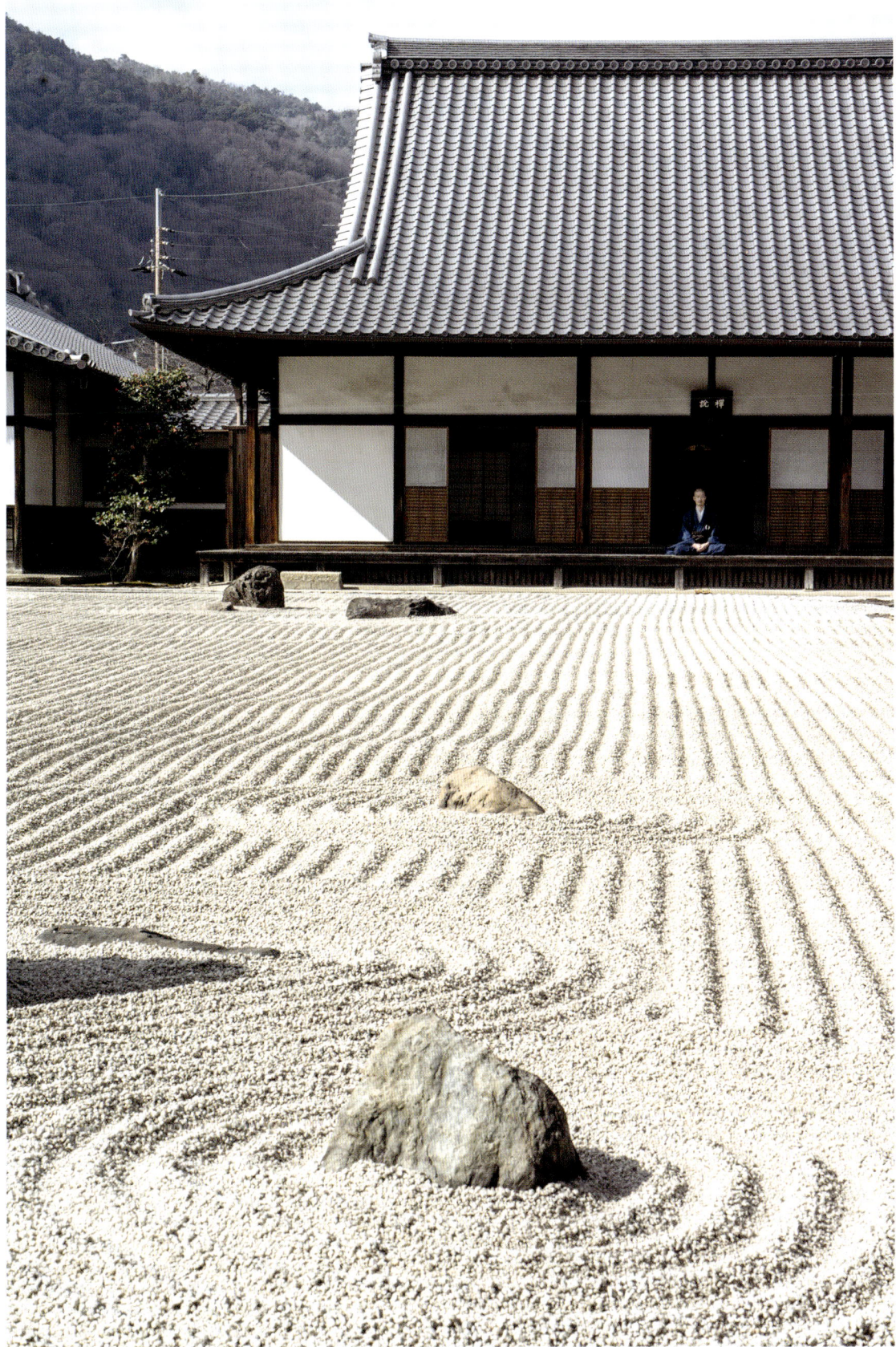

6-2 *Ginkaku-ji*

What would you say if people asked you: Which is your favorite garden in Kyōto? It's a hard question, as there are countless spectacular gardens in this world capital of temples and gardens, and different people have their favorites. I usually say the Ginkaku-ji. It's historically important as well as unique and sublime. That's just my own feeling.

The Kōgetsu Dai (Facing the Moon Platform) at the Ginkaku-ji (→) is almost six feet high. (See 3-2.) You can also glimpse (↓) the eastern end of the Brocade Mirror Pond and Searching East Hall. (See "Garden Plan Example: The Ginkaku-ji," in appendices.)

The garden of the East Mountain Palace—the original version of this temple, whose formal name is Jishō-ji, as mentioned earlier—was created after 1482 by art directors Zen'ami and Sōami for the eighth *shōgun* of the Muromachi government, Yoshimasa Ashikaga.

From the Ginkaku-ji to the nearby Nanzen-ji, there is a narrow path called Tetsugaku no Michi (Philosopher's Path) along a canal called Sosui, channeling water from Lake Biwa east to the city. The path is so called because philosopher Kitarō Nishida (1870–1945), known for his theory of "the self-identity of absolute contradiction," used to contemplate such things while strolling along it. My guess is that the path was named this way after the Philosophenweg in Heidelberg, Germany.

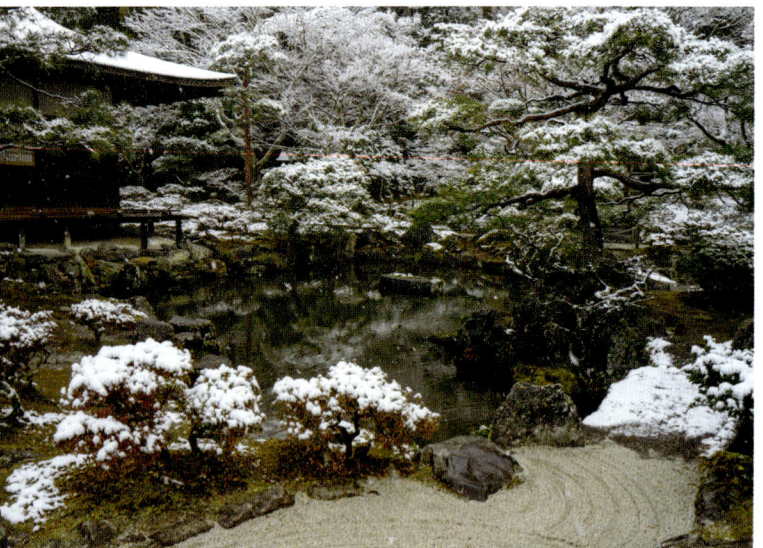

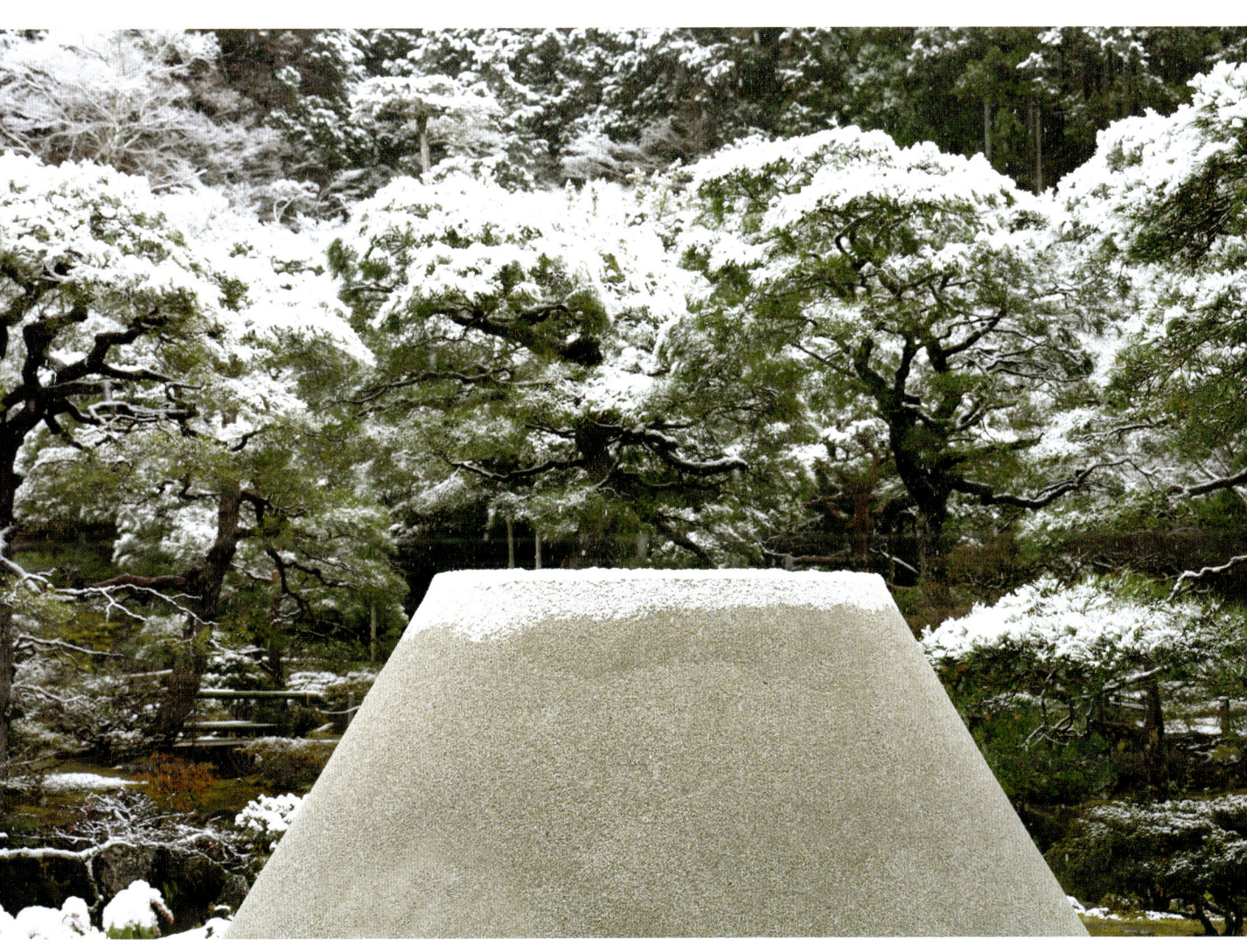

6-3 *Ryōsoku-in, Kennin-ji*

The Kennin Monastery, the oldest Zen temple in Kyōto, was founded in 1202 by Myōan Eisai, who went to China twice and brought Zen teachings to Japan for the first time. Eihei Dōgen, who studied and went to China with Myōzen, Eisai's successor, stayed at this monastery before and after he visited China.

The Ryōsoku-in is one of the subtemples of the Kennin-ji. It was founded in 1358 by Ryūzan Tokuken, the thirty-fifth abbot of the Kennin-ji. This temple became known as a place for Zen studies and produced a number of noted authors of Chinese-style Zen poems, characterized as the Five Mountains literature (poetry and prose), written by Kyōto and Kamakura monastics. The Kennin-ji used to have thirty-four subtemples, but only fourteen of them survived the persecution of Buddhism that occurred after the Meiji Restoration of 1868 when nationalist forces attempted to expurgate Buddhism in favor of Shintōism.

Here (→) you see a garden in front of the *shoin* or audience hall. The garden with a passage around the pond, rimmed by rocks, is called Hangeshō no Niwa (Lizard's Tail Garden). The same garden may be seen (↓) from the abbot's quarters, going directly down to the pond below. This is rather exceptional, as a flat garden is commonly viewed from the abbot's quarters.

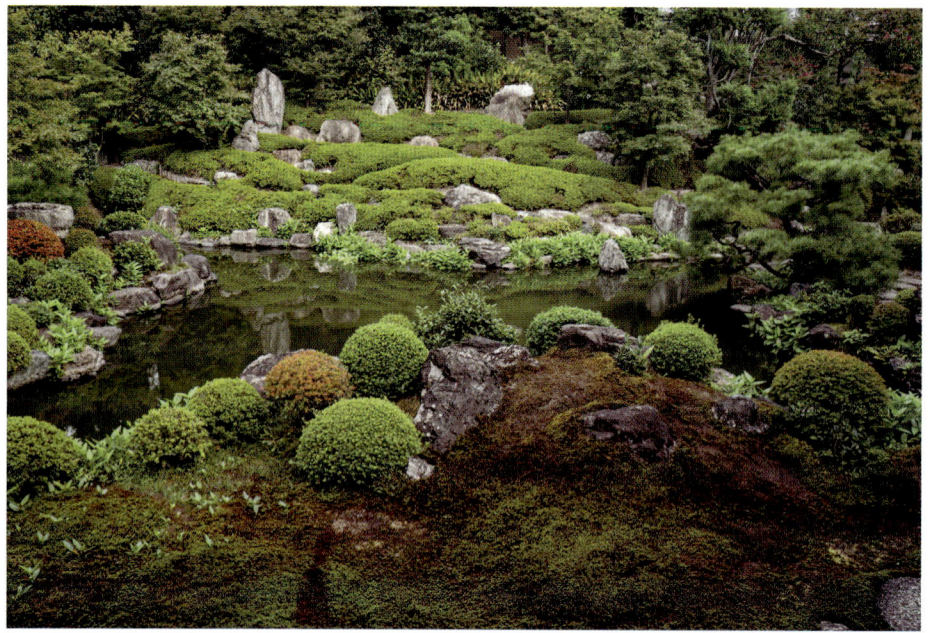

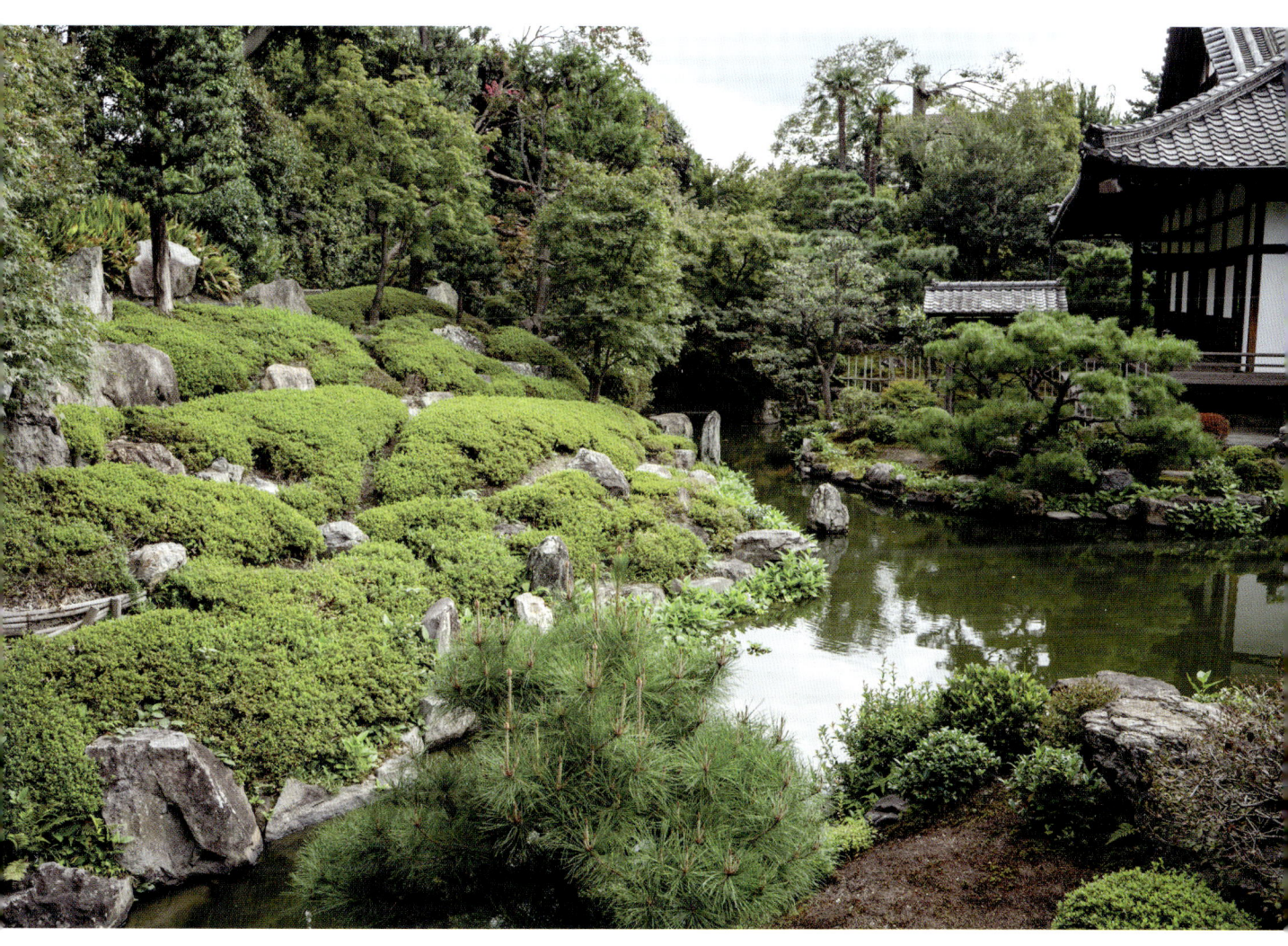

6-4 *Tenryū-ji*

The Tenryū Monastery garden overlooking the Sōgen Pond (↓) features the *shakkei* (borrowed landscape) of Mount Kame (meaning Turtle), diminutive seeming in the foreground, and Mount Arashi (meaning Storm), farther away. Mountains are timeless. Stones and sand are timeless. Ponds are timeless. The colors and shapes of plants, on the other hand, change every day, every moment. Seasons constantly change. Spring (↓) and autumn (→) are captured here, but the cycle of seasons is timeless. (See also 1-4, 4-4.)

Japanese Zen buildings seem to be sturdy and long-lasting, yet they often have a history of destruction and rebuilding. For example, most of the buildings of this monastery were originally constructed in the 1340s. They caught fire, mostly due to war, in 1358, 1367, 1373, 1380, 1416, 1447, 1815, and 1864. The Meiji government confiscated the majority of land around the Tenryū-ji in the 1870s. The great abbot's quarters was rebuilt in 1889. Temples are developed and redeveloped, and gardens are built and rebuilt over the generations.

In the northwestern part of the Tenryū-ji compound, there is a well-kept imperial mausoleum enshrining Kameyama, who founded this villa and also initiated the development of the Nanzen Monastery. Thus, you might find subtle connections between these highest-ranking monasteries.

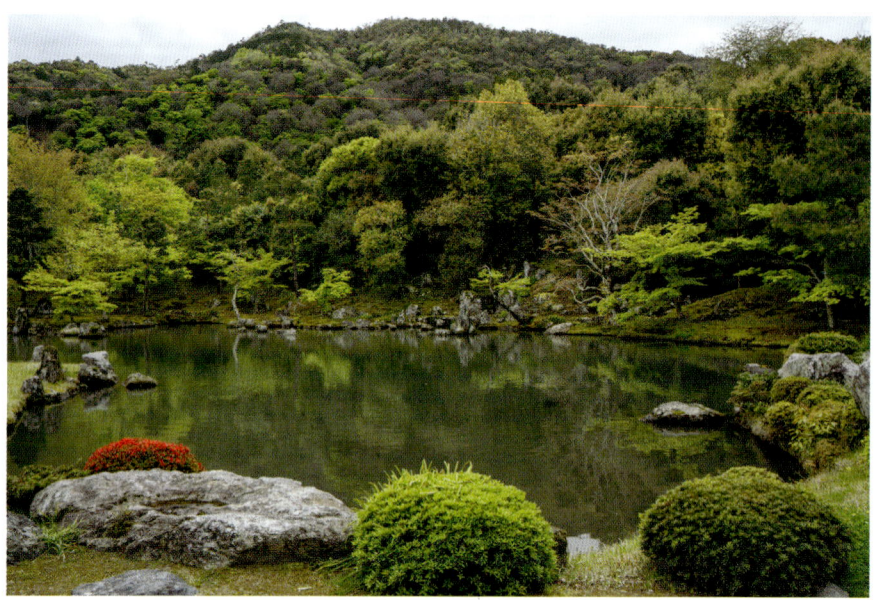

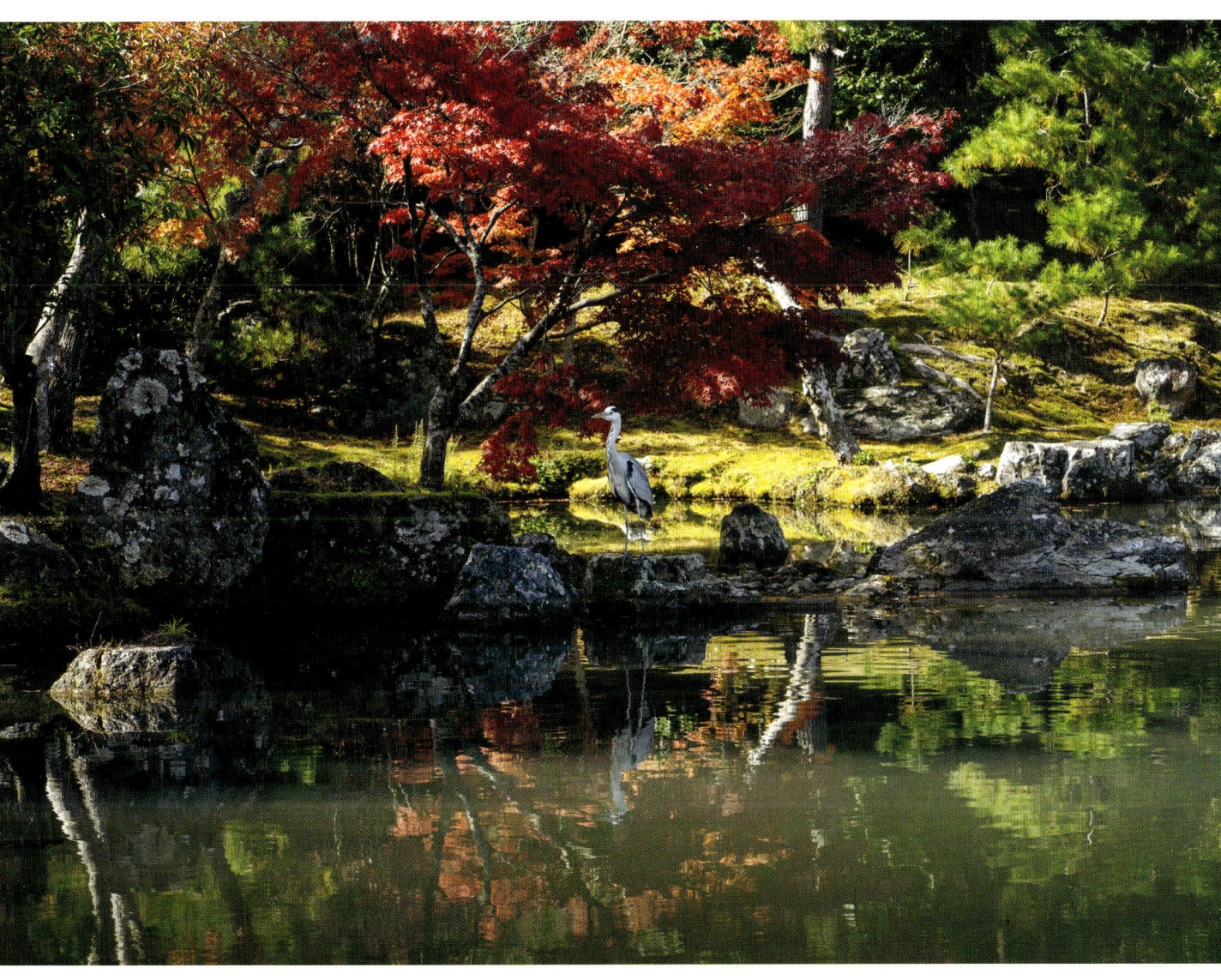

6-5 *Taizō-in, Myōshin-ji*

The Myōshin Monastery, situated in the western part of the capital city, is known as the strictest Zen training center. The Taizō-in is one of its forty-six subtemples. Founded in 1404 by Muin Sōin, the third abbot of the Myōshin-ji, it was burned during a military conflict but restored in 1597. Surprisingly, instead of buddhas or bodhisattvas, Zen master Muin Sōin is the main figure enshrined in this temple.

This spacious temple is known for Motonobu's Garden, attributed to the painter Motonobu Kanō (1476–1559); the Yokō En (Lingering Fragrance Garden), created in 1966 by Kinsaku Nagane; and the Yin and Yang Gardens by an unidentified landscaper.

The Yin Garden (→) has a flat field of dark sand, representing a vast sea. Here you may enjoy a large body of water without a drop of moisture. The surface is drawn each day by an accomplished Zen practitioner pulling a wooden rake called a *kumade* 熊手, literally meaning "bear's paw." Contemplating it, you see straight lines, then circular lines that are waves. You see the concentration of the raker. You experience the practice of the meditator. You see the life of one who is dedicated to dharma.

The Yang Garden (↓) has brightly reflective white sand with an island of rocks and rounded bushes.

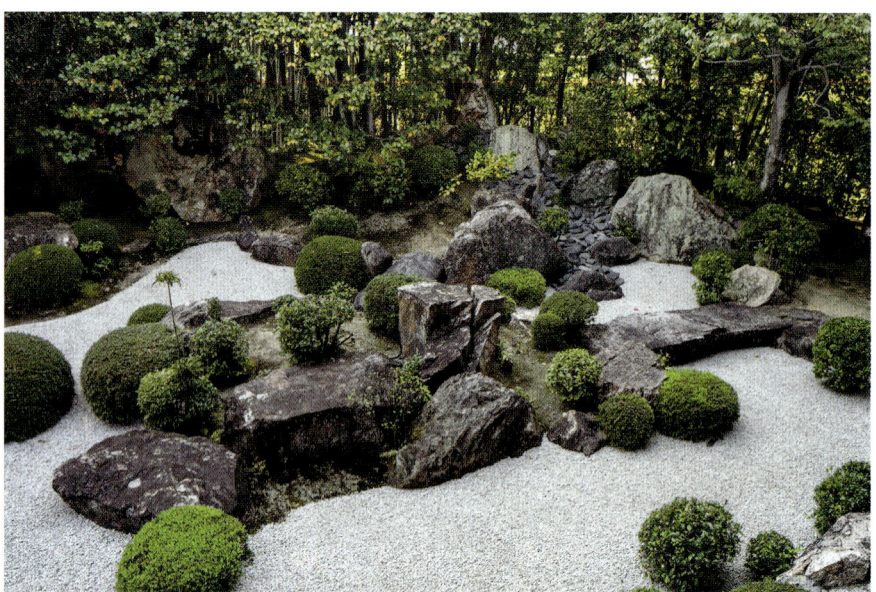

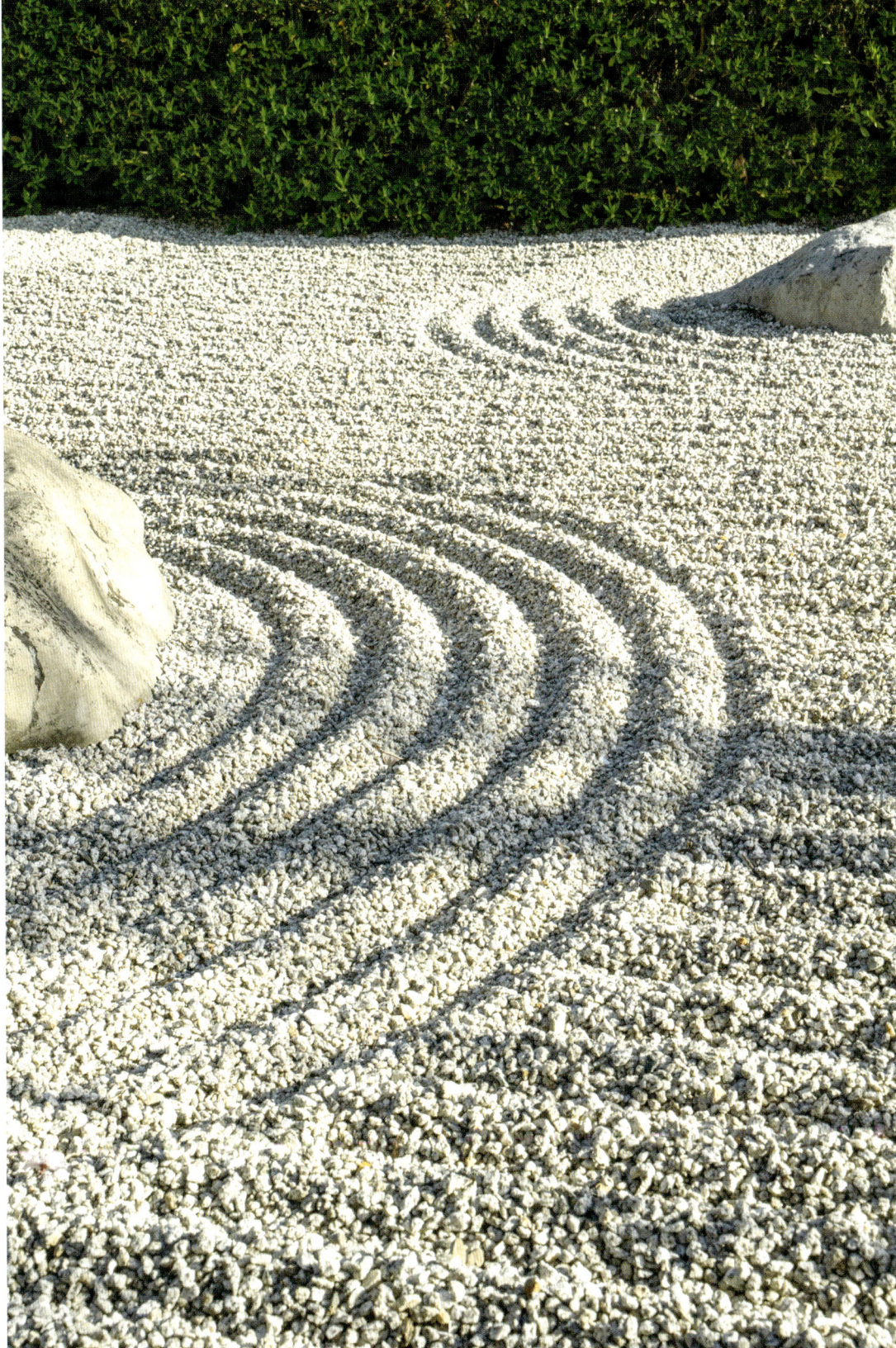

無盡藏 Inexhaustible
mujinzō

INEXHAUSTIBLE MEANS that dharma embodies all things without limit. A single camellia blossom with a few leaves set in a bamboo vase in the alcove of a tea room is enough to represent the symphony of spring. Behind the mask, the face of a protagonist in a *Noh* play—who would be a male performer enacting a female role—slowly leans forward, and his hand, grasping a folded fan, subtly tips up; this is enough to express the tremendous grief of his female character. Each motion of a *Noh* actor embodies years of training, centuries of tradition. All of this is present in one small gesture.

One blossom is all blossoms. One brush line is the life of the artist. A dewdrop on a blade of grass embodies the vastness of awakening.

Extremely small is extremely large. Extremely large is extremely small.

—ATTRIBUTED TO SENGCAN

A student asked Shimen, "What is the point I should keep in mind?" The master said, "Day and night, keep your inexhaustible lamp on."

—SHIMEN

This is the timeless moment to attain buddha ancestors' infinite life. All of you aspire and practice within this timelessness. Endeavoring to follow the way, you must actualize one phrase. When timelessness is realized, you are powerful. When timelessness is realized, you are alive.

—DŌGEN

Beings are numberless; I vow to awaken with them. Delusions are inexhaustible; I vow to transform them. The dharma is boundless; I vow to comprehend it. The awakened way is incomparable; I vow to embody it.

—FOUR ALL-EMBRACING VOWS, A MAHĀYĀNA CHANT

7-1 *Nanzen'-in, Nanzen-ji*

Built in 1292, the Nanzen'-in is the original temple of the Nanzen Monastery, and there is a legend that former emperor Kameyama is the one who decided on the strolling style of its garden. (See 2-3.) It is also said that Musō Soseki was later involved in the landscape design of this temple. As he was the abbot of the Nanzen-ji for a short time in 1235, it is not inconceivable. Interestingly, the upper pond adjacent to the waterfall is called the Sōgen Pond, the same name as the one at the Tenryū-ji that Soseki definitely designed. (See 1-4, 4-4, 6-4.)

The view here (↓) is from the abbot's quarters, built in 1703. The Sōgen Pond has the shape of a dragon.

By the way, it is an unspeakable pleasure for me to contemplate and write about Zen gardens in Kyōto. There are so many spectacular cities worldwide—Venice, Florence, Paris, Vienna, Amsterdam, San Francisco . . . I leave my heart in many cities, and when I imagine myself to be there, then I can go there without actually going—they are so vivid to me. People often ask me, "What is your most favorite city in all the world?" I sometimes say, "I can tell you the second most beloved city of mine." "What is it?" "Kyōto." "What is the first?" "The city where I am at the moment."

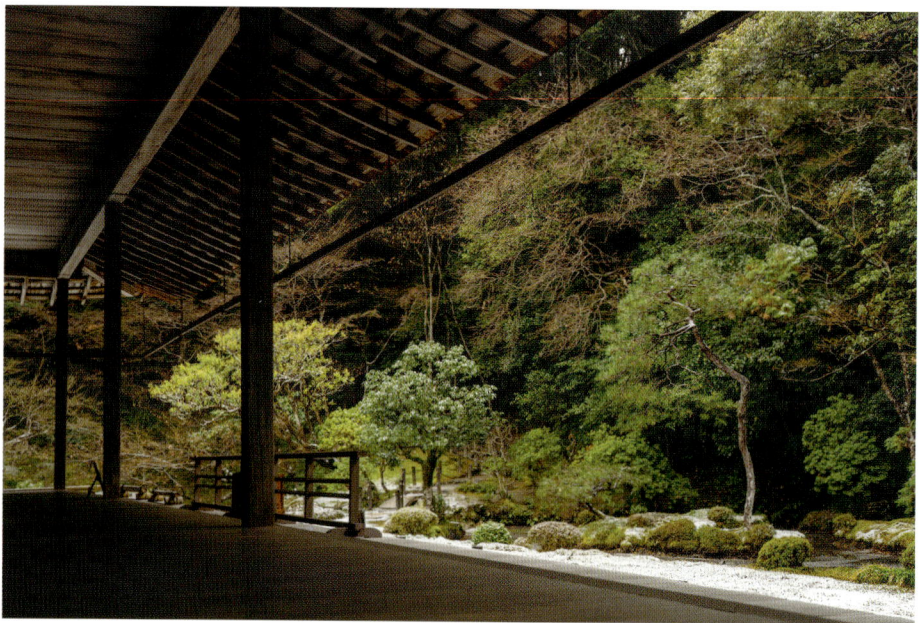

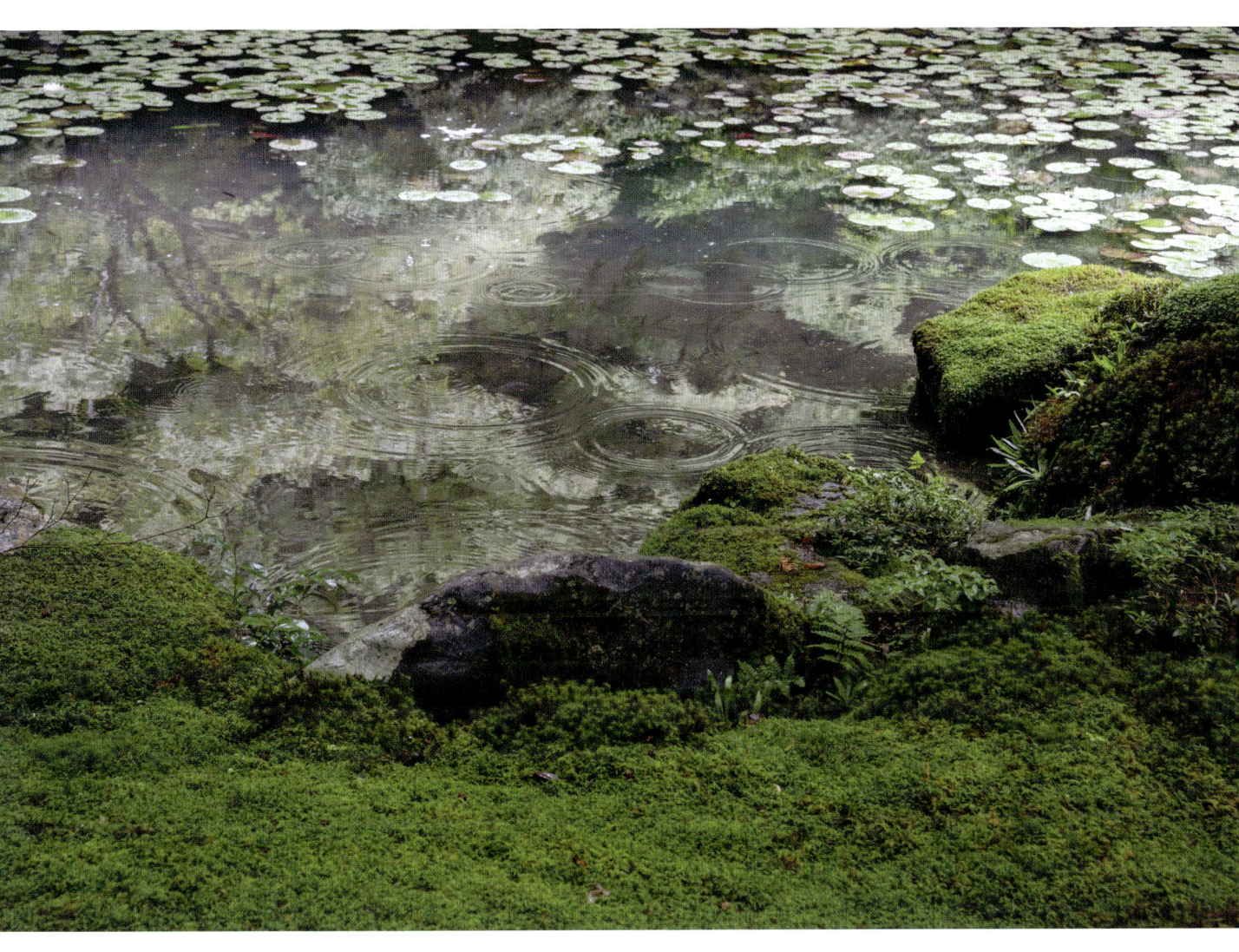

7-2 *Ikkyū-ji*

These (→)(↓) are views of the main garden to the south of the abbot's quarters at the Ikkyū-ji, situated to the south of Kyōto. This temple's original iteration, called the Myōshō-ji, was founded by Nampo Jōmin, who revitalized the Rinzai School. After the temple burned down during a war, Zen monk Ikkyū Sōjun built a grass hut here in 1456 when he was sixty-two and called it the Shūon'-an, meaning "Hut for Repaying the Benefaction" (of Jōmin). It is now known as the Ikkyū-ji.

Ikkyū is believed to have been an illegitimate son of Emperor Gokomatsu. He became a monk at age six. From his youth he was known for his talent in writing poetry. Later, he become famous for his eccentric and flamboyant lifestyle, often breaking precepts and visiting pleasure quarters. An anthology of his Chinese-style poems is titled *Kyōun Shū* (Crazy Wind Anthology). In 1474, at the age of eighty, he was appointed abbot of the Daitoku Monastery by an imperial order to restore the temple compound destroyed by war. He wouldn't live there but commuted from the Shūon-an instead.

According to legend, this garden was built by Jōzan Ishikawa, founder of the Shisen-dō (see 1-1, 4-5), and his associates in the seventeenth century.

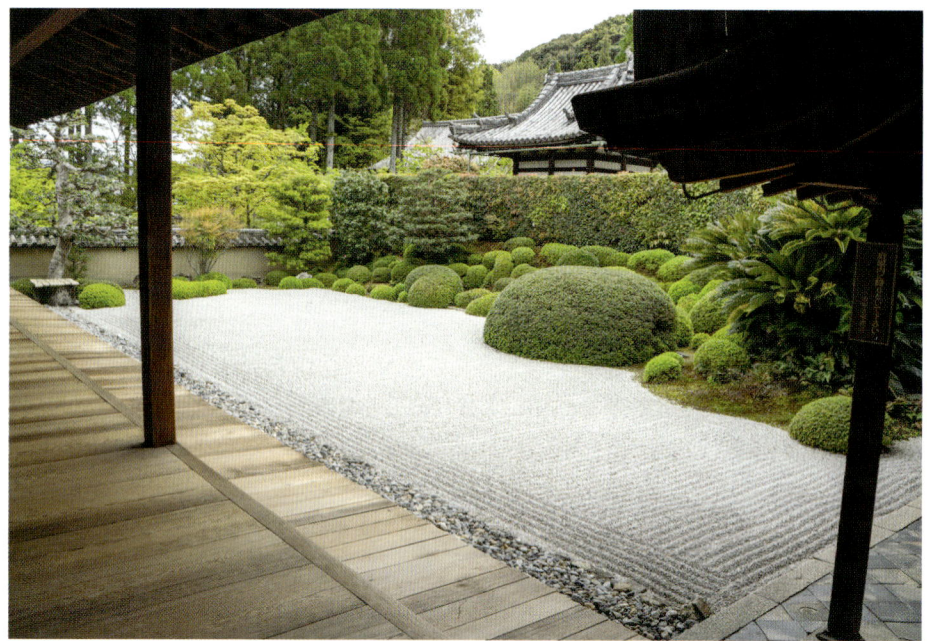

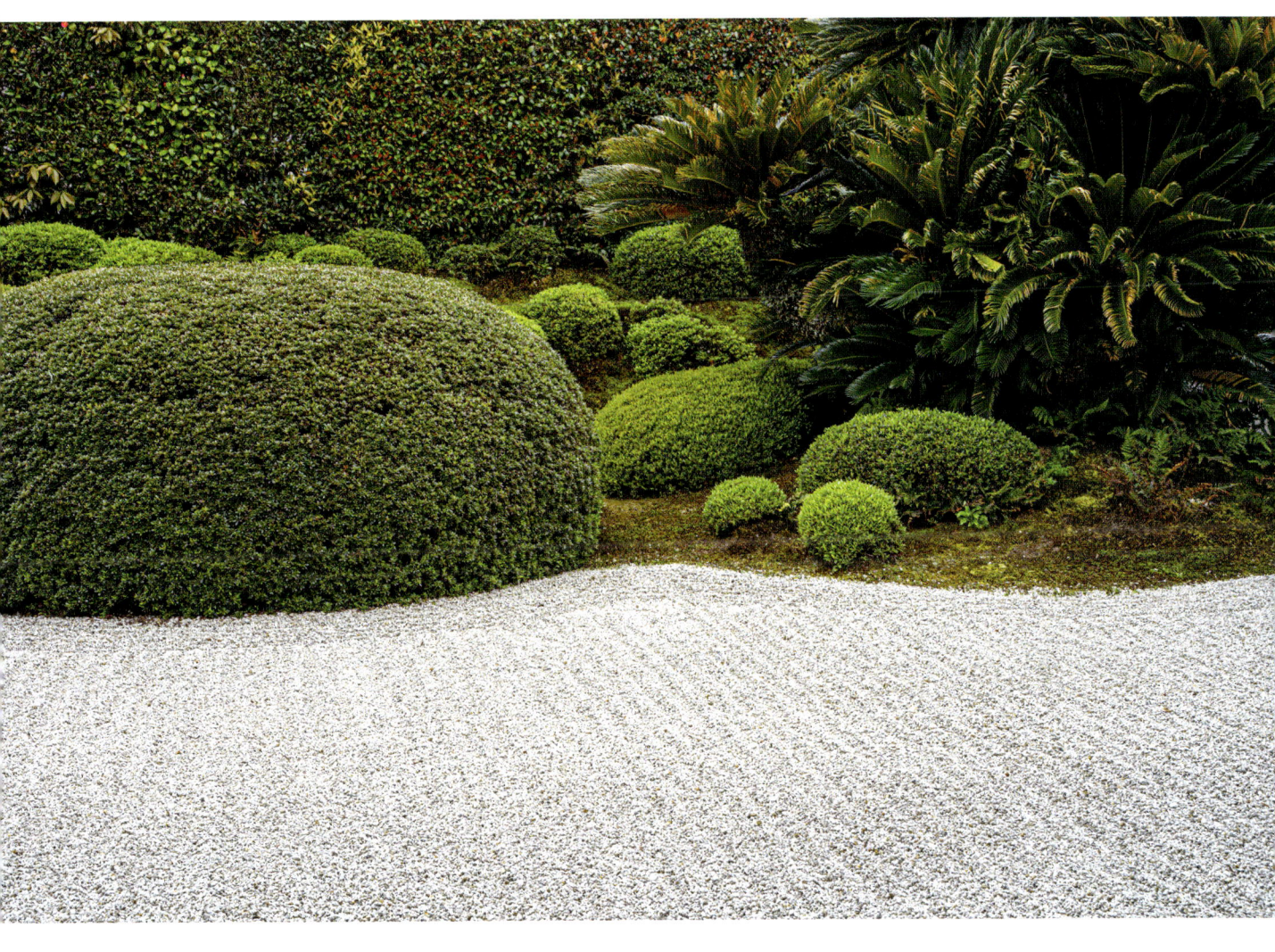

7-3 *Kompuku-ji*

The Bashō Hut at the Kompuku Temple in northern Kyōto (just south of the Shisen-dō) was in disrepair. In the fourth month of 1776, the *hokku* poet Buson Yosa and his associates decided to restore it. (*Hokku* is an earlier common name for *haiku*.) They formed a *sūtra* copying group and made a plan to have *hokku* meetings twice a year. In the following month Buson wrote "A Plan for Rebuilding the Bashō Hut in Eastern Kyōto."

In the winter of 1777, at the age of sixty-two, perhaps on the memorial day of Bashō—the twelfth day of the tenth month—Buson wrote this verse.

I will also die
and be by this monument
—withered pampas grass.

Withered Pampas Grass (*Kareobana*) is the title of the memorial anthology for Bashō edited by his student Kikaku. This verse can be seen as Buson's death poem. A stone monument to commemorate Bashō was erected at the Kompuku-ji.

The stone path (→) turns to the right after you enter the main gate. The faraway view of mountains (↓) is on the western side of the temple.

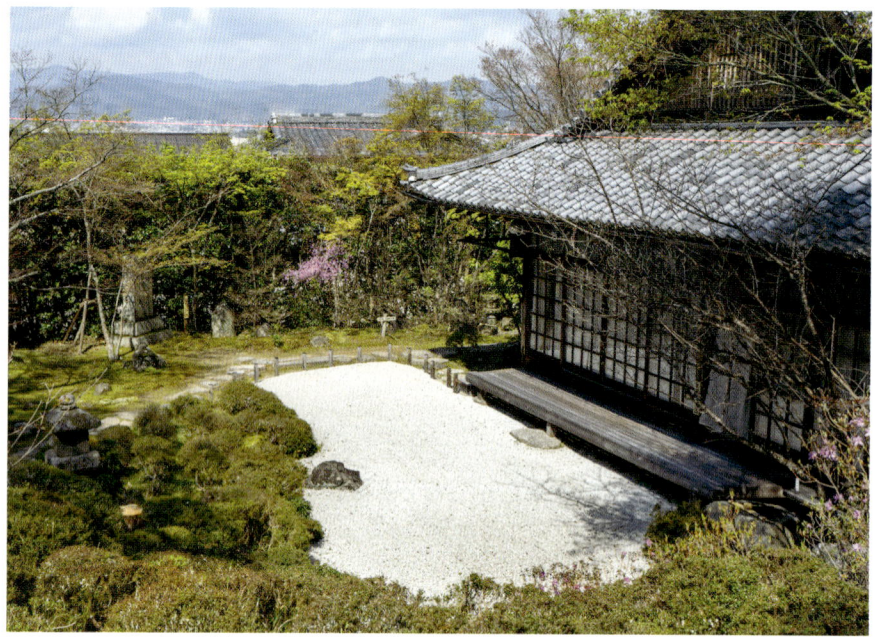

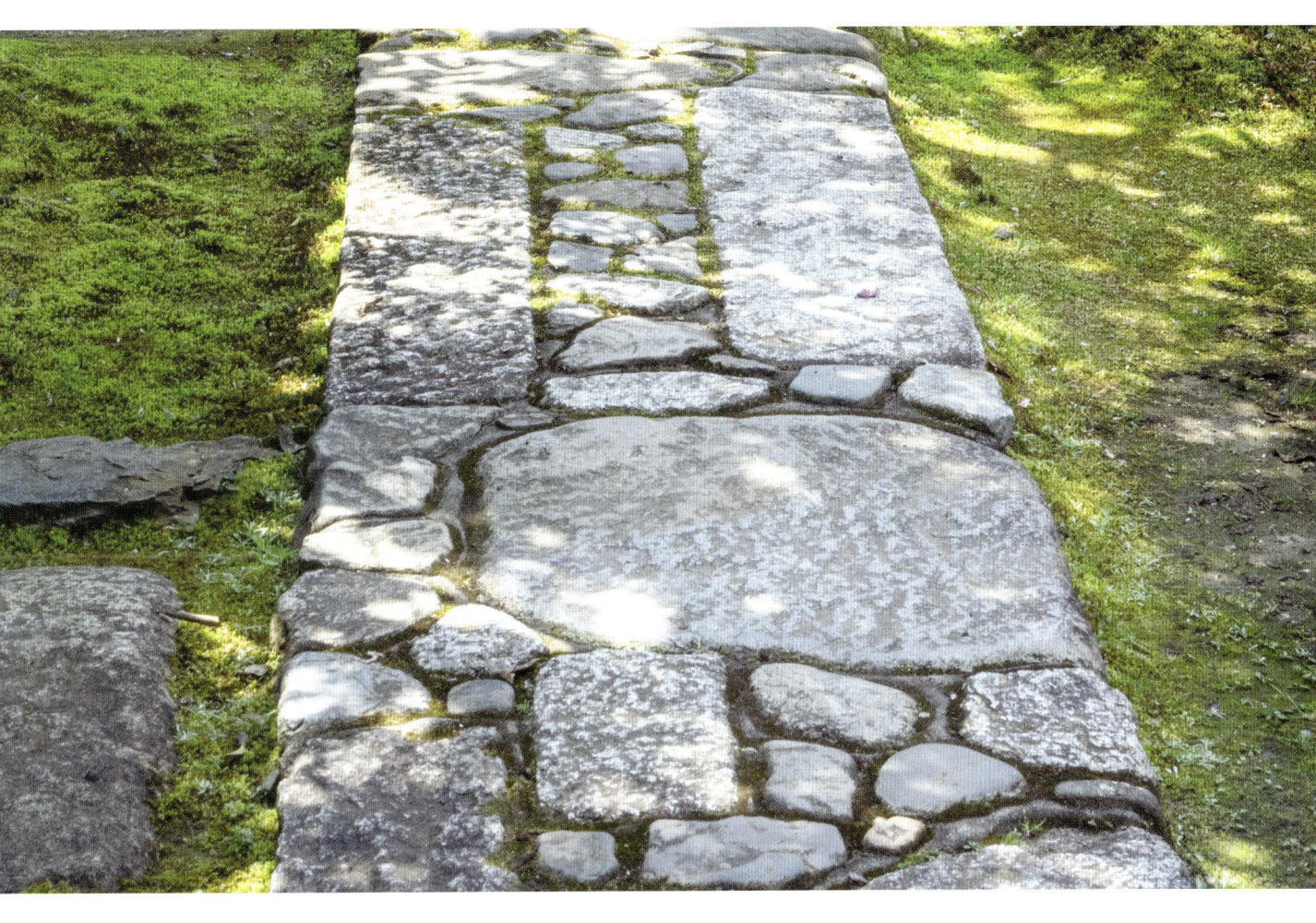

7-4 *Ryōan-ji*

The dry landscape garden of the Ryōan-ji consists of fifteen rocks in five groups. As discussed earlier, its landscape designer and date of creation are not known. The temple has been destroyed by fire three times, and no record remains of the designing and building of the garden. We can only guess that it was put in place around the turn of the sixteenth century. (See p. 3. Also 4-1 and 5-5.)

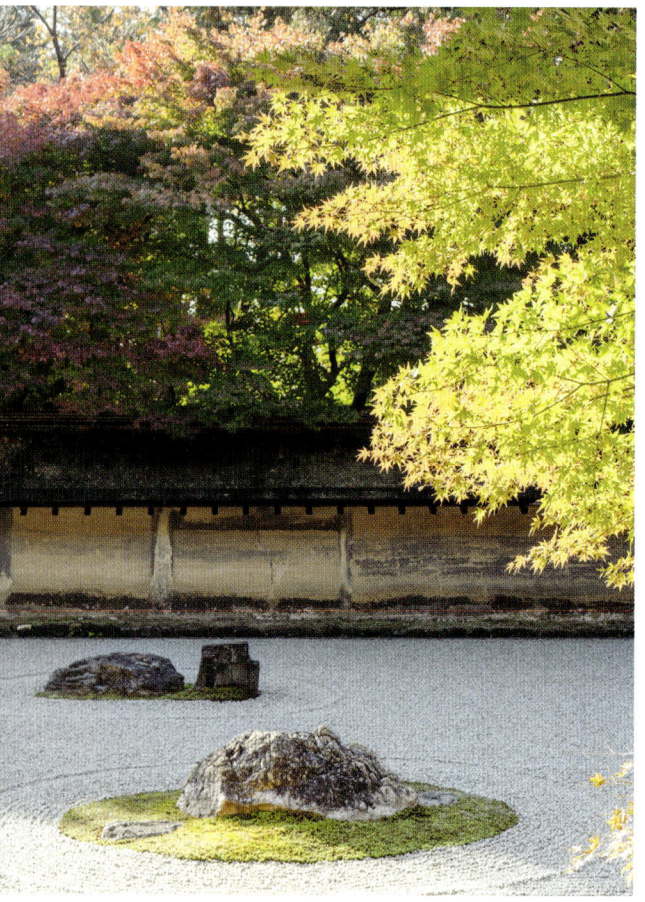

The first record of this garden, characterizing it as "a tigress carrying her cubs across the river," was in *Tōzai Rekiran Ki* (East and West Pilgrimage Record), published in 1681. Since then, there have been multiple theories on the meaning of the arrangement of these stones.

The most recent one seems to be from an article published in the scientific magazine *Nature*, titled "Visual structure of a Japanese Zen garden: The mysterious appeal of a simple and ancient composition of rocks is unveiled."[*] The authors computed the perceptional local axes of symmetry and concluded: "We believe that the unconscious perception of this pattern contributes to the enigmatic appeal of the garden."

[*] Gert J. Van Tonder, Michael J. Lyons, and Yoshimichi Ejima, *Nature*, September 26, 2002.

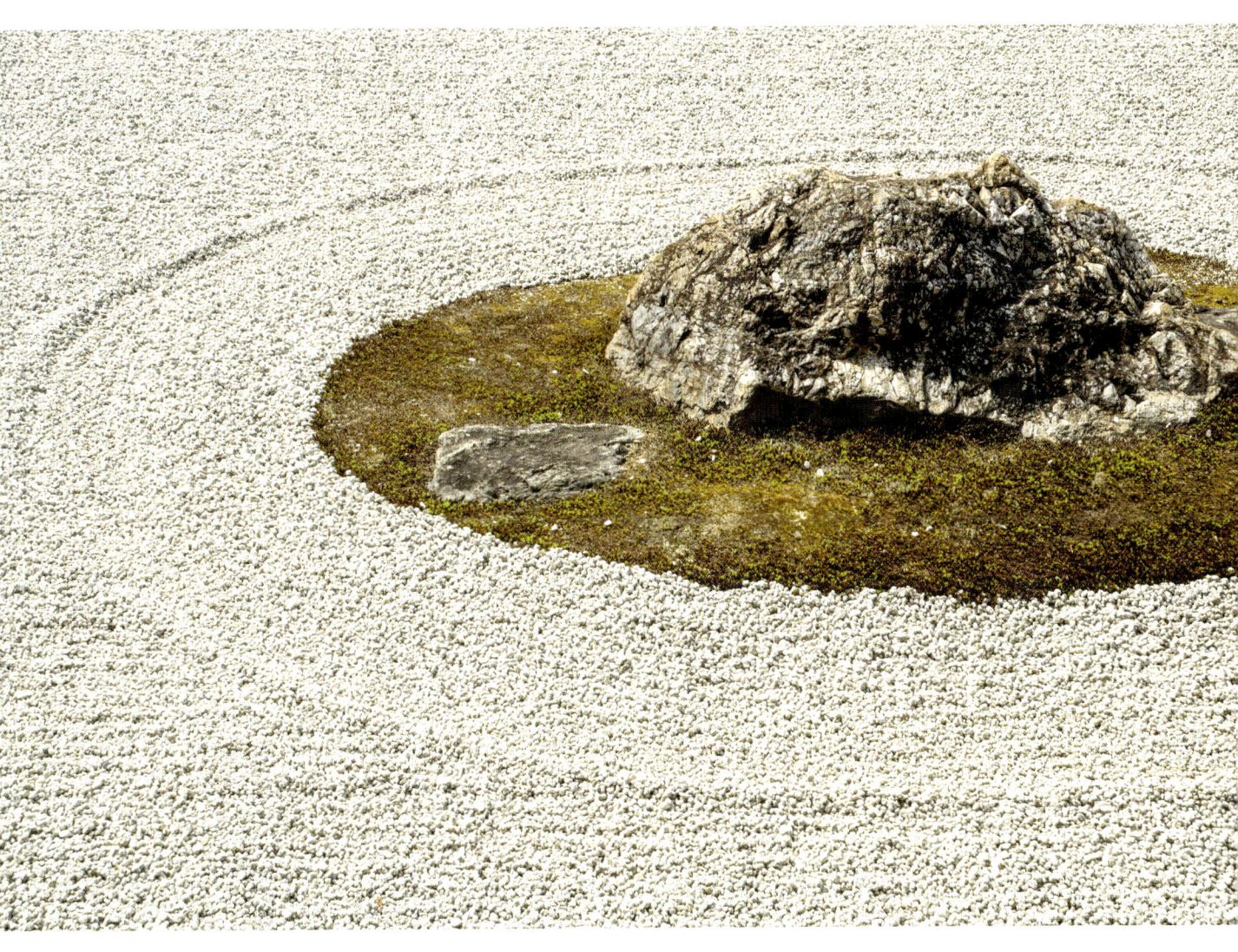

7-5 *Tōfuku-ji*

Tokiyori Hōjō, the fifth regent of the Kamakura government, had a crucial role in the development of Zen in Japan. In 1254, Tokiyori invited Enni Ben'en to be abbot of the Jufuku Monastery in Kamakura. Ben'en was a student of Myōan

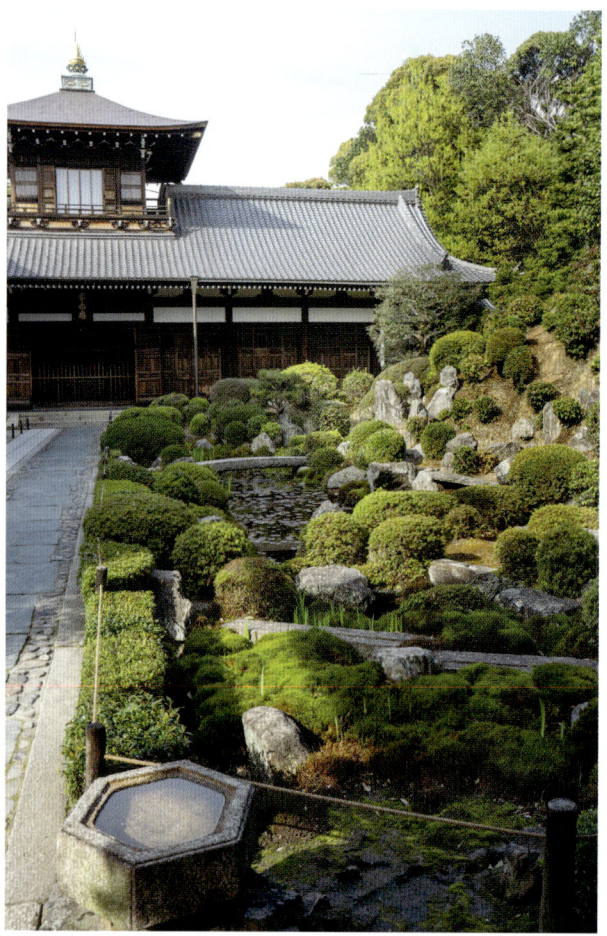

Eisai, the first monk to go to Song Dynasty China who brought Zen teachings to Japan. Ben'en himself had studied in China from 1235 till 1241. Thereafter, leaders of the *shōgun* government as well as emperors studied with Zen teachers of the Rinzai School and helped develop a nationally supported Zen practice and culture.

Michi'ie Kujō, the highest-ranking imperial courtier of the time, wanted to build the largest Zen monastery. Thus, he constructed the Tōfuku Monastery in a southern suburb of Kyōto and wanted Ben'en to be the abbot. When Ben'en passed away, he became the first Japanese Zen master to be presented with the title of national teacher. The photo (←) here shows the garden with well-cropped bushes and standing rocks leading toward the Founder's Hall, which enshrines Ben'en. It is situated in the very back of the monastery. The other photo (→) shows the Tsūten (Reaching Heaven) Bridge with the abbot's quarters in the back. (See "Temple Plan Example: The Tōfuku-ji," in the appendices.)

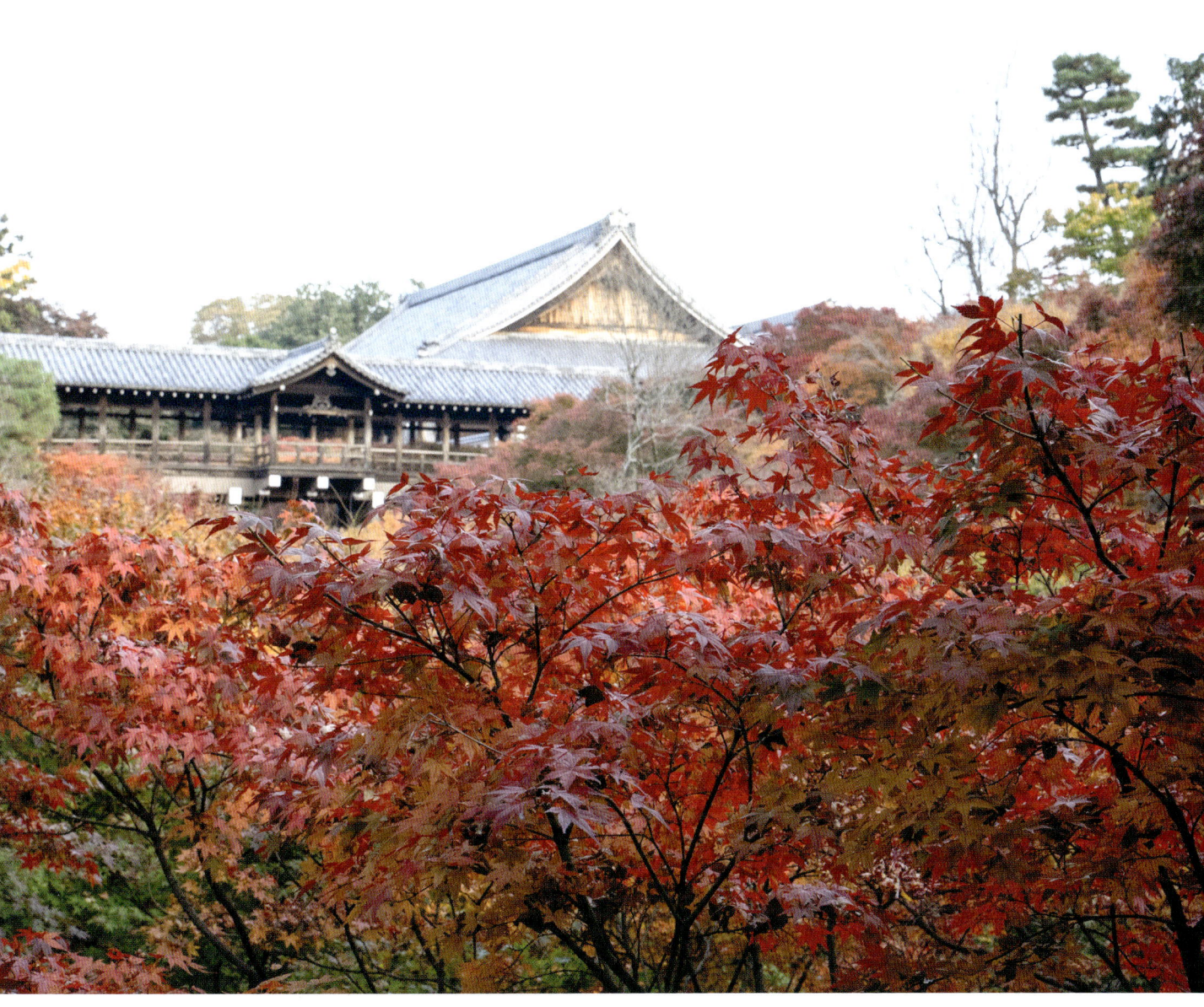

Appendices

Masters Quoted in Part Two

Bashō: Bashō Matsuo, 1644–1694, Japan, poet.

Dizang: Dizang Guichen, 867–928, China, Zen master of the Qingyuan lineage.

Dōgen: Eihei Dōgen, 1200–1253, Japan, Zen master regarded as the founder of the Sōtō School of Zen.

Dongshan: Dongshan Liangjie, 807–869, China, Zen master regarded as a cofounder of the Caodong School.

Hakuin: Hakuin Ekaku, 1685–1768, Japan, Zen master regarded as the restorer of the Rinzai School.

Kyorai: Kyorai Mukai, 1691–1704, Japan, poet, a student of Bashō.

Layman Pang: Pangyun, 740–808, China, lay practitioner of Zen in the Nanyue lineage.

Linji: Linji Yixuan, d. 867, China, Zen master, regarded as the founder of the Linji School.

Nanquan: Nanquan Puyuan, 748–834, China, Zen master of the Nanyue lineage.

Sengcan: Jianzhi Sengcan, d. 606, China, Zen master, the Third Chinese Ancestor of the Zen School.

Shimen: Shimen Huiche, c. tenth–eleventh centuries, China, Zen master of the Caodong School.

Shitou: Shitou Xiqian, 700–790, China, Zen master of the Qingyuan lineage.

Su Dongpo: 1036–1101, China, a poet.

Yuanwu: Yuanwu Keqin, 1063–1135, China, Zen master of the Linji School, compiler of the *Blue Cliff Record*.

Yunmen: Yunmen Wenyan, 864–949, China, Zen master regarded as the founder of the Yunmen School.

Ze'ami: Zeami Motokiyo, 1363–1443, Japan, the establisher of the *Noh* play.

Zhaozhou: Zhaozhou Congshen, 778–897, China, Zen master in the Nanyue lineage.

The Sūtra on the Heart of Realizing Wisdom beyond Wisdom

Avalokiteshvara, who helps all to awaken,
moves in the deep course of
realizing wisdom beyond wisdom,
sees that all five streams of
body, heart, and mind are without boundary,
and frees all from anguish.

O Shāriputra,
[who listens to the teachings of the Buddha],
form is not separate from boundlessness;
boundlessness is not separate from form.
Form is boundlessness; boundlessness is form.
The same is true of feelings, perceptions, inclinations, and discernment.
O Shāriputra,
boundlessness is the nature of all things.
It neither arises nor perishes,
neither stains nor purifies,
neither increases nor decreases.
Boundlessness is not limited by form,
nor by feelings, perceptions, inclinations, or discernment.
It is free of the eyes, ears, nose, tongue, body, and mind;
free of sight, sound, smell, taste, touch, and any object of mind;
free of sensory realms, including the realm of the mind.

It is free of ignorance and the end of ignorance.
Boundlessness is free of old age and death,
and free of the end of old age and death.
It is free of suffering, arising, cessation, and path,
and free of wisdom and attainment.

Being free of attainment, those who help all to awaken
abide in the realization of wisdom beyond wisdom
and live with an unhindered mind.
Without hindrance, the mind has no fear.
Free from confusion, those who lead all to liberation
embody profound serenity.
All those in the past, present, and future,
who realize wisdom beyond wisdom,
manifest unsurpassable and thorough awakening.

Know that realizing wisdom beyond wisdom
is no other than this wondrous mantra,
luminous, unequaled, and supreme.
It relieves all suffering.
It is genuine, not illusory.

So set forth this mantra of realizing wisdom beyond wisdom.
Set forth this mantra that says:

Gaté, gaté, paragaté, parasamgaté, bodhi! Svaha!

Translated by Kazuaki Tanahashi
and Joan Halifax Rōshi

Engraving Trust in the Heart

The utmost way is not difficult.
Just be free of preferences.
Without attachment or aversion,
all becomes transparent.

Missing the way by a hair's breadth,
you separate earth from sky.
If you want to see the way as it is,
do not affirm or deny it.

Dividing things by opposites
is a disease of the mind.
By not seeing the subtle essence,
you lose your serenity.

The circle of the way is boundless space.
There is nothing lacking, nothing extra.
Grasping and discarding
will not bring you there.

Do not pursue external conditions,
nor abide in futile asceticism.
Maintain a peaceful heart,
letting the way be invisible.

Stillness and motion return to stillness.
Stillness turns into motion.
If you are caught in either,
how can you know they are inseparable?

If oneness does not prevail,
the opposites cannot flow freely.
Let existence hide existence.
Pursuing boundlessness betrays
    boundlessness.

Too many words and thoughts
do not accord with the way.
Free from words and thoughts,
returning to the source,
you go beyond teachings to awakening.

Awakening even for a moment
takes you beyond thoughts on emptiness.
Ideas about emptiness change,
as all of them are illusory.

Pursuing the truth is useless.
Just stop looking.
Do not harbor dualistic views;
refrain from following them.

The slightest idea of right and wrong
fragments the mind.
Two views come from one view;
don't cling to even one view.

When the single mind is not yet born,
the myriad things are undivided:

no separation, no myriad things,
no birth, no mind.

Pursuing the subject, the object vanishes.
Chasing the object, the subject is obscured.
Object is object because of the subject.
Subject is subject because of the object.

How are they related?
Their source is the same boundlessness.
Without boundary, the two are
    indistinguishable,
each embracing the myriad forms.

Not discriminating between coarse and fine,
how can you be attached to either?
The great way is relaxed,
neither easy nor difficult.

Those with a narrow view are filled with
    doubt,
going in circles quickly or slowly.
When grasping overtakes you,
you are sure to go astray.

Surrender with ease.
The essence neither leaves nor stays.
If your nature is in accord with the way,
you wander freely without fear.

Caught in thoughts, you betray reality.
Trapped in delusion, you miss the point.
Weary with what is not clear,
what is the use of being near or far?

Do not favor the single path
or disfavor the six sense objects.

The objects of our senses are not
    unwholesome.
They are inseparable from authentic
    awakening.

The wise do not make things happen.
Fools are caught by doing.
Things are no more than things.
Don't be deceived by attachments.

To reveal the mind with the mind—
is it not a great mistake?
Delusion divides stillness from turmoil.
Enlightenment does not pick and choose.

All things have two sides.
Mistakenly, you waver between this and that.
Dreams, phantoms, blossoms of illusion—
why try to grasp them?

Gain and loss, right and wrong—
let go of them right now.
When your eyes are not shut,
then all dreaming ceases.

If your mind makes no distinctions,
all things are as they are.
Thusness is subtle,
being free from all conditions.

Seeing all things as equal,
you return to suchness.
Bring to an end all causes,
and let go of all comparisons.

Motion in stillness is not motion.
Stillness in motion is not stillness.

When neither happens,
neither is there.

In the ultimate freedom,
there are no doctrines.
When your mind merges with impartiality,
both making and being made disappear.

While doubts exhaust the pure heart,
genuine trust is plain and simple.
In it nothing remains,
and nothing is remembered.

Space illuminates itself,
not requiring mental effort.
In the realm beyond thinking,
thoughts and feelings are not measured.

In the dharma world of true thusness,
there is no self, no other.
To explain it briefly:
just say, "Not two."

Nonduality has no distinctions.
It leaves out nothing.
The wise in the ten directions
abide in the original source.

This source is timeless.
One moment is ten thousand years.

Time exists and does not exist.
The ten directions are right here.

The extremely small is vast;
it leaps beyond boundaries.
The extremely large is minute;
you cannot define it.

Existence is itself nonexistence.
Nonexistence is itself existence.
If reality is not like this,
it will never continue.

One is inseparable from all.
All is inseparable from one.
If you realize this,
you go beyond thinking.

Trust in the heart is not-two.
Not-two is trust in the heart.
Words, unspoken,
go beyond past, present, and future.

Attributed to Jianzhi Sengcan
Translated by Kazuaki Tanahashi
and Joan Halifax Rōshi

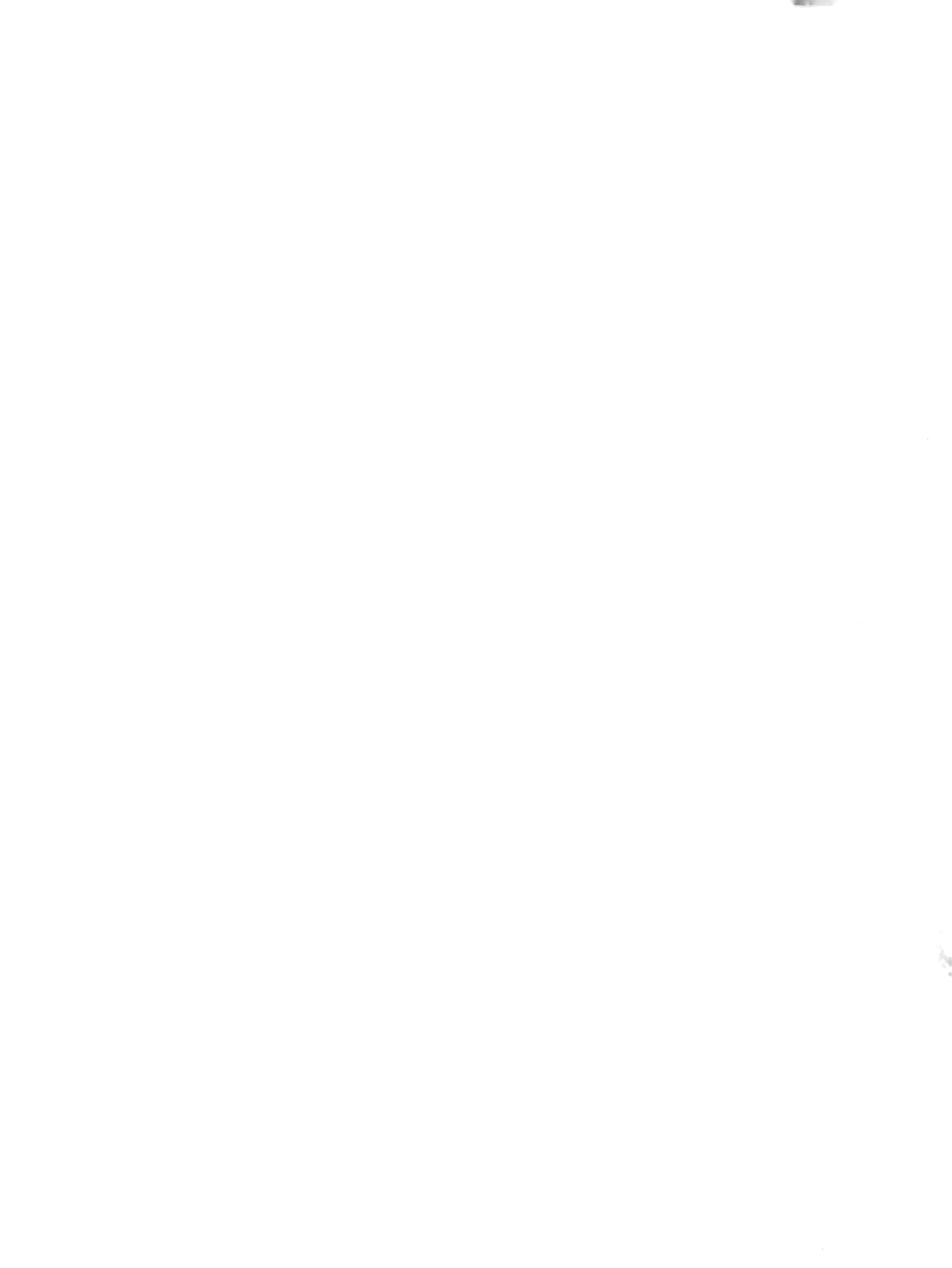

Map of Japan

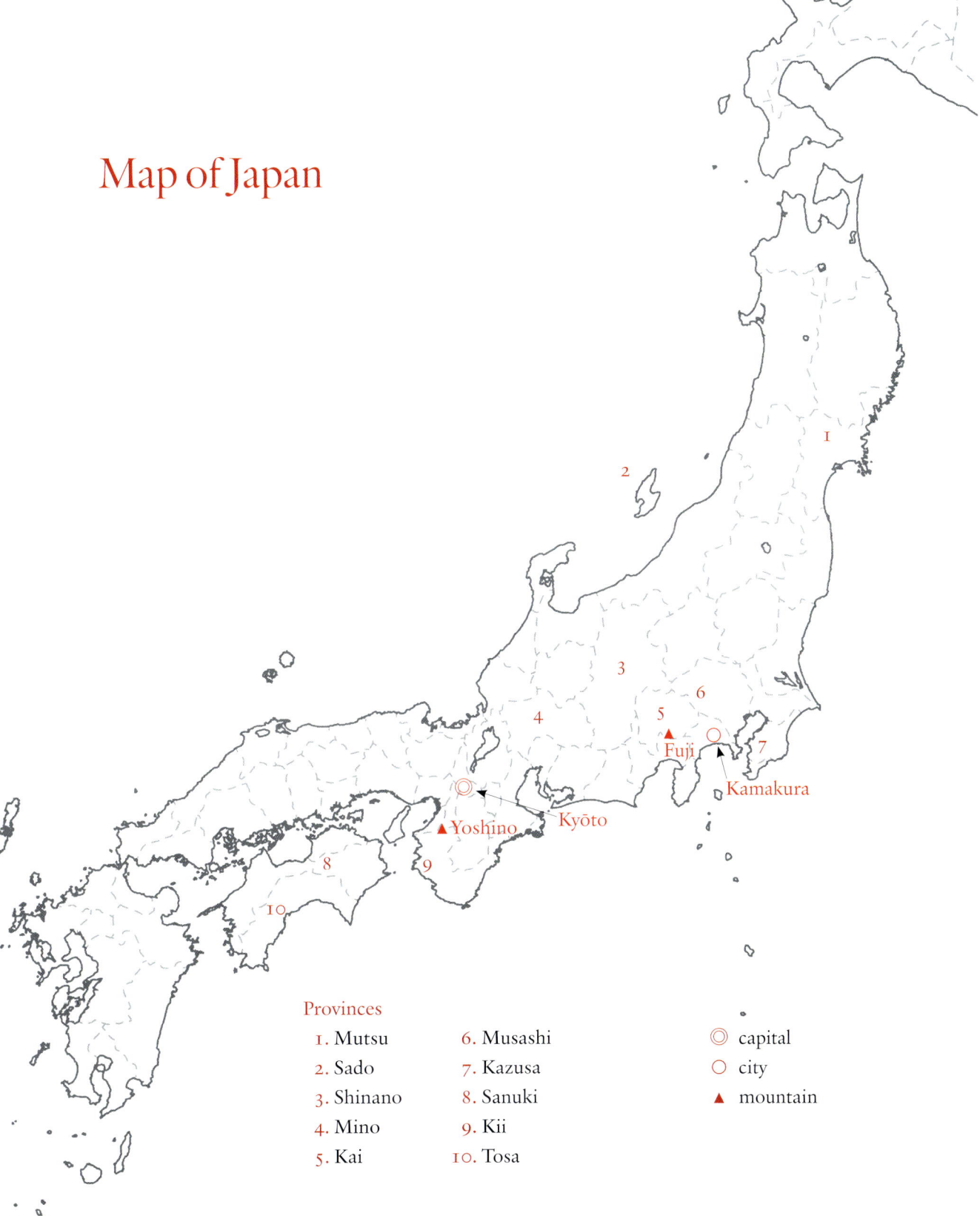

1

2

3

5

6

▲ Fuji

○

7

◎

▲ Yoshino

Kyōto

Kamakura

4

8

9

10

Provinces

1. Mutsu
2. Sado
3. Shinano
4. Mino
5. Kai

6. Musashi
7. Kazusa
8. Sanuki
9. Kii
10. Tosa

◎ capital
○ city
▲ mountain

Zen Temples in Kyōto Selected

Rinzai School

Above Five Mountains

Nanzen-ji: Nanzenji Fukuchi-chō, Sakyō-ku. Open year-round.

Five Mountains

Tenryū-ji: Susukinobaba-chō, Saga-Tenryūji, Ukyō-ku. Open year-round.

Shōkoku-ji: Shōkoku-ji Monzen-chō, Kamigyō-ku. Open year-round.

Kennin-ji: Komatsu-chō, Higashiyama-ku. Open year-round.

Tōfuku-ji: Hon-machi, Higashiyama-ku. Open year-round.

Manju-ji: Hon-machi, Higashiyama-ku. Not open to the public.

Subtemples of Above Five Mountains

Nanzen'-in, Nanzen-ji: Nanzenji Furoyama-chō, Sakyō-ku. Open year-round.

Konchi-in, Nanzen-ji: Nanzenji Fukuchi-chō, Sakyō-ku. Open year-round.

Tenju-an, Nanzen-ji: Nanzenji Fukuchi-chō, Sakyō-ku. Open year-round.

Subtemples of Five Mountains

Rinsen-ji, Tenryū-ji: Tsukurimichi-chō, Saga Tenryū-ji, Ukyō-ku. Visitable with approval by the Tenryū-ji.

Hōgon'-in, Tenryū-ji: Susukinobaba-chō, Saga Tenryū-ji, Ukyō-ku. Open on selected days.

Tōji-in, Tenryū-ji: Tōji-in Kita-machi, Kita-ku. Open year-round.

Ryōsoku-in, Kennin-ji: Komatsu-chō, Higashiyama-ku. Open on selected days.

Kōmyō-in, Tōfuku-ji: Hon-machi, Higashiyama-ku. Open year-round.

Others

Daitoku-ji: Murasakino Daitoku-ji-chō, Kita-ku. Open year-round.

Enkō-ji: Ichijō-ji Kotani-chō, Sakyō-ku. Open year-round.

Ginkaku-ji: Ginkaku-ji-chō, Sakyō-ku. Open year-round.

Ikkyū-ji: Takigisatonouchi, Kyōtanabe City. Open year-round.

Kinkaku-ji: Kinkaku-ji-chō, Kita-ku. Open year-round.

Kompuku-ji: Ichijō-ji Saitaka-chō, Sakyō-ku. Open year-round.

Kōrin'-in, Daitoku-ji: Murasakino Daitoku-ji-chō, Kita-ku. Open year-round.

Myōshin-ji: Hanazono Myōshin-ji-chō, Ukyō-ku. Open year-round.

Ōbai-in, Daitoku-ji: Murasakino Daitoku-ji-chō, Kita-ku. Open on selected days.

Ryōan-ji: Ryōan-ji Goryōnoshita-chō, Ukyō-ku. Open year-round.

Ryōgen'-in, Daitoku-ji: Murasakino Daitoku-ji-chō, Kita-ku. Open year-round.

Saihō-ji: Matsuo Jingatani-chō, Nishikyō-ku. Visitable with reservation by mail or online.

Taizō-in, Myōshin-ji: Hanazono Myōshinji-chō, Ukyō-ku. Open year-round.

Tōrin'-in, Myōshin-ji: Hanazono Myōshin-ji-chō, Ukyō-ku. Open on selected days.

Zuihō-in, Daitoku-ji: Murasakino Daitoku-ji-chō, Kita-ku. Open year-round.

SŌTŌ SCHOOL

Shisen-dō: Ichijōji Monguchi-chō, Sakyō-ku. Open year-round.

Map of Zen Temples in Kyōto

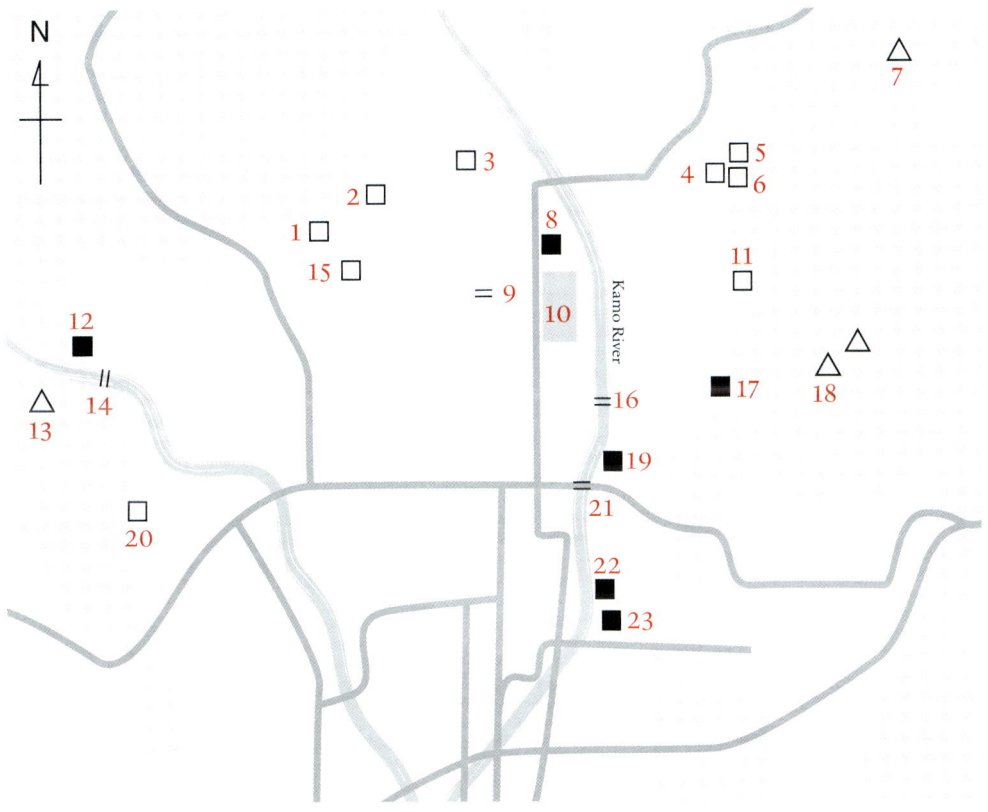

N

Kamo River

3
5
2
4 6
1 8
15 11
9
12 10
14
13 16
19
20 21
22
23
17
18
7

1. Ryōan-ji
2. Kinkaku-ji
3. Daitoku-ji
4. Kompuku-ji
5. Enkō ji
6. Shisendō
7. Mt. Hiei
8. Shōkoku-ji
9. Ichijō Bridge
10. Kyōto Imperial Palace

11. Ginkaku-ji
12. Tenryū-ji
13. Mt. Arashi
14. Togetsu Bridge
15. Myoshin-ji
16. Sanjō Bridge
17. Nanzen-ji
18. Mt. Higashi
19. Kennin-ji
20. Saihō-ji

21. Gojō Bridge
22. Manju-ji
23. Tōfuku-ji
Not shown: Ikkyū-ji (south)

◼ Nanzen-ji,
   Five Mountain Monastery
◻ Temple
△ Mountain
= Bridge
   Mountains and hills

1. Founder's Hall
2. Fumon'-in (subtemple)
3. Gekka (Under the Moon) Gate
4. Aizen (Rāgarāja) Hall
5. Ryōgin'-in (subtemple)
6. Gaun (Lying Cloud) Bridge
7. Sengyoku (Jewel Washing) River
8. Tsūten (Reaching Heaven) Bridge
9. Shoin (Study Hall)
10. Engetsu (Lying Moon) Bridge
11. Nikka (Under the Sun) Gate
12. Bell Tower
13. *Sūtra* Treasury
14. Abbot's Quarters
15. Kitchen
16. Zendō (Meditation Hall)
17. Main (Buddha) Hall
18. Kōmyō-in (sub-temple)
19. Daie (Great Wisdom) Hall, Office
20. *Tōsu* (Toilet)
21. Sammon (Monastery Gate)
22. Thirteen-story Stūpa
23. Imperial Messenger Gate
24. Shion (Thinking Far) Pond
25. Bathhouse
26. Five Shintō Shrines
27. Bell Tower

Temple Plan Example

The Tōfuku-ji

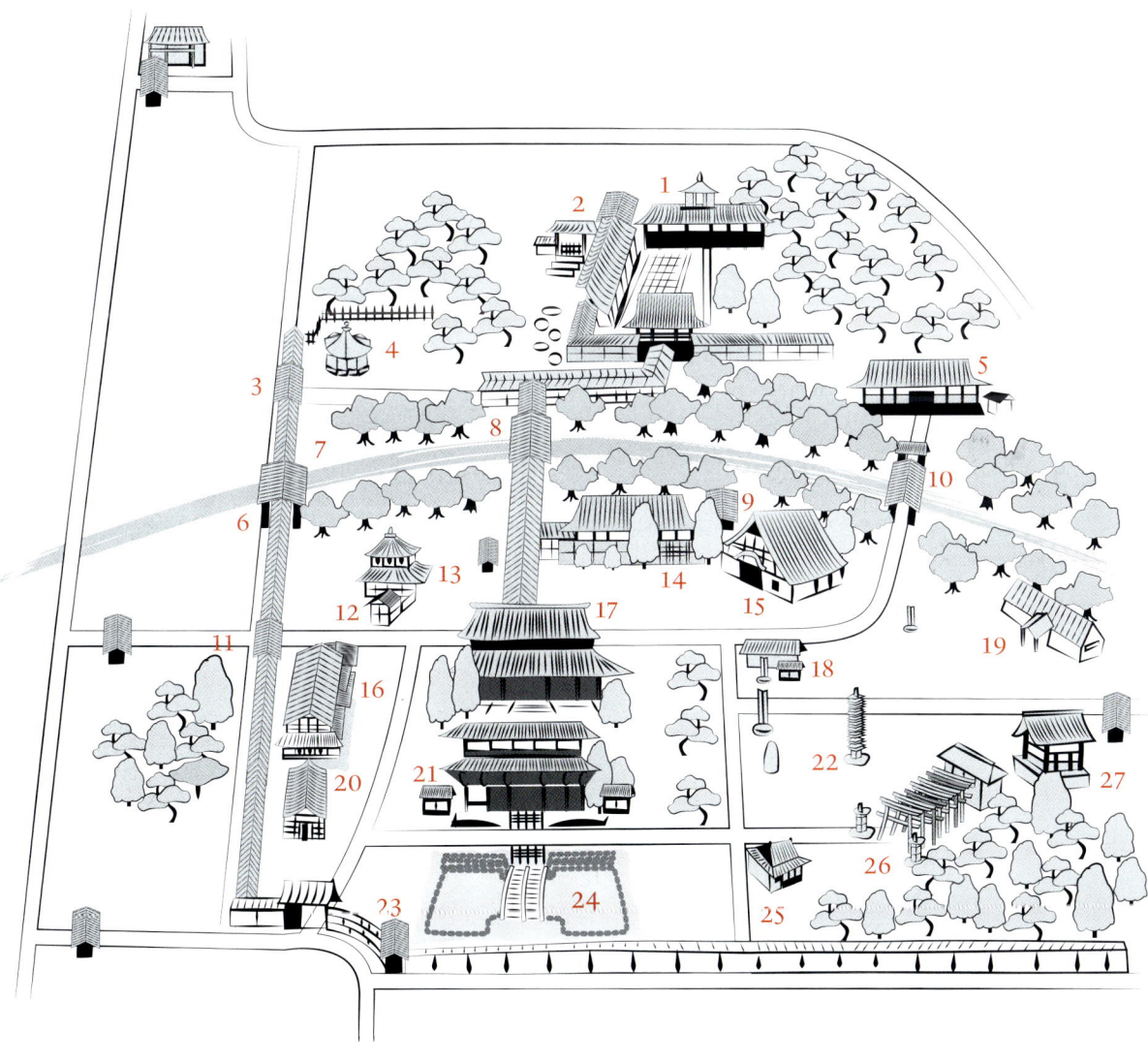

1. Main Gate
2. Gingaku-ji Hedge
3. Walkway
4. Kitchen
5. Abbot's Quarters
6. Tōgu (Searching East) Hall
7. Middle Gate
8. Tō (Chinese) Gate
9. Ginsha Dan (Silvery Sand Bank)
10. Hakkaku (White Crane) Island

11. Senkei (Immortal Laurel) Bridge
12. Kōgetsu (Facing the Moon) Platform
13. Senshū (Immortal's Sleeves) Bridge
14. Ginkaku (Silver Pavilion)
15. Ryūhai (Dragon's Back) Bridge
16. Bunkai (Dividing Border) Bridge
17. Kinkyō (Brocade Mirror) Pond
18. Sengetsu (Cleansing the Moon) Waterfall

Garden Plan Example

The Ginkaku-ji

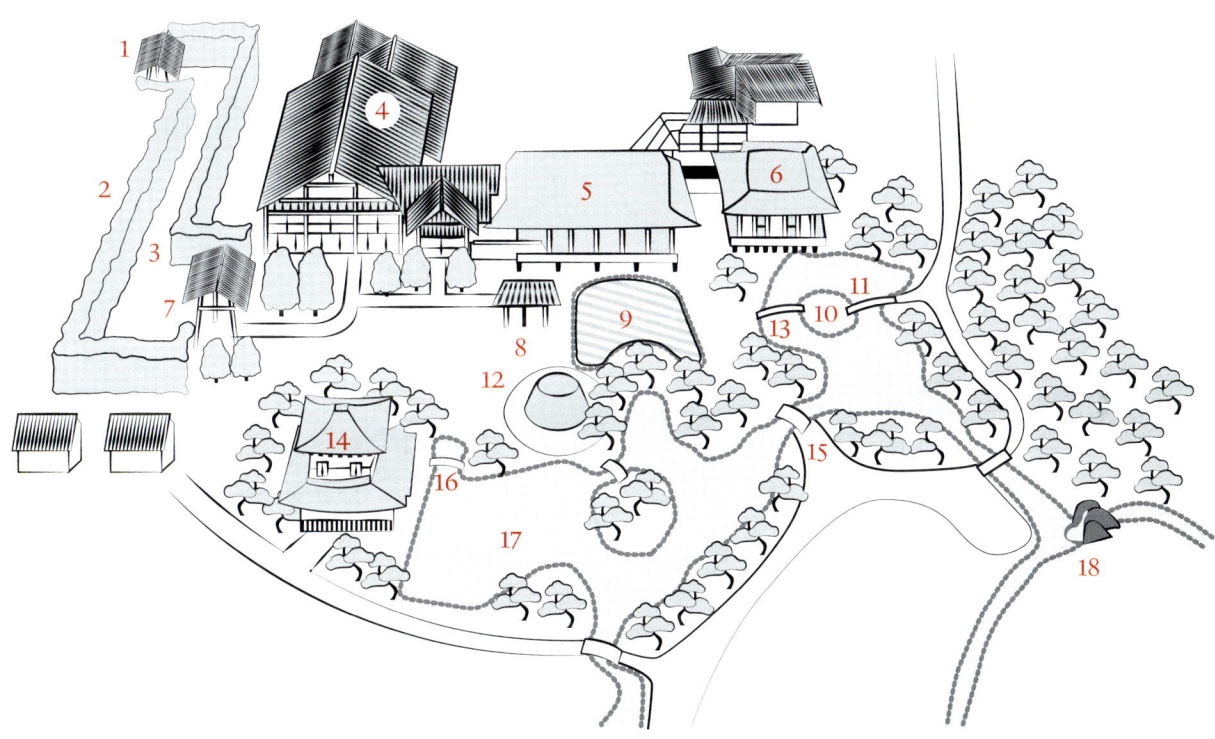

Stone Formations

Dry Waterfall, Saihō-ji

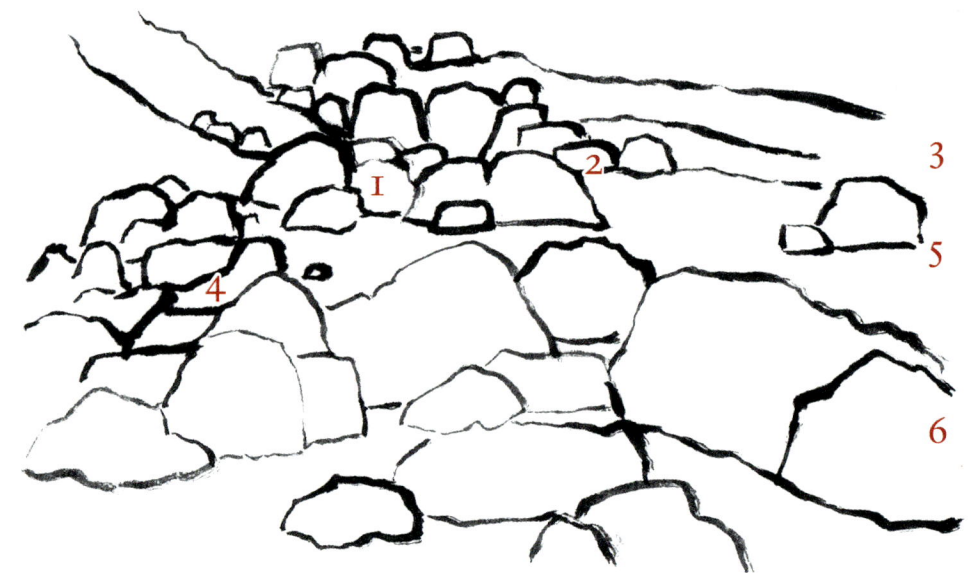

Konchi-in, Nanzen-ji

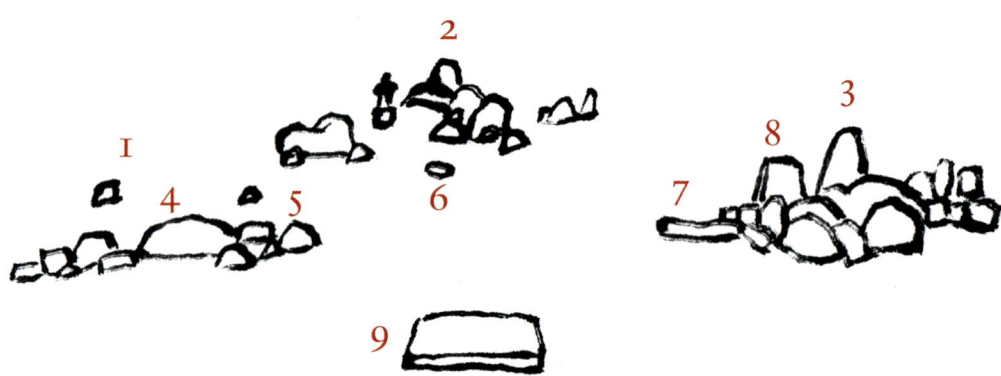

KEY TO DRY WATERFALL, SAIHŌ-JI

1. Zazen Stone
2. Zazen Stone
3. Upper Section
4. Carp Stone
5. Middle Section
6. Lower Section

KONCHI-IN, NANZEN-JI

1. Turtle Island
2. Hōrai (Immortals) Mountains
3. Crane Island
4. Turtle Shell Stone
5. Turtle Head Stone
6. Turtle Stone
7. Crane Nect Stone
8. Feather Stone
9. Bowing (Place) Stone

OTHER STONE TYPES

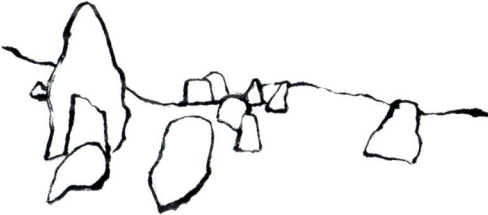

Mount Sumeru, Nine Mountains,
and Eight Seas Stones

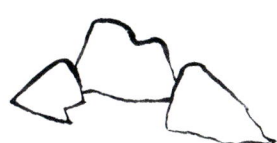

Tigress and Her Cubs Stones

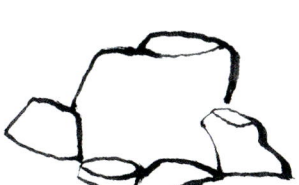

Trinity Buddha Stones

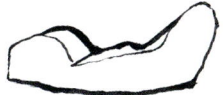

Boat Stone

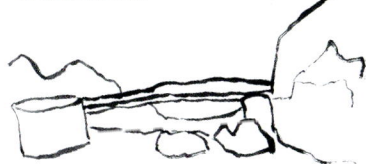

Stone Bridge

Reference: Nomura Kanji. *Zen Dera to Karesansui* [Zen Temples and Dry Landscape].

Bibliography

ENGLISH

Davidson, A.K. *The Art of Zen Gardens*. Los Angeles: Jeremy P. Tarcher, 1983.

Dougill, John, and John Einarsen. *Zen Gardens and Temples of Kyōto*. North Clarendon, VT: Tuttle Publishing, 2017.

Keane, Marc Peter. *The Art of Setting Stones & Other Writings from the Japanese Garden*. Berkeley, CA: Stone Bridge Press, 2002.

Keene, Donald. *Yoshimasa and the Silver Pavilion*. New York: Columbia University Press, 2003.

Mansfield, Stephen. *Japanese Stone Gardens*. North Clarendon, VT: Tuttle Publishing, 2009.

Musō Soseki. *Sun at Midnight: Poems and Letters*. Translated by W. S. Merwin & Sōiku Shigematsu. Port Townsend, WA: Copper Canyon Press, 1989.

Saito Katsuo and Wada Sadaji. *Magic of Trees and Stones: Secrets of Japanese Gardening*. New York, San Francisco, Tokyo: Japan Publications Trading Company, 1964.

Scheidegger, Ildegarda. *Bokutotsusō: Studies on the Calligraphy of the Zen Master Musō Soseki*. Bern, Switzerland: Peter Lang, 2005.

Takei Jirō and Marc P. Keane. *Sakuteiki: Visions of the Japanese Garden*. North Clarendon, VT: Tuttle Publishing, 2008.

Tanahashi Kazuaki. *The Heart Sutra: A Comprehensive Guide to the Classic of Mahayana Buddhism*. Boston: Shambhala Publications, 2014.

Tanahashi Kazuaki. *Zen Chants: Thirty-Five Essential Texts with Commentary*. Boston: Shambhala Publications, 2015.

GUIDEBOOKS WE RECOMMEND

Morgan, Kate, and Rebecca Melner. *Kyōto*. Oakland, CA: Lonely Planet, 2018.

Treib, Marc, and Ron Herman. *A Guide to The Gardens of Kyōto*. Novato, CA: ORO Editions, 2019.

Japanese

Arima Raitei and Kuga Natsumi. *Koji Junrei: Kyōto no. 11: Ginkaku-ji* [A Pilgrimage to Old Temples in Kyōto, no. 11: Ginkaku-ji]. Kyōto: Tankōsha, 2007.

Arima Raitei and Umehara Takeshi. *Koji Junrei: Kyōto no. 21: Kinkaku-ji* [A Pilgrimage to Old Temples in Kyōto, no. 21: Kinkaku-ji]. Kyōto: Tankōsha, 2008.

Fujita Shūgaku and Shimoshige Akiko. *Koji Junrei: Kyōto no. 36: Saihō-ji* [A Pilgrimage to Old Temples in Kyōto, no. 36: Saihō-ji]. Kyōto: Tankōsha, 2009.

Hatano Hiroshi. *Hidensho wo Yomu "Sakuteiki"* [Reading "Sakuteiki" (Notes on Garden Making): The Secret Guide for Garden Design]. Tōkyō: Seibundō Shinkōsha, 2015.

Hirata Seikō, and Gen'yū Sōkyū. *Koji Junrei: Kyōto no. 9: Tenryū-ji* [A Pilgrimage to Old Temples in Kyōto, no. 9: Tenryū-ji]. Kyōto: Tankōsha, 2007.

Hisamatsu Shin'ichi. *Zen to Bijutsu* [Zen and Fine Arts]. Kyōto: Shibunkaku, 1976.

Imae Hidefumi. *Kyōto Hatsu: Niwa no Rekishi* [Start from Kyōto: The History of Gardens]. Kyōto: Sekai Shisōsha, 2020.

Kawase Kazuma. *Musō Kokushi: Muchū Mondō Shū* [Dialogues in Dreams]. Tōkyō: Kōdansha, 2000.

Kizu Masayo. *Chūgoku no Teien: Sansui no Renkinjutsu* [Chinese Gardens: The Alchemy of Landscape]. Tōkyō: Tōkyōdō Shuppan, 1994.

Kumakura Isao and Takenuki Genshō. *Musō Soseki* [Zen Master Musō Soseki: Life and Legacy]. Tōkyō: Shunjūsha, 2012.

Masuno Shummyō. *Zen to Zen Geijutsu toshite no Niwa* [Zen and Gardens as Zen Art]. Tōkyō: Mainichi Shimbunsha, 2008.

Matsuyama Daikō. *Kokoro wo Utsusu Kyōto, Zen no Niwa Meguri* [Strolling in Kyōto around Zen Gardens That Reflect the Heart]. Kyōto: PHP Kenkyūsho, 2016.

Miyamoto Kenji. *Nihon Teien no Mikata* [How to Appreciate Japanese Gardens]. Kyōto: Gakugei Shuppansha, 1998.

Mizuno Hidehiko. *Kyōto Zekkei Teien* [Spectacular Landscape Gardens in Kyōto]. Tōkyō: Dempasha, 2017.

Mizuno Katsuhiko. *Kyōto Chatei Haiken* [Viewing Tea Gardens in Kyōto]. Kyōto: Mitsumura Suiko Shoin, 2013.

Nomura Kanji. *Zen Dera to Karesansui* [Zen Temples and Dry Landscapes]. Tōkyō: Takarajimasha, 2015.

Ono Masaaki. *Zukai: Niwashi ga Yomitoku Sakuteiki, Sansui narabini Nogata no Zu* [Illustrated Guide: *The Notes of Garden-Making Interpreted by a Gardener: Artistic and Natural Landscape Design*]. Kyōto: Gakugei Shuppansha, 2016.

Rurubu-sha. *Pocket Guide Kyōto*. Tōkyō: JTB, 2003.

Shinji Isoya. *Nihon no Teien* [The Japanese Gardens]. Tōkyō: Chūōkōron Shinsha, 2005.

Shōgakukan. *Toki wo Koeru Zen no Sekai: Musō Kokushi no Niwa* [The Timeless World of Zen: The Garden of National Teacher Musō]. Tōkyō: Shōgakukan, 2006.

Takada Myōho and Sen Sōshitsu. *Koji Junrei: Kyōto no. 17: Daitoku-ji* [A Pilgrimage to Old Temples in Kyōto, no. 17: Daitoku-ji]. Kyōto: Tankōsha, 2007.

Tanaka Sendō. *Cha no Yu Meigenshū* [The Collection of Famous Quotes on Tea Ceremony]. Tōkyō: Kadokawa Shoten, 2010.

Ugaya Yuri. *Shikake ni Kandōsuru Kyōto Meiteien* [Impressive Tricks of Famous Kyōto Gardens]. Tōkyō: Seibundō Shinkōsha, 2018.

Yamaguchi Yūsuke. *Mu no Geijutsu* [The Fine Art of Nothingness]. Tōkyō: Risōsha, 1939.

Yanagida Seizan. *Musō Kokushi Goroku* [Recorded Sayings of Zen Master Musō]. Tōkyō: Kōdansha, 1983.

Acknowledgments

Who saved Kyōto from the atomic bomb? Legend holds Edwin Reischauer, an expert on Japan, wept hard upon seeing the city on the list of potential targets at a military strategic meeting, and thus the city was removed from consideration. Dr. Reischauer, later an ambassador to Japan, however, denied the story in his book *My Life between Japan and America*, saying, "I probably would have done this if I had ever had the opportunity, but there is not a word of truth to it. . . . The only person deserving credit for saving Kyōto from destruction is Henry L. Stimson, the Secretary of War at the time, who had known and admired Kyōto ever since his honeymoon there several decades earlier." My utmost gratitude goes to Secretary Stimson and all those who helped save the thousand-year-old city, and so we are here today.

When Japan surrendered unconditionally to the United States and the Allied Forces in 1945, I was eleven years old. That year my mother sent me to Kyōto to live with my father's father to finish primary school. Then I rode to my middle school on an aged bicycle. The city was dusty and depressed, with large streets destroyed for fire lanes and mounds of rubbish lying around. There were no tourists.

The hospitality of the citizens of Kyōto, including laborers and the caretakers of the gardens, monks and nuns, abbots, and administrators of the temples, has created and maintained the sublime beauty of the art and culture of gardens and many forms of architecture. Thank you.

It's been a privilege to work with Mitsue Nagase. She has taken over 10,000 photographs of Zen gardens of the city over the course of three years. For me it's been an unmatched opportunity to study and enjoy the landscapes. My thanks to Joan Halifax Rōshi for cotranslating Zen chants with me and inviting me to colead pilgrimages organized by the Upaya Zen Center annually. I would like to thank Bernd Schellhorn, an expert on Zen temple–style vegetarian cooking, for being with us when Mitsue and I conceived this book in Kyōto and for his continuous support. My gratitude goes to Bruce Mingzhou Guo for giving me an opportunity to help design a series of Zen-inspired gardens in Northern California.

Dr. Susan O'Leary was as always very kind and gave me excellent editorial advice.

Dr. Linda Hess helped me translate the seven characteristics of Zen art. Roberta Werdinger has been helpful to check my writing. Thanks to Yuka Saitō for working on the bibliography. Thanks to the tea master John McGee for the Ingrid Bergman story.

Mitsue Nagase and I thank Lora Zorian and Gopa & Ted2 for the extraordinary book design. Matt Zepelin has guided us throughout the production process, including excellent editing with Sami Ripley. We have enjoyed working with Nikko Odiseos and the staff at Shambhala Publications. Our gratitude also goes to Victoria Shoemaker for representing us.

Kazuaki Tanahashi

When I first met Kaz in 2010, I asked him for his advice on how to continue working as a professional photographer. "Take on the challenge to publish books" was his answer. Looking back to that particular moment twelve years later, I am stunned to see how this book on Zen Gardens manifested—and that I was given a chance to collaborate with him. I appreciate Kaz from the bottom of my heart for his extraordinary generosity and trust.

My deep gratitude goes to my late father for introducing me to the magical world of photography, and to my mother for her continuous encouragement. My husband Bernd has been a driving force behind this project. He has accompanied me to all the gardens depicted in this book. Without his support, I could not have pushed myself this far.

John Einarsen, an amazing photographer and a dear friend, has been a true inspiration, as well as my Miksang mentors Michael Wood and Julie DuBose.

Susan O'Leary guided me on how to express myself through the medium of words, and Ken Rodgers kindly offered his remarkable skill to edit my text. Mana Tanakadate created maps and illustrations. I am so grateful for their contributions.

If I were to list everyone to whom I owe words of appreciation, the list would be endless. Among them, my heartfelt gratitude goes to Aki Kimoto for her warm friendship and kindness over decades and Natalie Goldberg for giving me a firm push when I needed it.

Most of the images appearing in this book were photographed during the recent pandemic. Even though the temple gates remained open, hardly any visitors came, so I could experience the gardens radiating their gentle powers, surrounded by utmost tranquility, as originally intended. So, last but not least, I would like to express my admirations to the gardens' creators and caretakers.

Mitsue Nagase

Index

About the Authors

KAZUAKI TANAHASHI, born in 1933 in Japan, is an artist, Buddhist scholar, and activist who once lived in Kyōto. While residing in the United States since 1977, he has visited gardens in the ancient capital almost every year for two decades. His many publications include *Painting Peace: Art in a Time of Global Crisis*, *Penetrating Laughter: Hakuin's Zen and Art*, and *Brush Mind*. www.brushmind.net.

MITSUE NAGASE, born in 1967 in Japan, started studying photography in Vancouver, Canada. While living in the United States, her interest in Zen Buddhism led her to study Miksang, a contemplative approach to photography, which she now teaches in workshops. Her photographs have been published in various magazines and books and have been exhibited in Japan and internationally. For more information and to see her recent works visit www.mitsuenagase.com.